0 km   50

0 miles   50

LANZAROTE
Pages 80–95

ISLA DE ALEGRANZA

ISLA DE MONTAÑA CLARA

ISLA GRACIOSA

LANZAROTE

Arrecife

ISLA DE LOS LOBOS

• Puerto del Rosario

FUERTEVENTURA

Las Palmas
• de Gran Canaria

rucas

GRAN CANARIA

• Maspalomas

FUERTEVENTURA
Pages 66–79

GRAN CANARIA
Pages 40–65

EYEWITNESS TRAVEL
CANARY ISLANDS

EYEWITNESS TRAVEL

CANARY ISLANDS

MAIN CONTRIBUTORS: PIOTR PASZKIEWICZ
& HANNA FARYNA-PASZKIEWICZ

LONDON, NEW YORK,
MELBOURNE, MUNICH AND DELHI
www.dk.com

Produced by Hachette Livre Polska Sp. z o.o.,

SENIOR GRAPHIC DESIGNER Paweł Pasternak
CONTRIBUTORS Piotr Paszkiewicz, Hanna Faryna-Paszkiewicz, Małgorzata
Wiśniewska, Barbara Sudnik, Eligiusz Nowakowski
CONSULTANT Carlos Rubio Palomera
GRAPHIC DESIGNERS Paweł Kamiński, Paweł Pasternak, Piotr Kiedrowski
EDITOR Robert G. Pasieczny
TYPESETTING AND LAYOUT Ewa Roguska, Piotr Kiedrowski
CARTOGRAPHERS Magdalena Polak, Dariusz Romanowski,
Olaf Rodowald
PHOTOGRAPHERS Paweł Wójcik, Bartłomiej Zaranek
ILLUSTRATORS Monika Sopińska, Bohdan Wróblewski

Dorling Kindersley Limited
TRANSLATOR Magda Hannay
EDITORS Irene Lyford, Michelle de Larrabeiti, Matthew Tanner
SENIOR DTP DESIGNER Jason Little
PRODUCTION CONTROLLER Melanie Dowland

Printed and bound in China
by L-Rex Printing Company Limited, China

First American Edition, 2003

10 11 12 13 10 9 8 7 6 5 4 3 2 1

Published in the United States by DK Publishing,
375 Hudson Street, New York, New York 10014

Reprinted with revisions 2006, 2008, 2010

Copyright © 2003, 2010 Dorling Kindersley, London

Published in Great Britain by Dorling Kindersley Limited.

A CATALOG RECORD FOR THIS BOOK IS AVAILABLE
FROM THE LIBRARY OF CONGRESS

ISSN 1542-1554

ISBN 9780-7566-6134-2

FLOORS ARE REFERRED TO THROUGHOUT IN ACCORDANCE WITH EUROPEAN
USAGE; IE THE "FIRST FLOOR" IS THE FLOOR ABOVE GROUND LEVEL.

Front cover main image: Valle de Agaete, Gran Canaria

We're trying to be cleaner and greener:

- we recycle waste and switch things off
- we use paper from responsibly managed forests whenever possible
- we ask our printers to actively reduce water and energy consumption
- we check out our suppliers' working conditions – they never use child labour

Find out more about our values and best practices at www.dk.com

---

**The information in this
Dorling Kindersley Travel Guide is checked regularly.**
Every effort has been made to ensure that this book is as up-to-date
as possible at the time of going to press. Some details, however,
such as telephone numbers, opening hours, prices, gallery hanging
arrangements and travel information are liable to change. The
publishers cannot accept responsibility for any consequences arising
from the use of this book, nor for any material on third party
websites, and cannot guarantee that any website address in this
book will be a suitable source of travel information. We value the
views and suggestions of our readers very highly. Please write to:
Publisher, DK Eyewitness Travel Guides, Dorling Kindersley,
80 Strand, London, WC2R 0RL, Great Britain.

◁ **Viewing point by Los Roques at Teide National Park**

CONTENTS

HOW TO USE
THIS GUIDE **6**

**Madonna from a church façade
at Santiago del Teide**

INTRODUCING
THE CANARY
ISLANDS

DISCOVERING THE
CANARY ISLANDS **10**

PUTTING THE
CANARY ISLANDS ON
THE MAP **12**

A PORTRAIT OF THE
CANARY ISLANDS **14**

THE CANARY ISLANDS
THROUGH THE YEAR **24**

**Children at the carnival in Las
Palmas de Gran Canaria**

Golden sandy beach near Corralejo, on Fuerteventura

Façade of the parish church in Vega del Río de Palmas

TRAVELLERS' NEEDS

Exotic fruits grow in abundance on the Canary Islands

SURVIVAL GUIDE

Traditionally decorated pot from La Orotava

MAP OF FERRY ROUTES
Inside back cover

Aquatic life of the Canary Islands
(see pp18–19)

HOW TO USE THIS GUIDE

This guide will help you to get the most out of your visit to the Canary Islands. It provides recommendations on places to visit, as well as detailed practical information. The section *Introducing the Canary Islands* gives an overview of the geographical position of the islands, their natural environment, their culture and their history. Individual sections describe the main historic sites and star attractions on each of the archipelago's seven inhabited islands. Help with accommodation, restaurants, shopping, entertainment and recreational activities can be found in the *Tourist Information* section, while the *Survival Guide* provides useful practical information and advice for visitors.

THE CANARY ISLANDS AREA BY AREA

Each of the seven inhabited islands has a section devoted to it. Towns and sights of interest on each of the islands are shown on the relevant map.

Colour-coded thumb tabs identify pages devoted to individual islands.

1 Introduction
This section provides a brief overview of each island, describing its history, geographical features and cultural characteristics as well as main tourist attractions.

A locator map indicates the position of the island within the archipelago.

2 Island Map
This shows the main roads and topography of the island. It also locates all the places that are later described in detail.

Boxes contain information about events and people associated with an area.

3 Detailed Information
All the major towns and places of interest are described, listed and numbered to correspond with the island's map. Each entry provides information on the star sights and local attractions.

4 Major Towns
At least two pages are devoted to each major town, with detailed descriptions of historic remains and local curiosities that are worth seeing.

A Visitors' Checklist provides tourist and transport information, including opening hours of tourist attractions, admission charges, and details of local festivals and market days.

A Town Map shows the location of all the main sights within the town centre and provides tourist information on post offices and car parks.

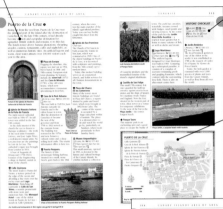

5 The Canary Islands' Star Sights
Two pages are devoted to each major sight. They include an area map and, in the case of larger towns, a street map of the town centre.

An Area Map indicates the main sights, which are numbered for easy reference.

Tourist Information details length of suggested tour plus good stopping places.

6 National Parks
Separate pages in the guide are devoted to the national parks on the islands. Topographic maps in these sections indicate the star sights and any other special features of the park.

Photographs illustrate the most interesting areas and the most scenic spots within the park.

Maps show the area's main roads, walking trails and topography, as well as useful tourist information.

INTRODUCING THE CANARY ISLANDS

DISCOVERING THE CANARY ISLANDS

The archipelago of the Canary Islands has seven main islands – Gran Canaria, Tenerife, Lanzarote, Fuerteventura, La Gomera, La Palma and El Hierro. Each island has a unique personality, from the golden desertscapes of Fuerteventura to the lush greenery of La Palma; the black volcanic beaches of El Hierro to the ruddy red hues of Lanzarote. Indelible cultural marks left by conquerors from North Africa, Portugal, Britain and Spain make this mixture of islands a place like no other on earth.

Camel ride in the Montañas del Fuego

GRAN CANARIA

- **Pine-clad mountains**
- **Historical Las Palmas**
- **Exciting theme parks**
- **Buzzing nightlife**

Visitors arrive at the Canaries' third largest island in their thousands. Some come for the incredibly healthy climate and invigorating mountain walks on trails such as those found in the area around **Roque Nublo** *(see p62)*. Others delve into the history, mirroring the footsteps of Christopher Columbus in **La Vegueta** *(see p48)*, the old quarter of **Las Palmas** *(see pp44–9)*. But most seek little more than that sacred trinity of sun, sand and sea. This can be interspersed with daytime strolls in pretty villages such as **Puerto de Mogán** *(see pp58–9)*, or a visit to one of the many theme parks such as **Aquasur** in Maspalomas *(see p60)*. At night, the scores of bars and clubs of the southern resorts offer lively entertainment.

The picturesque harbour at Puerto de Mogán, Gran Canaria

White sands and clear azure sea at Papagayo beach in Lanzarote

FUERTEVENTURA

- **Glorious beaches**
- **World-class watersports**
- **Los Lobos nature reserve**

Like a vast play park for sand lovers old and young, the coast of Fuerteventura has more beaches than any other Canary Island. The two main resorts – **Corralejo** *(see pp70–71)* in the north, and **Morro Jable** *(see p76)* in the south – are where most visitors gather. Here you'll find world-class windsurfing as well as sensational snorkelling opportunities. Lying a few kilometres from Corralejo is the small volcanic island of **Los Lobos** *(see p71)*. The whole island is a nature reserve and makes for a very peaceful day's excursion.

LANZAROTE

- **Dramatic volcanic scenery**
- **Underground grottoes**
- **Secluded coves**

Lanzarote is a varied island of dramatic volcanic scenery, pristine white villages and beautiful, broad beaches. Lava plays a big role in the island's attractions, which include the volcano-fuelled barbecue in **Timanfaya National Park** *(see pp92–3)*. The island differs from the others largely due to César Manrique's environmental and conservational efforts, chronicled at the **Fundación César Manrique** *(see p85)*. At **Jameos del Agua** *(see p86)* there are underground grottoes illuminated and furnished by him. Lanzarote's resorts are contained and few in number, but amenities are still abundant. Hidden coves like those around **Papagayo** *(see p94)* are a magnet for holidaymakers.

TENERIFE

- **Pico del Teide – Spain's highest peak**
- **Pretty towns of Masca and La Orotava**
- **Animal fun at Loro Parque**

The most celebrated of the islands, Tenerife offers all the highs and lows of a sub-tropical paradise. Ride a cable car up the world's third largest volcano, towering high above the lunar landscape of **Parque Nacional del Teide** *(see pp118–19)*. Take a boat trip to watch whales and dolphins frolic, or visit the world famous **Loro Parque** *(see pp114–15)*, home of tigers, penguins, gorillas and much more. In the capital, **Santa Cruz** *(see pp100–3)*, visit the **Museo de Bellas Artes** *(see p101)* or bag some bargains in the shopping zone. The pretty town of **La Orotava** *(see pp108–11)* offers the Tenerife of old, with Canarian mansions and cobbled streets; while at **Masca** *(see p116)* whitewashed cottages cling to the mountainside.

Whitewashed houses cling to the mountainside in Masca, Tenerife

LA GOMERA

- **Breathtaking hikes**
- **Ancient forests**
- **Tiny fishing villages**
- **Intriguing customs and traditions**

Certainly not an island for the neon-loving dance set, Tenerife's nearest neighbour is a green, hilly outcrop scarred with deep ravines and fertile valleys. A walker's paradise, La Gomera is etched with hiking trails. In the ancient laurel forests of the **Parque Nacional de Garajonay** *(see pp130–31)* you might hear the distant whistling of Silbo, La Gomera's unique whistling language. On an island of tiny fishing villages and clusters of mountainside cottages, **Valle Gran Rey** *(see p128)* bears the closest

resemblance to a holiday resort, but only just. Here you'll find a shingle beach and several bars catering for the mainly Spanish visitors. For culture-seekers, the pretty harbour town and capital of **San Sebastián** *(see p126)* has a museum and visitor centre showcasing legacies of Christopher Columbus's time here.

EL HIERRO

- **Fragrant pine forests**
- **Dramatic coastline**
- **Giant lizards**

Known locally as "La Isla Chiquita" (the Small Island), El Hierro is by far the least commercialized (and least visited) of the islands. Its appeal lies mostly with nature lovers keen to enjoy a varied landscape of speckled meadows, the aromatic pine forests and junipers of **El Sabinar** *(see p137)*, and the wild coastline hammered by

crashing waves, such as at **Roques de Salmor** *(see p136)*. The solitude also suits a shy reptile indigenous to El Hierro. Efforts to conserve these giant lizards can be seen at **Lagartario** *(see p137)*.

Colourful balconies overhang the streets of Santa Cruz de La Palma

LA PALMA

- **Lush mountain trails**
- **Unrivalled stargazing**
- **Fine Canarian architecture**

This lush green gem is the most verdant of all the Canary Islands, and a major draw for hikers and botanists. The vast **Caldera de Taburiente** *(see pp150–51)* is one of the largest volcanic craters on earth, and the view from its rim is spectacular. The vista overhead is also out of this world; the skies above La Palma are among the clearest anywhere so the stargazing opportunities are unbeatable. The capital, **Santa Cruz de La Palma** *(see pp144–5)*, offers fine Canarian architecture at every turn.

Waves crashing onto rocks on the northern shore of El Hierro

Putting the Canary Islands on the Map

Dotted in a gentle curve, the archipelago of the Canary Islands lies in the Atlantic Ocean to the west of Morocco in Saharan Africa. The seven main islands are inhabited with a total population of more than 2 million – the majority living on the larger islands of Gran Canaria and Tenerife. The total area of these volcanic islands is 7,447 sq km (2,875 sq miles) and encompasses a surprisingly rich variety of landscapes, from beaches and desert-like areas to dramatic mountain ranges and green woods. Hot winds from the Sahara ensure that the islands enjoy a warm climate all year round with temperatures averaging 18° C (64° F) in winter and 24° C (75° F) in summer.

Satellite View of Tenerife
This satellite picture shows how Mount Teide, with its volcanic crater, dominates the centre of this rocky island. At 3,718 m (12,195 ft), Teide is the highest peak in the Canaries and Spain.

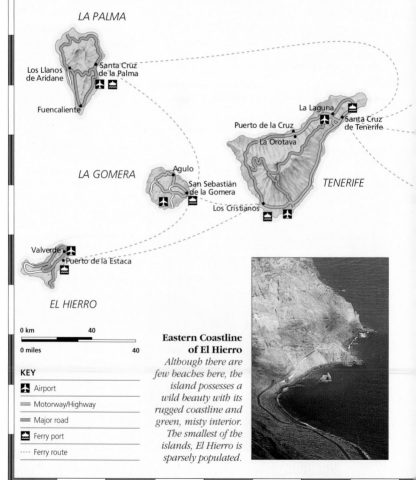

LA PALMA

Los Llanos de Aridane

Santa Cruz de la Palma

Fuencaliente

La Laguna

Puerto de la Cruz

Santa Cruz de Tenerife

La Orotava

LA GOMERA

Agulo

San Sebastián de la Gomera

TENERIFE

Los Cristianos

Valverde

Puerto de la Estaca

EL HIERRO

0 km   40

0 miles   40

KEY

✈ Airport

▬ Motorway/Highway

▬ Major road

⛴ Ferry port

---- Ferry route

Eastern Coastline of El Hierro
Although there are few beaches here, the island possesses a wild beauty with its rugged coastline and green, misty interior. The smallest of the islands, El Hierro is sparsely populated.

↑ *Cádiz*

Bird's-eye View of Haria

Set in a beautiful valley on Lanzarote, Haria is typical of Canary villages. Its cluster of low, white houses nestles in the shadow of picturesque yet forbidding volcanoes.

ISLA DE ALEGRANZA

ISLA DE MONTAÑA CLARA

ISLA GRACIOSA

Tinajo
San Bartolomé
LANZAROTE
Arrecife
Playa Blanca

Corralejo   *ISLA DE LOS LOBOS*

FUERTEVENTURA

Puerto del Rosario

Betancuria

Tuineje

Galdar   Las Palmas de Gran Canaria
Agaete   Arucas
Telde
anta Lucia

Morro Jable

• Maspalomas

GRAN CANARIA

Location of the Islands

Although just 100 km (62 miles) from Africa, the Canary Islands belong to Spain – a country over 1,100 km (680 miles) away. The islands' population of over 2 million, is swollen each year by more than 7.5 million tourists.

WESTERN EUROPE AND NORTH AFRICA

IRELAND   UNITED KINGDOM

FRANCE

ANDORRA

PORTUGAL
AZORES   SPAIN
BALEARICS

MADEIRA

MOROCCO

WESTERN SAHARA   ALGERIA

MAURITANIA

The Formation of the Canary Islands

Along with other Atlantic islands, such as Madeira, the Azores and the Cape Verde Islands, the Canaries are of volcanic origin. They emerged from the sea millions of years ago: Lanzarote and Fuerteventura are believed to be the oldest at between 16 and 20 million years old, with Gran Canaria, Tenerife and La Gomera appearing around 8–13 million years ago. The remaining islands are much younger. Most of the islands lie in the shadow of a central volcanic cone surrounded by smaller cones and areas of solidified lava.

Near El Golfo (see p91) *on Lanzarote is a crater filled with seawater. A black sand beach separates the ocean from the grey-green waters of the lake.*

La Geria's vineyards *on Lanzarote (see p94) flourish in the fertile volcanic soil. Semi-circles of stones protect the vines from the prevailing winds, and the resulting grapes are used to produce the amber-coloured Malvasía wine.*

THE ORIGIN OF THE ISLANDS

The Canary Islands are the tips of volcanoes pushed up from the floor of the Atlantic Ocean by the movement of the Earth's crust. As the crust buckled along fault lines, hot liquid rock or magma burst up through the cracks.

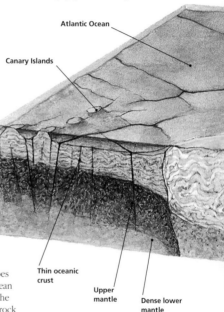

Atlantic Ocean

Canary Islands

Thin oceanic crust

Upper mantle

Dense lower mantle

Los Azulejos *on Gran Canaria show the beauty of the multi-coloured volcanic rocks. Their varied chemical compositions, including copper salts and iron hydrites, create a stunning palette of colours from grey and brown, through ochre and red, to blue and green.*

Malpaís *means "badlands" and refers to this almost
completely barren landscape on Fuerteventura (see p78).
Only the most desert-hardened flora and fauna survive here.*

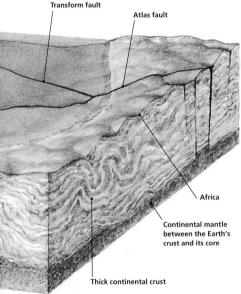

- Transform fault
- Atlas fault
- Africa
- Continental mantle between the Earth's crust and its core
- Thick continental crust

Around La Restinga *on El Hierro, the fields of lava assume fantastic shapes. Fat tongues of lava, that resemble solidified tar, are created by under-water volcanic eruptions. As the flowing lava rapidly cools it forms large areas of magma nodules.*

EVOLUTION OF VOLCANIC ISLANDS

The islands in this archipelago
are at various stages in their
geological evolution. Tenerife,
El Hierro, Lanzarote and La
Palma are still volcanically
active, with the latter
experiencing its most recent
eruption in 1971.

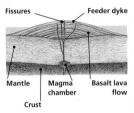

- Fissures
- Feeder dyke
- Mantle
- Magma chamber
- Basalt lava flow
- Crust

1 **The islands of** *La Gomera, El
Hierro and La Palma are
really the tops of volcanoes that
rise from the ocean's bed. They
consist of basalt rock produced
by solidified lava. Below, the
Earth's crust bends under the
weight of the islands.*

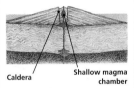

- Caldera
- Shallow magma chamber

2 **When the magma** *chamber
empties during an eruption,
the top of the cone collapses
downwards. This creates a crater,
known as a caldera – such as
the Caldera de Taburiente on
La Palma. This stage of an
island's evolution is marked by
abundant flows of lava.*

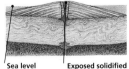

- Sea level
- Exposed solidified magma chamber

3 **When the eruption** *has
ended, the volcano begins to
erode. The mountains of Gran
Canaria are in the early stages
of erosion, while Fuerteventura's
volcanic chambers, with their
solidified lava, are typical of a
more advanced stage of evolution.*

Flora of the Canary Islands

The flora of the Canary Islands is unique. La Gomera, for example, is home to a rare ancient forest that is now a UNESCO world heritage site. More than half of the islands' 1,800 species are indigenous, and the unusual character of these exceptional plants has long attracted the attentionof botanists. They are the relics of the old Mediterranean flora, which became extinct throughout the region because of changes in climate. The local flora that remains has survived because of the fairly stable and relatively humid climate of the Canary Islands, along with a variety of colourful, exotic imported plants.

Canary Island pine *is one of the native species, growing at altitudes of over 1,000 m (3,280 ft). Its needles reach over 30 cm (12 in) in length.*

Canary palm (Phoenix canariensis), *another indigenous species, inhabits scrublands and semi-desert regions. It bears edible fruit, but is regarded mainly as an ornamental plant.*

Viper's bugloss (Echium wildpretii)

Canary Islands juniper

The basalt slopes *of volcanoes are not conducive to plant growth. The few species found here are often indigenous plants, which have evolved to be able to retain water.*

This type of spurge olive has silvery leaves.

THE DRAGON TREE

One of the most unusual plants in the Canaries, the dragon tree *(Dracaena draco)* erupts into swollen branches that end in tufts of spiky leaves. Its red sap (known as dragon's blood) and its fruit were used in Roman times to make a medicinal powder, and it was used in pigments, paints and varnishes. One specimen at Icod de los Vinos, on Tenerife, known as *Drago Milenario*, is said to be 1,000 years old.

Balsamic spurge *grows in semi-desert areas. Its juice is sometimes made into chewing gum, but it is also valued as an ornamental plant.*

PLANT ZONES

Coastal zones, *mostly rocky, are home to plants that can tolerate salt and temperature variations.*

Semi-desert *plants, found above 400 m (1,300 ft), store water within their fleshy leaves and stalks.*

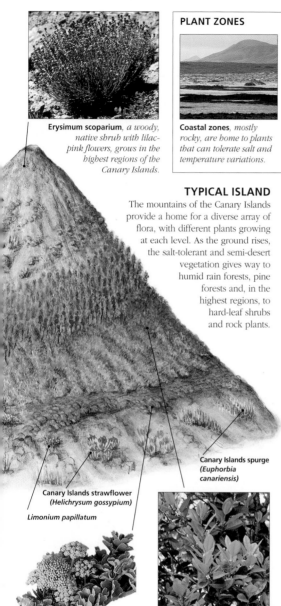

Erysimum scoparium, *a woody, native shrub with lilac-pink flowers, grows in the highest regions of the Canary Islands.*

TYPICAL ISLAND

The mountains of the Canary Islands provide a home for a diverse array of flora, with different plants growing at each level. As the ground rises, the salt-tolerant and semi-desert vegetation gives way to humid rain forests, pine forests and, in the highest regions, to hard-leaf shrubs and rock plants.

Low shrubs *are found above 500 m (1,650 ft), particularly in areas with a low annual rainfall.*

Canary Islands spurge (Euphorbia canariensis)

Canary Islands strawflower (Helichrysum gossypium)

Limonium papillatum

Laurel forests *cover the northern slopes of the islands, where humidity is constantly high.*

Pine woods *occur at up to 2,000 m (6,560 ft). Their undergrowth consists mainly of shade-loving shrubs.*

Canary samphire (Astydamia latifolia) *is found on the coastal basalt rocks of the Canary Islands. This native genus, with its distinctive fleshy, green leaves flowers from December until April.*

Canary Islands holly *is an evergreen shrub, and one of the most common inhabitants of the laurel forests. Its bark has medicinal properties.*

Areas above *2,000 m (6,560 ft) feature cushion-like shrubs. Rock grass covers the highest slopes.*

The Underwater World

Despite the Canary Islands' favourable position on the edge of the tropics, the waters around the islands are relatively cold. This explains the relative lack of coral reefs, which would normally occur at such latitudes. Nevertheless, the sea conditions are congenial to many species of fish, mammal and seaweed. Divers in coastal and offshore waters will find a rich variety of marine life, including several species of whales and dolphins, shoals of small cardinal fish, huge crabs, colourful parrot-fish and tiny seahorses.

Long-finned pilot whales *(blackfish) belong to the dolphin family. The coastal waters of Tenerife are home to the world's second-largest colony of these mammals.*

SEA LIFE

The ocean floor around the Canary Islands is mainly composed of rock with occasional patches of sand. This environment, illustrated here, is one reason for the richness of the local fauna, which includes some 600 species of seaweed.

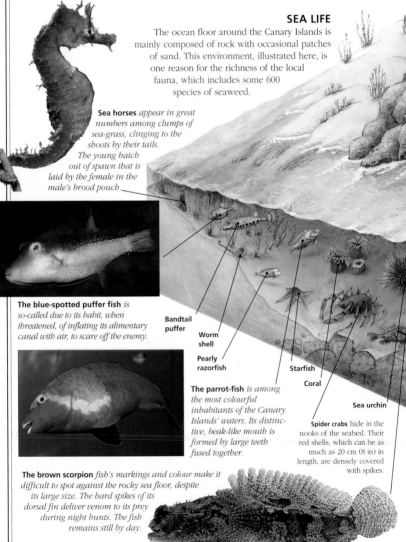

Sea horses *appear in great numbers among clumps of sea-grass, clinging to the shoots by their tails. The young hatch out of spawn that is laid by the female in the male's brood pouch.*

The blue-spotted puffer fish *is so-called due to its habit, when threatened, of inflating its alimentary canal with air, to scare off the enemy.*

Bandtail puffer

Worm shell

Pearly razorfish

Starfish

Coral

Sea urchin

The parrot-fish *is among the most colourful inhabitants of the Canary Islands' waters. Its distinctive, beak-like mouth is formed by large teeth fused together.*

Spider crabs hide in the nooks of the seabed. Their red shells, which can be as much as 20 cm (8 in) in length, are densely covered with spikes.

The brown scorpion *fish's markings and colour make it difficult to spot against the rocky sea floor, despite its large size. The hard spikes of its dorsal fin deliver venom to its prey during night hunts. The fish remains still by day.*

The Moroccan octopus *is a common sight in the areas of rocky seabed that lie around the Canary Islands. It catches its prey with its tentacles, which are armed with suckers.*

This small mollusc is the Murex trunculus, used since antiquity for 2,000 years to make purple dye. It hides inside its thick, striped shell, and eats putrefied matter, including other, dead molluscs.

Limpet

Chiton

DIVING AND SNORKELLING IN THE CANARIES

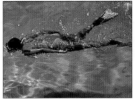

The Canary Islands provide very attractive diving grounds. Here, beginners can gain experience, while more advanced divers can explore the underwater caves off Gran Canaria, La Palma and El Hierro and the coral reefs near Lanzarote. The water is at its clearest between November and February. The water temperature of 15–20° C (59–68° F) is also conducive to diving and snorkelling. However, strong currents, particularly at greater depths, can present difficulties for divers.

The conger eel *has a blackish body, with paler belly, large head and wide mouth. It is active at night, hiding in caves and cracks during the day.*

The moray eel, *with its elongated, snake-like body and sharp teeth, is one of the fiercest predators of the coastal waters. This marine creature, which can be up to 3 m (10 ft) long, inhabits caves and cracks in the rocks.*

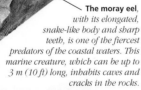

Cardinal fish *with their scarlet bodies are small, fast-moving fish that may be seen mostly at the entrances to underwater caves. The male carries the spawn in his mouth.*

Crafts of the Canary Islands

The inhabitants of the Canary Islands are enthusiastic about keeping alive their strongly rooted tradition of local handicrafts. These include embroidery, lace-making, basket-weaving, ceramics and woodcarving. Different islands specialize in particular crafts: La Gomera is known for its basketware and pottery that is made without using a wheel, while Tenerife is also a centre for traditional, Guanche-style pots, El Hierro produces beautifully woven rugs and bags and the town of Ingenio *(see p64)* Gran Canaria, produces some of the best embroidery in the islands.

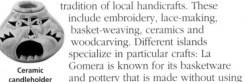
Ceramic candleholder

Potter at work in La Orotava workshop, Tenerife

POTTERY

Thanks to archaeological discoveries, we now know that pottery was one of the best-developed crafts of the Guanches – the indigenous people of the Canary Islands. Using local clay, they made vessels of various shapes and sizes, which they used for cooking, storing food and carrying water.

Although locally made pottery can be found on all the islands, there are a few centres that pride themselves on their ceramic workshops. La Gomera, Tenerife and La Palma are particularly well known for traditional pottery. Produced from dark clay, without the use of a potter's wheel, this is the most popular style of pottery, and it is regarded as a classic reinterpretation of Guanche work. Other islands also make pieces that are based on original Guanche designs copied from archaeological finds and produced by traditional methods.

As on the Spanish mainland, there are tiles, plates and vases in the multi-coloured style of the Moorish inspired *azulejos,* for sale in pottery shops.

Colourful displays of pottery adorn many local village shops and most markets will have at least one stall selling ceramics. Workshops where you can view the pots being made also offer an array of wares that makes choosing difficult.

Ornamental water vessel

EMBROIDERY

Practised mainly by the women, the skills and styles of Canary Islands' embroidery are passed down from mother to daughter. The craft of embroidery is a source of great pride in the areas that specialize in it. Gran Canaria is famous for embroidery, particularly the villages of Ingenio *(see p64)* and Agaete *(see p57)*, as is La Orotava *(see pp 108–11)* on Tenerife. Original patterns, hand-embroidered onto silk or linen, are among the most exquisite souvenirs that visitors can take home. Richly embroidered bed linen, tablecloths and napkins are among the most popular items. The only drawback is their often very high price, which is a reflection of the skill and time taken by the embroiderer.

Clothing, especially the islands' national costumes, is decorated with embroidery. White shirts, blouses and aprons are all adorned with open-work frills that are threaded with ribbons. Modern, somewhat garish copies of these clothes are on sale in craft markets.

Traditional embroidery in Betancuria Museum, Fuerteventura

LACE-MAKING

Lacework is among the most beautiful and the most striking of the Canary Islands' handicrafts. The subtlety of the designs and colours reflects the continuation of European and Mediterranean traditions.

There are several small, specialized co-operatives on the islands, producing lace tablecloths and curtains. These are very popular among the islanders as well as tourists. Unlike embroidered items, lacework is not too expensive.

The beautiful openwork tablecloths and placemats are always produced in white and beige. Their designs usually consist of symmetrical patterns with abstract or floral motifs, featuring circles and suns linked together to create uniform compositions.

Experts regard the lace produced in Vilaflor, on Tenerife, as being the most beautiful and best quality.

Lace tablecloth from San Bartolomé on Lanzarote

WEAVING

Weaving is another traditional handicraft that continues to thrive in the Canary Islands, and there are many established weavers' shops still working in the islands today. As in past centuries, simple hand-looms are still used to produce carpets, which are based on traditional designs. Long and narrow, often with randomly mixed colours,

Weaver's workshop, producing striped carpets

these carpets are very popular with the local population. You will also find carpets with regular stripes or with more sophisticated designs, based on traditional local patterns. Hand-woven cloth is still used to make rugs, tapestries and bags and, until recently, some elements of the local national costumes were also hand-woven.

Long, multi-coloured striped carpet

The islands of La Palma and La Gomera are known for their woven products.

OTHER HANDICRAFTS

Always very popular with tourists are items woven from palm leaves or willow. These include baskets and bowls, which are not designed to last forever, but are nevertheless very reasonably priced. Also for sale are the wide-brimmed hats that are an indispensable part of farm workers' clothing.

On religious feast days, the women of the islands wear small hats with an upturned brim. This local fashion has helped to further a demand for these locally produced, plaited straw hats, which are light and airy to wear.

Highly regarded for their artistic merit are local carpentry and woodwork products. The tradition of adorning the surfaces of wooden gates, doors and shutters with carved motifs goes back many centuries. Old gates and shutters, as well as church ornaments, are often masterpieces of woodcarving. The distinctive wooden balconies and oriels, with their carved brackets and balustrades, are based on historic designs. Local trees, including pine, chestnut and beech, provide timber for many household items such as bowls, spoons and ladles.

The *timple* – a small, wooden, five-stringed instrument resembling a ukulele – is a popular souvenir from the Canary Islands. The village of Telde on Lanzarote is renowned for producing these instruments.

***Timple*-maker at work**

Canary Islands Carnivals

Often compared to the extravaganzas in Rio de Janeiro and New Orleans, the Santa Cruz carnival in Tenerife takes place each year in the 10–14 days before Ash Wednesday. It is one of the largest carnivals in Europe, with a spectacular display of costumes and Latin American music. In Gran Canaria, festivities start when the Tenerife carnival ends. The Carnival Fiesta in Lanzarote takes place at the beginning of March, with one in Fuerteventura two weeks later. Although street parties were banned under the Franco regime, the tradition of holding carnivals – renamed "winter festivals" – survived on the islands, re-emerging in their full glory after Spain's return to democracy in 1975.

A candidate for the coveted title of "Carnival Queen"

Colourful procession in the streets of Santa Cruz de Tenerife

THE CARNIVAL QUEEN

The carnival begins with the election of its queen. Accompanied by colourful carnival crowds, the hopeful candidates arrive in front of the jury on their lavishly decorated floats.

The contestants are usually local beauties, but any girl may take part in the competition. The beauty and grace of the prospective queens are emphasized by their magnificent costumes. The queen's dress must be unique and command general admiration.

The newly elected queen, accompanied by her equally beautiful ladies-in-waiting, reigns over all the carnival festivities. Her float takes the place of honour in all the parades and the happy "sovereign" looks down from her throne, greeting her cheering carnival subjects as she passes by.

STREET PARADES

Each carnival has a different theme, which dictates the character of the street parades, the costumes worn by revellers and the choice of decorations. Street processions are held every day during the carnival.

Organized marchers are accompanied by floats with tableaux of historical or allegorical scenes. Although just for fun, a considerable amount of care goes into creating the music and costumes for the parades.

THE STAGE

Another essential element of each carnival is the stage, which is usually built in the town centre. A main venue for night-time revels, this is where the spectacular carnival shows are held each evening, the bands and acrobatic displays attracting huge crowds. Keenly fought competitions are held here, such as one for the best formation dancing team. Comedy shows also attract large audiences. The same stage provides a venue for classical concerts, including programmes of choral works.

Drag show on the stage in Las Palmas de Gran Canaria

CHILDREN

Carnival means fun and games for everyone, not just the adults – children also enjoy the festivities with many events just for them. They march in separate "small" parades and participate in their own stage shows and competitions. Little girls compete for the title of "Carnival Princess".

Children's costumes, made specially for the occasion, are often tiny masterpieces of dressmaking. They include traditional Spanish folk dresses, Brazilian samba costumes, fairy-tale and circus figures. Pint-sized participants, thrilled with the excitement and their roles, quickly enter into the spirit of carnival.

Children's dancing display, in colourful costumes

CARNIVAL COSTUMES AND MAKE-UP

It often takes months to make the extravagant costumes and masks and to design and construct the floats, so as soon as one carnival ends, the Canarios begin planning the next.

The general aim is always originality, and the ideas for carnival costumes are often unique. The shapes and forms of the outfits are inspired by many cultures, but one indispensable element is an unusual hair-style – the more extravagant the better.

Another important factor is the make-up, which often sets the theme and is an integral component of the costume. Carnival events often include exhibitions of the most unusual or spectacular body paintings.

DRAG QUEENS

Another notable feature of the Canary Islands' carnivals is the drag queens. Mixing with the masquerading crowds they are conspicuously tall as they walk on their high-heeled, platform shoes. At night-time, drag queens flaunt their costumes and demonstrate their dancing skills. The one judged most striking and beautiful becomes queen.

A Medusa costume, with equally lurid make-up

MASQUERADERS

In contrast with the carnival in Rio de Janeiro, where the main procession consists only of organized groups, in the Canary Islands almost everybody wears a mask and costume. Since the masquerade fever also affects tourists, the parade inevitably turns into a huge fancy-dress ball, with druids, pirates, samurai warriors and comedy figures, such as Charlie Chaplin or Disney cartoon characters, packing the streets and squares. The ever-popular game of pretending to be someone else creates a great sense of euphoria and encourages masqueraders to let their hair down and party.

THE BURIAL OF THE SARDINE

The Santa Cruz carnival ends with a grand funeral procession, called *El Entierro de la Sardina* (the burial of the sardine). This ritual is rooted in the past when carnival was the one occasion when people could deride such powerful institutions as the church. Today, crowds still dress up as clerical figures.

Carried at the head of the procession is an enormous papier-mâché sardine. The "mourners" wail and laugh as they escort the fish to the sea. Here it is set alight and hundreds of fireworks inside it create an explosive display.

Carnival reveller, dressed as a pirate

THE CANARY ISLANDS THROUGH THE YEAR

The inhabitants of the Canary Islands are deeply devoted to tradition – a fact that is reflected in the numerous religious feast days, or fiestas, that they celebrate. Some of these traditions go back to the time of the Guanches *(see pp30–31)*. Fiestas are normally associated with the cult of saints, and in particular with various patron saints. In agricultural areas, fiestas mark the end of the harvest. During

Tenerife 1996 carnival souvenir

the fiesta, people abandon their work to pray, dance and join colourful parades. Fiestas in the Canary Islands tend to last for several days, some for as long as two or three weeks. In the Islands' larger cities such fiestas are often accompanied by music, theatre and cinema festivals, and some have an international flavour. Of the other events on the islands, sporting events, and particularly *lucha canaria* and soccer, attract enormous crowds.

Flowering apple trees at the foot of Roque Nublo, Gran Canaria

SPRING

Although the year-round mild climate of the Canary Islands gives the impression of perpetual spring, true spring weather is most noticeable between March and May. Then the landscape is at its greenest. This is also the season of intense rainfall, particularly on Tenerife.

MARCH

Fiesta del Almendro en Flor *(early Mar)* all islands. The fiesta of almond blossom, is celebrated on a grand scale in the towns of Tejeda and Valsequillo, Gran Canaria.

There are displays of classic folk dancing, and almonds, wines and sweets are distributed by each village.
Rally El Corte Inglés *(Mar/Apr)*, Gran Canaria. Car rally attracting international competitors.
Semana Santa *(Mar/Apr)*, all islands. Holy Week, with a Good Friday procession.

APRIL

Fiesta de Juventud *(5 Apr)*, Lajita, Fuerteventura. Feast day of the Virgin Mary.
Fiesta de los Pastores *(25 Apr)*, La Dehesa, El Hierro. The annual feast of the island's shepherds.
Fiesta de Ansite *(29 Apr)*,

Bunch of ripe bananas

Gran Canaria. Music and dancing mark the final uprising of the Guanches against the Spanish and Spain's victory over the island.

MAY

Festival de Ballet y Danza *(May)*, Las Palmas de Gran Canaria. Concerts and dance performances.
Fiesta del Queso del Flor *(30 Apr–7 May)*, Santa María de Guía, Gran Canaria. Much eating of cheese in this small town famed for its production.
Feria del Caballo *(1 May)* in Valsequillo is an annual horse market.
Romería de San Isidro *(15 May)* in Uga, Lanzarote. Elaborate procession.

Traditional fiesta procession on El Hierro

AVERAGE DAILY HOURS OF SUNSHINE

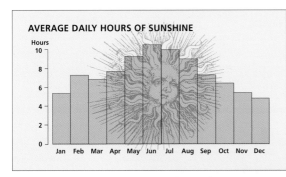

Hours

10

8

6

4

2

0

Jan Feb Mar Apr May Jun Jul Aug Sep Oct Nov Dec

Hours of Sunshine

The islands differ considerably in their daily hours of sunshine: Lanzarote and Fuerteventura enjoy about 12 hours of sunshine per day in August; northern parts of Tenerife and Gran Canaria can sometimes be cloudy, while the southern regions of the islands bask in sunshine.

SUMMER

In summer, temperatures in the islands can reach 35° C (95° F). During July and August, there is very little rainfall, except in the region of Las Palmas de Gran Canaria. In August, the crowds of foreign tourists are swollen by holidaymakers from the Spanish mainland. This is when most fiestas take place.

Crowded beaches of Puerto del Carmen, Lanzarote

Gathering cochineal insects on a prickly pear plantation

JUNE

Corpus Christi *(Jun)*, all islands. Celebrations include processions, and are at their most colourful in Las Palmas, Gran Canaria, and La Laguna, and La Orotava, Tenerife.
Festival Internacional de Música Popular *(Jun)*, Las Palmas. Folk music and dancing performed by both local and visiting groups.
Día de San Juan *(24 Jun)*, Las Palmas de Gran Canaria.

Commemorates the town's foundation with a big party.
Bajada de Nuestra Señora de las Nieves *(every 5 years, end Jun)*, Santa Cruz de la Palma. Amazing costumes, and a lavish procession at this important festival.
Día de San Pedro y San Pablo *(29 Jun)*, is the feast of St Peter and St Paul.

JULY

Bajada de la Virgen de los Reyes *(every 4 years, early Jul)*. El Hierro. A fabulous procession and party.
Festival Internacional Canarias Jazz & Mas Heineken *(three weeks in Jul)*, all islands. Jazz concerts by international musicians.
Fiesta de San Marcial del Rubicon *(one week in Jul)*, Femés and Yaiza. Celebrates Lanzarote's patron saint.
Día de San Buenaventura *(14 Jul)*, Bentacuria, Fuerteventura. The town's patron saint processes through the streets.
Fiesta del Carmen *(16 Jul)*, Gáldar, Gran Canaria. Party and procession in honour of

the patron saint of fishermen.
Día de Santiago Apóstol *(25 Jul)*, Santa Cruz, Tenerife. Celebrates Spain's patron saint and the town's defeat of the English and Nelson.

AUGUST

Bajada de la Rama *(4 Aug)*, Agaete, Gran Canaria. This colourful fiesta has its roots in the Guanches' rain dance.
Día de San Bartolomé *(24 Aug)*, in San Bartolomé, Lanzarote. Processions, music and dancing honour the saint.
Fiesta de San Ginés *(25 Aug)*, Arrecife, Lanzarote. Feast of St Gines, the patron saint of the town of Arrecife.

Bajada de Nuestra Señora de las Nieves, La Palma

AVERAGE MONTHLY RAINFALL

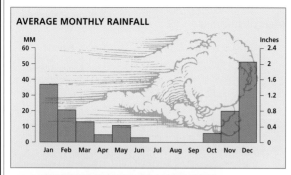

MM
60
50
40
30
20
10
0

Inches
2.4
2
1.6
1.2
0.8
0.4
0

Jan Feb Mar Apr May Jun Jul Aug Sep Oct Nov Dec

Rainfall
The average monthly rainfall in the Canary Islands rarely exceeds 50 mm (2 in). La Palma and La Gomera have the highest rainfall, Lanzarote and Fuerteventura the lowest. The rain is more frequent in Tenerife and Gran Canaria, particularly on the northern shores of the islands.

Fiesta of San Miguel Arcangel in Tuineje

AUTUMN

Autumn does not differ much from summer, except that high daytime temperatures give way to somewhat cooler nights. Large temperature differences may be felt at higher altitudes on Tenerife or Gran Canaria, where you can find yourself suddenly enveloped in fog, with a rapid drop in temperature.

SEPTEMBER

Encuentro Internacional Tres Continentes *(Sep)*, Agüimes, Gran Canaria. Exciting international theatre festival, with European, Latin American and African groups.
Columbus Week *(1–6 Sep)*, San Sebastián, La Gomera. Shows and processions celebrate Christopher Columbus.
Fiesta de la Virgen del Pino *(6–8 Sep)* Teror, Gran Canaria. The island's most important celebration includes an evening procession with offerings of

produce to the patron saint of Gran Canaria.
Fiesta del Charco *(7–11 Sep)*, San Nicolás, La Palma. Participants jump into a pool of salt water to catch fish.
Romería de Nuestra Señora de Los Dolores *(21 Sep)*, Lanzarote. A pilgrimage to the sanctuary of Los Dolores (St Mary of the Volcanoes), in Mancha Blanca.

Fishing, an all-year-round occupation in the Canary Islands

Fiesta de la Virgen de la Peña *(3rd Sat in Sep)*. Celebration of the patron saint of Fuerteventura.
Fiesta del Santísimo Cristo *(late Sep)* La Laguna, Tenerife. A spectacular fiesta featuring firework displays, a vintage car rally and *lucha canaria* tournaments.

OCTOBER

Bajada de la Virgen de Guadelupe *(5 Oct)*, La Gomera. Fishermen carry a statue of the Virgin Mary from Puntallana to San Sebastián by sea.
Fiesta de la Naval *(6 Oct)*, Las Palmas, Gran Canaria. Festival to celebrate victory over Sir Francis Drake.
Romería de Nuestra Señora de la Luz *(mid- Oct)*, Las Palmas, Gran Canaria. Procession of boats at sea celebrate the Virgin.
Festival Internacional de Cine de Las Palmas *(Oct–Nov)*, Gran Canaria. Film festival attracting many international movie stars.

NOVEMBER

International Ecological Film Festival Puerto de la Cruz, Tenerife. Shows films that are devoted mainly to the Canary Islands.
Feast of the Teide Volcano *(16 Nov)* Guía de Isora, Tenerife. Celebrates Spain's highest mountain.
Atlantic Rally for Cruisers *(last Sun in Nov)*, Gran Canaria. A transatlantic rally for yachts from Las Palmas to the Caribbean.

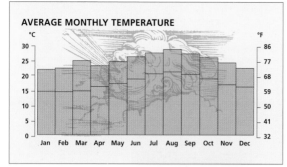

AVERAGE MONTHLY TEMPERATURE

Temperature
The chart shows the average minimum and maximum monthly temperature. The mild climate of the Canary Islands produces average temperatures of between 18° C (64° F) in the winter and 24° C (75° F) in the summer months.

WINTER

Many people decide to spend the winter months on the Canary Islands, not least because of the mild climate at this time of the year. For this reason, the height of the tourist season on the Canary Islands is from December to February. Although the peak of the Teide volcano is sometimes covered with snow, the coastal areas remain warm.

DECEMBER

Día de Santa Lucía *(13 Dec)*, Gran Canaria. Churches and villages are illuminated for this celebration.
Santos Inocentes *(28 Dec)*, all islands. This is the Spanish equivalent of April Fools' Day, when tricks are played.
Carrera de San Silvestre *(31 Dec)*, Maspalomas, Gran Canaria. This is the annual New Year's Eve run.
Noche Vieja *(31 Dec)* is the New Year's Eve celebration.

Gale-stricken ship listing off the coast of Lanzarote

JANUARY

Festival de Música de Canarias *(Jan/Mar)*, most islands. Classical music concerts with international orchestra and soloists.
Soccer Tournament *(Jan/Feb)*, Maspalomas, Gran Canaria. For European clubs.
Día de los Reyes *(6 Jan)*, all islands. The three kings throw sweets to the children at this Epiphany celebration with colourful processions.

FEBRUARY

Festival de Opera *(Feb/Mar)* most islands. An international opera festival held principally in Las Palmas' Teatro Pérez Galdós and Tenerife's Teatro Guimerá.
Carnival *(Feb/Mar)*, all islands. Several weeks of partying and masquerades commence with the election of the carnival queen.
Romería de la Virgen de Candelaria *(2 Feb and 15 Aug)*, Candelaria, Tenerife. Candlemas. The Feast of the Virgin Mary, the patron saint of the islands, is celebrated in style to commemorate the day on which the Virgin appeared to the Guanches.

PUBLIC HOLIDAYS

Año Nuevo New Year's Day (1 Jan)
Día de los Reyes Epiphany (6 Jan)
Jueves Santo Maundy Thursday (Mar/Apr)
Viernes Santo Good Friday (Mar/Apr)
Día de Pascua Easter (Mar/Apr)
Fiesta de Trabajo Labour Day (1 May)
Día de las Islas Canarias Canary Islands Day (30 May)
Corpus Christi (early Jun)
Asunción Assumption of the Virgin Mary (15 Aug)
Día de la Hispanidad National Day (12 Oct)
Todos los Santos All Saints' Day (1 Nov)
Día de la Constitución Day of the Constitution (6 Dec)
Inmaculada Concepción (8 Dec)
Navidad Christmas (25 Dec)

Drag queen in procession during carnival

THE HISTORY OF THE CANARY ISLANDS

The early history of the Canary Islands is shrouded in myth and legend. Some believed the islands to be the lost land of Atlantis, which, according to Plato, was destroyed by an earthquake. To others they were known as the Fortunate Islands, poised at the edge of the world, whose inhabitants knew no sorrow.

It is believed that the first inhabitants of the Canary Islands came from North Africa, and probably arrived here around 3,000 BC. Although scholars disagree about the origins of the islands' early dwellers, one prominent theory is that they were Neolithic people from the Cro-Magnon era. Typically they were tall and well-built with narrow skulls.

Around the second century BC, the islands became populated by the next wave of arrivals – the Guanches. Their origins have also not been clearly established. It is believed that prior to the conquest of the islands by Spain in the 15th century, the Guanche population of the islands consisted of some 30,000 in Gran Canaria and Tenerife, over 4,000 in La Palma, over 1,000 in El Hierro and a few hundred in Fuerteventura and Lanzarote.

The ancients knew about the islands: their sailors used to visit them and information about the archipelago can be found in the writings of Roman historians. In AD 150, a fairly accurate map by the

Idol from Tara – a statuette from the time of the Guanches

Egyptian geographer, Ptolemy, represented the islands as the edge of the world. Following the fall of the Roman Empire, Europe forgot the Canaries for over 1,000 years.

CONQUEST OF THE CANARY ISLANDS

The Canary Islands were rediscovered by Mediterranean sailors. In 1312, Captain Lanzarotto (or Lancelotto) Malocello, a native of Genoa, reached the furthest north-east island, where he encountered the native population, the Guanches. The island was subsequently named after him – Lanzarote.

Throughout the 14th century, Italians, Portuguese and Catalans sent their ships to the islands to bring back slaves and furs.

The rapid process of the islands' conquest began in 1402, when the Norman knight, Jean de Béthencourt, arrived in Lanzarote. Two years later, he returned with the backing of the Castilian crown. Encountering little resistance, the conquistadors took over the sparsely populated islands of El Hierro, La Gomera and Fuerteventura.

TIMELINE

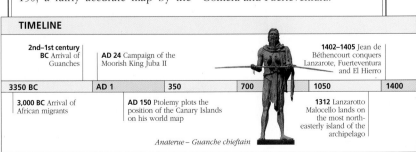

2nd–1st century BC Arrival of Guanches

AD 24 Campaign of the Moorish King Juba II

1402–1405 Jean de Béthencourt conquers Lanzarote, Fuerteventura and El Hierro

| 3350 BC | AD 1 | 350 | 700 | 1050 | 1400 |

3,000 BC Arrival of African migrants

AD 150 Ptolemy plots the position of the Canary Islands on his world map

1312 Lanzarotto Malocello lands on the most north-easterly island of the archipelago

Anaterue – Guanche chieftain

◁ **Christopher Columbus, discoverer of the Americas**

The Guanches

Guanche clay pot

The ancient inhabitants of the Canary Islands were known as the Guanches from the words "guan", (meaning "man") and "che", (meaning "white mountain"), referring to the snow-capped Teide volcano on Tenerife. According to Spanish historical records, the Guanches were tall, strongly built, blue-eyed and blond-haired. Their origins and date of arrival on the islands are still unknown, as is the language they spoke. Their society was based on a tribal structure, with a king or chieftain at its head. They worshipped Abor – a powerful god who could bring rain and stop the flow of lava. Their tools and weapons were produced from roughly cut wood, stone and bone.

Rock Carvings
These rock carvings, many of which have been pre-served, once adorned caves inhabited by the Guanches.

Guanche family in their cave

Rock Paintings
Cave paintings bear testimony to the artistic skill of the Guanches. Cueva Pintada, near Gáldar on Gran Canaria, is decorated with striking red, white and black geometric patterns.

Quern
The Guanches used querns (mills) made from lava to grind barley, to make their staple, a porridge known as gofio.

DAILY LIFE OF THE GUANCHES
One of three small mosaics in the town park in Santa Cruz de Tenerife illustrates the life of the Guanche tribe during peacetime. In a landscape and climate similar to that of the present day, the Guanches cultivated land and raised animals.

Cave Dwelling
The Guanches lived in natural caves, such as Cueva de Belmaco, or in grottos carved into the rocks. Caves also served as granaries and as places of worship, and were also used to bury the dead.

Domestic Animals
Goats and sheep are the only animals that can find food in the hard mountainous terrain of the Canary Islands. The Guanches depended on these animals to supply them with skins, milk and meat.

Shepherds fought daily battles for better grazing grounds for their flocks of sheep and goats. In the face of external dangers, they would unite and become warriors.

Guanche Chief
Guanches were led into battles by their tribal kings, known as "guanarteme" in Gran Canaria and as "menceyes" in Tenerife and La Palma.

CHES Y VALLE DE OROTAVA

Long, strong poles or spears were used as weapons in battles and were also useful when traversing the difficult mountainous terrain.

REMAINS OF THE GUANCHE CULTURE

Apart from the caves, the early indiginous population lived in somewhat primitive, low huts built of stone, such as those that have been partially reconstructed in the ethnographic park Mundo Aborigen, in Gran Canaria. The bodies of the tribal elders were mummified, and you can see them today in Canary museums, along with stone and bone ornaments, clay pots and woven bags.

The mummified skull *of a Guanche is one of many such items housed in the Museo de la Naturaleza y el Hombre, located in Tenerife.*

Circular Guanche tombs in Mundo Aborigen

Founding of Santa Cruz de Tenerife

THE 15TH CENTURY

The Portuguese followed in the foot-steps of the Spanish conquistadors in the mid-15th century. The rivalry between the two seafaring powers lasted until 1479, when the Alcáçovas Treaty gave the Canary Islands to Spain, who, in return, let Portugal annex the Azores, the Cape Verde Islands and Madeira.

Mosaic depicting the ship of Christopher Columbus

The following years brought a new wave of bloody conquests: 1483 saw the fall of Gran Canaria, followed five years later by La Gomera and, in 1496, La Palma. In 1495, following three years of intense battles, Tenerife, which had put up the fiercest resistance, fell into the hands of the Spanish. The Guanches, deprived of their land and forced into slavery, were soon dying out. Those who survived were forcibly converted to Christianity and became assimilated.

In 1541, Girolamo Benzoni, an Italian visiting the islands, noted that the Guanches were "nearly extinct" and that their language had not survived the century following their subjugation by Spain.

THE SUGAR ERA

The 16th century brought about a rapid growth in the numbers of European settlers on the islands, particularly in Gran Canaria and Tenerife. Sugar cane, imported from Madeira, was used to produce sugar, which quickly became the main export from each island. Large sugar-cane plantations sprang up, employing European workers and African slaves, despite the ban on the slave trade introduced by Spain in 1537. This industry resulted in the transformation of the local ecosystem. Stripped of their trees, forests gave way to sugar-cane fields and bare slopes became prone to erosion.

The growth of the sugar industry was halted by the colonization of America and the Caribbean where sugar could be produced more cheaply.

Castillo San Miguel, guarding Garachico against pirates

TIMELINE

1478–1483 The Spanish, led by Juan Rejón and Pedro de Vera, occupy Gran Canaria

1494–1496 Occupation of Tenerife by Alonso Fernández de Lugo completes the conquest of the archipelago

1537 The Spanish introduce a ban on the slave trade, which is not observed in the Canary Islands

1450	1500	1550	1600

1479 The Alcáçovas Treaty gives the Canary Islands to Spain

Christopher Columbus stopped in the Canary Islands to provision his ships

1590 *Descripción de las Islas Canarias*, by Leonardo Torriani

THE WINE TRADE

The Canary Islands' economy was saved by the growing export demand for wine, which was produced mainly in Tenerife and Gran Canaria. So popular was the local *vino seco* that it was praised by the character Falstaff in Shakespeare's play, Henry IV part II. The Canary Islands' Company was founded in 1665 in London, and came to monopolize the Canary wine trade in Great Britain.

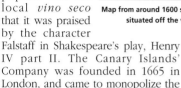

Map from around 1600 showing the Canary Islands situated off the west coast of Africa

At the turn of the 18th century, however, income from wine production fell drastically. One of the reasons was a plague of locusts from 1685 to 1687 that destroyed the vineyards. In addition, the emergence of competition from new brands of wine from Madeira and Málaga, and the War of the Spanish Succession, which Spain fought with England and Portugal, reduced the demand.

The closing years of the 18th century witnessed a further reduction in wine production and export. This led to the near total collapse of the economy on the islands. It was at this time that carmine – a natural dye obtained from cochineal insects – became a major export. To this day the islands are major exporters of cochineal, used to produce dye for the food industry.

THE ISLANDS UNDER ATTACK

Spanish rule of the Canary Islands was threatened almost from the start. Throughout the 16th and 17th centuries, pirates and slave traders, from Europe and the northwest coast of Africa, harassed the islands. Several castles were built during this period to defend port entries from French, Dutch and British fleets; they also provided shelter for the local population when under attack. The last attempt at conquering the Canary Islands was made in 1797 by Admiral Horatio Nelson, who launched an attack on Santa Cruz de Tenerife. He not only failed to take the town, but lost his arm in the battle. The Governor of Santa Cruz, in a truly magnanimous gesture, presented the vanquished enemy with some of the local wine.

Ornate Baroque altar from the church, Iglesia de Nuestra Señora de la Regla, in Pájara, Fuerteventura

1665 Establishment of the Canary Islands' Company, in London

British fleet attacking San Sebastián de la Gomera

1797 British fleet, commanded by Admiral Horatio Nelson, attacks Santa Cruz de Tenerife

1650	1700	1750	1800

1666 Peasants destroy English *bodegas* in Garachico

1706 Garachico destroyed by the eruption of Volcán Negra

1744 Benedict XIV permits Augustine monks to establish a university in La Laguna

El Tigre gun from Santa Cruz de Tenerife

19TH CENTURY ISLAND RIVALRIES

In 1821, the Canary Islands became a province of Spain, with its capital in Santa Cruz de Tenerife. This situation served to intensify the rivalry between the two most populated islands –

Casa de la Coroneles, seat of the Colonels who ruled Fuerteventura

Tenerife and Gran Canaria. In 1852, Queen Isabella II granted duty-free status to the Canary Islands.

In view of the growing domination of Tenerife in 1911, local rule was re-established on individual islands, thus weakening the control that Santa Cruz de Tenerife exercised over the whole archipelago. In 1927, the rivalry between Santa Cruz de Tenerife and Las Palmas de Gran Canaria led to the division of the archipelago into two provinces: the western province including the islands of

Manuel Velásquez Cabrera – fighter for Canary autonomy

Elected representatives of the first provincial government of Tenerife, in 1912

Tenerife, La Gomera, La Palma and El Hierro, and the eastern province including Gran Canaria, Fuerteventura and Lanzarote. This division remains in force to this day.

THE BANANA TRADE

The collapse of cochineal production in the 1870s led to a period of mass emigration of Canarios to Latin America. The archipelago's economy was saved by bananas, which at that time became the main export product. Their cultivation on an industrial scale was introduced by the French Consul, S. Berthelot, in 1855. Production peaked in 1913, when more than 3 million bunches of bananas were exported from Tenerife, Gran Canaria and La Palma.

The outbreak of World War I and the Allied blockade of the European continent ruined international trade, and banana exports dropped by more than 80 per cent. The ensuing harsh economic conditions resulted in a second wave of emigration.

THE FRANCO ERA

The proclamation of the Second Spanish Republic in Madrid, in 1931, led to increased tension. In 1936, fearing a coup d'état, the Republican government

TIMELINE

1852 Queen Isabella II proclaims the Canary Islands a free-trade zone

1882 Works commence on the construction of Las Palmas harbour (Puerto de la Luz)

1927 Division of the archipelago into two provinces

1850	1870	1890	1910	1930

1821 The Canary Islands proclaimed a province of Spain, with its capital in Santa Cruz de Tenerife

Emigrants Monument

1888 First steamer ferry service begins between the islands

1912 Formation of the first island-by island provincial government

1930 Building of an airport in Gran Canaria

"exiled" General Francisco Franco, a hero of the Moroccan wars, to Tenerife. In July 1936, Franco seized control of the islands, marking the beginning of the Spanish Civil War, which lasted until 1939. Franco's Spain was ostracized by the international community. This hampered economic development in the Canary Islands, and resulted in yet more inhabitants emigrating during the 1950s. Opening the borders to sun-seeking European tourists in the 1960s failed to improve the situation. Growing resistance to Franco fed on the fertile ground of revived Canary nationalism. The MPAIC movement, founded in 1963, became the vehicle of the islands' drive for independence. In the late 1970s, companies and military establishments on the Spanish mainland became targets for terrorist attacks by the nationalists.

General Francisco Franco, the ruler of Spain until 1975

THE CANARY ISLANDS TODAY

Changes following Franco's death in 1975 brought about the devolution of power in Spain and, in August 1982, the Canary Islands were granted autonomy. Local authorities are now in control of education, health services, and transport, leaving matters of defence, foreign policy and finances in the hands of the central government. In 1986, Spain became a member of the European Union (EU).

Today, tourism and related services account for some 80 per cent of the islands' revenue. However, on the smaller islands the economy still relies on agriculture and fishing. High unemployment and low wages continue to create problems. These, along with the need to protect the environment, present the greatest challenge to today's provincial authorities.

Golden beaches of Maspalomas, crowded with tourists

Mass tourism begins to develop in the 1960s

1986 Entry of Spain and the Canary Islands into the EU

2007 The Great Canary Telescope begins monitoring the stars

1950	1970	1990	2010	2030

1936 General Franco seizes control of the Canary Islands, leading to the outbreak of the Spanish Civil War

1982 The Canary Islands become an autonomous region of Spain

1992 Artist and architect César Manrique dies in a car crash *(see p85)*

Colourful carnival is the most popular fiesta on the islands

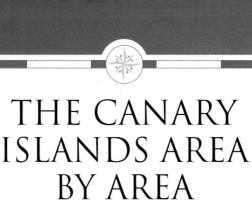

THE CANARY ISLANDS AREA BY AREA

The Canary Islands at a Glance

The Canary Islands are diverse enough to cater for all tastes, from the individual traveller to groups on package holidays. Those who shy away from the noisy modern resorts of Tenerife and Gran Canaria can find repose in the islands' interior. Fuerteventura can be recommended to admirers of beautiful windswept beaches, while Lanzarote offers a lunar landscape, spotted with craters and featuring curious architectural edifices built by the most famous Canary artist – César Manrique. The wild, lush island of La Gomera and the perpetually green La Palma provide a paradise for hikers. El Hierro attracts lovers of nature, regional cuisine and handicrafts.

Pico del Teide (see pp118–19), *the highest mountain in Spain and an active volcano, is one of few places on the Canary Islands where snow can sometimes be seen.*

In Santa Cruz de la Palma (see pp144–5) *stands a replica of the* Santa Maria, *the ship in which Christopher Columbus "discovered" the Americas.*

LA PALMA
(see pp140–51)

TENERIFE
(see pp96–121)

LA GOMERA
(see pp122–31)

EL HIERRO
(see pp132–39)

Hermigua (see p126), *nestles in a beautiful ravine, with steep slopes covered by the picturesque terraces of a banana plantation.*

El Sabinar (see p137), *a remote point on El Hierro, is named after the ancient juniper trees that grow here, twisted into strange shapes by ceaseless winds.*

| 0 km | 30 |
| 0 miles | 50 |

◁ **Yachts in Puerto Rico marina, Gran Canaria**

Haria (see p88), a small town lying in a valley, is reminiscent of a Saharan oasis with its low, whitewashed houses shaded by palm trees, acacias and rubber plants.

Goats are the most frequently encountered animals in Fuerteventura. Unsurprisingly, they are a symbol of the island.

LANZAROTE
(see pp80–95)

Orchids, in a host of fabulous colours, along with numerous species of exotic birds and butterflies from all over the world, attract tourists to Palmitos Parque (see p61).

FUERTEVENTURA
(see pp66–79)

GRAN CANARIA
(see pp40–65)

Ibis, a wading bird with a long, sabre-like beak, is one of the main attractions of Guinate Tropical Parque (see p88), one of many theme parks to be found throughout the larger islands.

Puerto Rico (see p60) is a modern resort on the south coast of Gran Canaria, offering facilities for all kinds of water sports and fishing and diving trips.

GRAN CANARIA

*L*ying at the heart of the archipelago and occupying an area of 1,533 sq km (599 sq miles), Gran Canaria is the third largest of the Canary Islands. It is one of the most densely populated islands, with 805,000 inhabitants – more than one third of the entire population of the archipelago. It is also the one of the most popular islands, attracting some 2.5 million visitors each year.

The centre of Gran Canaria is occupied by the rocky volcano summit of Pico de las Nieves *(see pp62–3).* The mountain sides, sloping towards the ocean, are criss-crossed by deep canyons.

The island is divided by a mountain range into two climatic zones. The northern part is more humid and fertile, with long stretches of banana plantations running along the coast, while the southern part is dry and hot.

Farmer with his donkey

The island's landscape displays similar diversity, with the northern and western coasts steep and rocky, and the eastern and southern slopes falling gently towards the sea. This diversity has given Gran Canaria the nickname of a "miniature continent".

Gran Canaria enjoys a mild climate throughout the year, with an average air temperature of 21° C (70° F). Water temperature, however, is somewhat lower than average for these latitudes, due to a cool current flowing from the Gulf of Mexico.

The island was conquered between 1478 and 1483 by the Spanish, led by Pedro de Vera, and fully colonized during the 1520s. Today it offers a multitude of tourist attractions. Las Palmas has museums and historic buildings alongside its own beach, the Playa de las Canteras, with its nightclubs, cafés and shops. In contrast, in the rugged environs of Pico de las Nieves hikers can follow the trails of the Guanches' culture.

Stage in a square in Puerto de Mogán

◁ **Tourists on the dunes around Maspalomas**

Exploring Gran Canaria

Gran Canaria is the second most frequently visited island of the archipelago (after Tenerife). Each year it receives over 2.5 million visitors, who are attracted by its fine scenery, consistently mild climate and numerous tourist attractions. The island's capital, Las Palmas, is situated in the northeast; it has a fascinating history *(see pp29–35)*, and its colonial past is reflected in its delightful old town and many museums. Sun-seekers favour the warmer, southern parts of the island, where sunshine is guaranteed all year round. Maspalomas is one of the largest, purpose-built tourist developments in Spain. At its heart is Playa del Inglés with its vast hotels, restaurants, bars, discotheques and, above all, golden sandy beaches.

LOCATOR MAP

GETTING THERE

Gran Canaria has scheduled flight connections with all the islands in the archipelago, and with mainland Spain, as well as charter flights from many European cities. There are regular ferries to Tenerife, Lanzarote and Fuerteventura. Gran Canaria has a good network of bus routes, but to reach some of the villages, particularly those at the centre of the island, you will need to hire a car. Most of the island's roads, major and minor, are well surfaced.

SEE ALSO

• *Where to Stay* pp156–8
• *Where to Eat* pp171–3

ATLANTIC OCEAN

SANTA CRUZ DE TENERIFE

LAS PALMAS DE GRAN CANARIA

Túmulo de la Guancha

Sardina

GÁLDAR ⓫

Cenobio de Valerón ⓾

SANTA MARÍA DE GUÍA DE GRAN CANARIA

Puerto de las Nieves

⓬ AGAETE

San Pedro

Fagajesto

El Risco

Tamadaba 1444m

Pinos de Gáldar 1377m

Parque Natural de Tamadaba

Mirador del Balcón

Acusa

Artenara

PICO

Puerto de la Aldea

Roque Bentaiga 1412m

Tejeda

LA ALDEA DE SAN NICOLÁS ⓭

Roque Nublo 1760m

El Juncal

Ayacata

Montaña de Sándara 1570m

Tasartico

Tasarte

Parque Rural del Nublo

Embalse de Soriá

Embalse de Chira

Las Casas de Veneguera

Mogán

Parque Natural de Pilancones

Playa de Tasarte

Lomo Central

Playa de Veneguera

Las Burrillas

El Sao

Palmitos Parque

PUERTO DE MOGÁN ⓮

Taurito

Monataña de la Data

PUERTO RICO ⓯

Arguineguín

Walking trail in the mountainous region of Presa de los Hornos, near Pico de las Nieves

KEY

▬▬	Motorway
▬	Major road
═	Minor road
▬	Scenic route
△	Summit

Village of Sardina, on the coast near Gáldar

SIGHTS AT A GLANCE

Agaete **12**
Agüimes **20**
Arucas **7**
Barranco de Guayadeque **22**
Caldera de Bandama **3**
Firgas **8**
Gáldar **11**
Ingenio **21**
La Aldea de San Nicolás **13**
Las Palmas de Gran Canaria pp44–51 **1**
Maspalomas **16**
Moya **9**
Puerto de Mogán **14**
Puerto Rico **15**
San Bartolomé de Tirajana **17**
Santa Brígida **4**
Santa Lucía **19**
Santa María de Guía de Gran Canaria **10**
Tafira Alta **2**
Telde **23**
Teror **6**
Vega de San Mateo **5**

Tours

Around Pico de las Nieves pp62–63 **18**

Orchids in Palmitos Parque, near Maspalomas

Las Palmas de Gran Canaria ●

Las Palmas town crest

The largest town of the archipelago, Las Palmas was founded on 24 June 1478 by the Spanish conquistadors. It soon became an important port for ships sailing around the African continent and heading for America. In the late 19th century, Sir Alfred Lewis Jones founded the Gran Canaria Coal Company here and the town began to flourish. The port became the main stopping point on the transatlantic route and a new town sprang up around it. In 1927, Las Palmas became the capital of the eastern province of the Canary Islands, encompassing Gran Canaria, Fuerteventura and Lanzarote.

The pretty marina in Las Palmas harbour

SIGHTS AT A GLANCE

CAAM ⑮
Casa Colon ⑬
Casa Museo Perez Galdos ⑪
Castillo de la Luz ①
Catedral de Santa Ana ⑭
Harbour ②
Hotel Santa Catalina ⑧
Muelle de Santa Catalina ⑤
Museo Canario ⑯
Museo Nestor ⑨
Parque Doramas ⑦
Parque Santa Catalina ④
Parque San Telmo ⑩
Playa de las Alcaravaneras ⑥
Playa de las Canteras ③
Teatro Perez Galdos ⑫

0 m   800
0 yards   800

Exploring La Isleta and Playa de las Canteras

Situated on a small, round peninsula, La Isleta is a residential quarter built on steep terrain, featuring narrow streets and renowned for its small local shops, bars and street vendors offering dried fish. The peninsula is separated from the modern part of Las Palmas by a narrow inlet.

Playa de las Canteras is a mixed district of hotels and offices. Scores of hotels and shops line the seaside promenade, Paseo de las Canteras, where there are also a great many bars and restaurants. This district has one of the town's biggest shopping centres – Las Arenas.

♠ Castillo de la Luz

C/Juan Rejón, s/n. **Tel** 928 464 757. ⬜ *10am–1pm, 6–9pm Mon–Fri; 10am–2pm Sat–Sun.* ⬛ *between exhibitions.*

On the south shore of La Isleta, near the harbour, stands Castillo de la Luz – the Castle of Light. This well-preserved fortress dates from the 16th-century, and was built to guard the town of Las Palmas against

pirates. It was restored in 1990, and is now used as a venue for art exhibitions.

⚓ Harbour

Las Palmas harbour boasts a long and glorious history and is an important factor in the prosperity of Gran Canaria. Around 1,000 ships use the harbour each month. The traffic was even heavier when the Canary Islands enjoyed duty-free status and the harbour was one of the most important in the world. The harbour area includes a marina, which is the starting

point for the annual Canary Islands to Barbados race.

⛱ Playa de Las Canteras

This stretch of yellowish-brown sand is almost 4 km (3 miles) long and in places 100 metres (300 yds) wide. This is the best beach in Las Palmas. It is well-served by cafés and restaurants. La Barra, a natural rock barrier protecting the beach against strong surf, makes bathing possible, even in rough conditions.

The long and sandy Playa de las Canteras

1. Castillo de la Luz
2. Harbour

Muelle del Sanapú

Muelle Pesquero

Muelle Grande

Muelle de León y Castillo

5. Muelle de Santa Catalina

Parque Santa Catalina

Base Naval

6. Playa de las Alcaravaneras

Muelle Deportivo

7. Parque Doramas

8.
9. seo Néstor

Pueblo Canario

Bus station
10. Parque San Telmo

Castillo de Mata

Casa Museo Pérez Galdós 11.

12. Teatro Pérez Galdós

Catedral de Santa Ana 14. 13. Casa de Colón

15. CAAM

16. Museo Canario

Key to Symbols *see back flap*

Colourful fun at the Santa Catalina Park carnival

Exploring Santa Catalina

The narrow streets of this district are filled with Indian shops, offering electronic goods, alcohol, tobacco products, jewellery and clothes. Shopping here is not quite as profitable these days, but it is still acceptable to haggle and get some bargains.

Santa Catalina has many hotels, most of which seem to face north, towards the long, golden sands of the popular Las Canteras beach.

🍀 Parque Santa Catalina

At the heart of the district is Santa Catalina Park, which has played an important role in the development of the town's mass tourism. During the 1960s it was the most popular meeting place for visitors to Las Palmas. Today the park is the centre of the city's nightlife, with numerous restaurants, bars, clubs and discotheques filled until the small hours by fun-loving guests. Horse-

drawn cabs line up in the park, ready to serve as taxis or take tourists on a sightseeing tour. There is also a tourist information office here.

At carnival time, a large stage is erected here and Santa Catalina Park becomes the focal point in Las Palmas for this great celebration.

⛴ Muelle Santa Catalina

On the south side of Avenida Marítima del Norte is the ferry terminal, which provides ferry and hydrofoil services to Tenerife and the other islands. This modern building can be seen from far away.

🏖 Playa de Alcaravaneras

South of the ferry terminal, within the district of Alcaravaneras, is the 1 km (0.5 mile) golden sand Alcaravaneras beach. This is the second longest of the Las Palmas beaches, after Las Canteras. The modern yacht marina of the **Real Club Náutico**, south of the beach, is packed with glamorous ocean-going boats.

Sunbathers on the golden sand at Playa de las Alcaravaneras

The exclusive Hotel Santa Catalina, in Ciudad Jardín

Exploring Ciudad Jardín

Ciudad Jardín is an oasis of peace in the bustling city of Las Palmas. This leafy residential district was created in the early 20th century by British residents, who dominated the economic life of the town at that time.

This "Garden Town", with its regular layout, now has many embassies and beautiful houses set in small buildings. These buildings display a variety of architectural styles. The district's main feature is the large Parque Doramas with its interesting statues.

♣ Parque Doramas

This beautifully landscaped park, featuring water cascades and a municipal swimming pool, is named after the Guanche chieftain Doramas, who, in the late 15th century, put up a fierce resistance to the Spanish invaders. His struggles are symbolized by the monument depicting Guanches tumbling over a precipice to escape capture.

⌗ Hotel Santa Catalina

C/Leon y Castillo, 227.
Tel 928 243 040. **Fax** 928 242 764.
www.hotelsantacatalina.com
Set among the sub-tropical greenery of the Parque Doramas stands the Santa Catalina Hotel. Originally built in 1890 for the British employees of the Grand Canary Island Company (see p33), the building was redesigned by Canary artist Néstor Martin Fernandez de la Torre (see below) between 1947 and 1952. Lovely views of the park can be enjoyed by non-resident visitors from the bar.

⌂ Museo Néstor

Pueblo Canario. **Tel** 928 245 135.
www.museonestor.com
◯ 10am–8pm Tue–Sat;
10:30am–2:30pm Sun, public holidays.

Opened in 1958, the museum exhibits works by Néstor, including sketches and erotic and symbolic paintings. One of the museum's highlights is the dome of the rotunda, which is decorated with eight murals illustrating Torre's *Poema del Mar* (Sea Poem).

Exploring in Triana

To the north of the motorway that encloses the area of La Vegueta lies Triana – the commercial district of town, marked to the north by **Bravo Murillo** street along which runs the old city wall. The street leads to the ruins of the old castle – **Castillo de Mata**. The centre of this regularly shaped area is cut across by the Boulevard **Calle Mayor de Triana**. The ground floors of its Modernist houses are occupied by shops. The bust of Christopher Columbus, unveiled in 1892, is one of many landmarks symbolizing the town's links with great geographic discoveries.

Tiled café in the Modernist kiosk in Parque San Telmo

♣ Parque San Telmo

San Telmo Park is reached via the **Calle Mayor Triana** Passage. At the edge of the park stands the small, 17th-century **San Telmo Chapel**, devoted to this patron saint of fishermen. On the opposite side is a Modernist **kiosk**, built in 1923 and decorated with ceramic tiles. Standing on the side of the park is the **Gobierno Militar** building where, on 18 July 1936, General Franco declared his opposition to the Republican government, signalling the start of the Spanish Civil War.

NÉSTOR MARTÍN FERNÁNDEZ DE LA TORRE

Néstor Martín Fernández de la Torre (1887–1938) was one of the most original artists to come from the Canary Islands.

Painting by Néstor in Museo Néstor (see above)

Born in Las Palmas, he studied in Paris where he became familiar with the work of Pre-Raphaelite, Symbolist and Secessionist artists. In 1910, he represented Spain in the World Exhibition in Brussels. He produced paintings, stage designs, theatre and opera costumes and interior designs, but was known principally for his murals. In 1934, he settled permanently in Gran Canaria, and devoted the last years of his life to developing and publicizing Canary art forms.

🏛 Casa Museo Pérez Galdós

C/Cano, 2. **Tel** *928 366 976.* ⭘
10am–2pm, 4–8pm Tue–Sat.
www.casamuseoperezgaldos.com

The Museum of Benito Pérez Galdós, the most distinguished writer from the Canary Islands, occupies the house in which he was born and where he lived until 1862. This five-storey building has a small patio adorned with a statue of the writer. The museum, which opened in 1964, still has the original interior décor. It contains objects associated with the writer's life, as well as photographs of many actors who appeared in his plays.

📽 Teatro Pérez Galdós

C/Lentini, 1. **Tel** *928 433 805.*

In the south of Triana, almost opposite Mercado Público, stands a theatre named after the respected writer Benito Pérez Galdós (1843–1920).

Built in 1919, this structure is the work of Miguel Martín Fernández de la Torre. The opulent interior decorations and the auditorium for 1,400 spectators were designed by his brother, Néstor Martín Fernández de la Torre. Today this is the best theatre in Las Palmas and one of the best in the Canary Islands.

Exploring La Vegueta

La Vegueta, the oldest district of Las Palmas, consists of a labyrinth of narrow streets, lined with historic houses with wooden balconies and beautiful patios. Equally

Patio of Casa Museo Pérez Galdós in Triana, with the writer's statue

charming are the old town squares, including **Plaza de Santo Domingo**.

Right at the edge of the district are large market halls selling a variety of goods, including fruit, fish, meat, cheeses, and local handicrafts.

⛪ Catedral de Santa Ana

Plaza Santa Ana.

The building of the cathedral began in 1497 and took 400 years to complete. The lengthy gestation affected both its architectural form and interior furnishings.

The Neo-Classical façade hides Gothic vaults resting on slender columns, altar retables, Baroque pulpits and sculptures by José Luján Pérez. The crypt contains the tomb of José de Viera y Clavijo, Canary traveller and the author of *Noticias de la Historia General de Canarias*. Another chapel is the resting place of diplomat Fernando de León y Castillo *(see p65).*

A lift in the south tower whisks visitors to the high viewing terrace, which offers outstanding views of the town and harbour.

🏛 Centro Atlántico de Arte Moderno (CAAM)

Los Balcones, 8–10.
Tel *902 311 824.* ⭘ *10am–9pm Tue–Sat; 10am–2pm Sun.* 📷

CAAM organizes exhibitions, mainly of avant-garde art. It also has its own collection of works by artists influential in shaping 20th-century Canary art. CAAM provides a venue for academic symposia on the subject of modern art and has an extensive library. In contrast to the 18th-century façade of this former hotel, the modern interior, designed by Francisco Sainz de Oiza and Martín Chirino, is light and airy.

🏛 Museo Canario

C/Dr Verneau, 2. **Tel** *928 336 800.*
⭘ *10am–8pm Mon–Fri; 10am–2pm Sat–Sun.* 📷
www.elmuseocanario.com

The Canary Islands' Museum was opened in 1879. A refurbishment carried out in the mid-1980s has transformed it into a modern establishment.

The collection includes such archaeological finds as statuettes of gods, pottery, jewellery and tools of the Guanches, as well as skulls, skeletons and mummies. The displays, which are diverse, also include models of historic houses. Among the star attractions are copies of the paintings discovered in Cueva Pintada de Gáldar, as well as *pintaderas* – terracotta "stamps" used for printing geometric patterns on clothes.

Façade of the cathedral of Santa Ana

Casa de Colón

In the oldest district of Las Palmas stands the palace of
the first governors of the island. According to tradition,
Christopher Columbus stayed here in 1492 during a break
in his voyage while one of his ships was repaired,
hence the name Casa de Colón, or Columbus House.
This charming building, with its beautiful wooden
balconies, was rebuilt in 1777. Since 1952 it has
housed a museum that includes models and artifacts
relating to voyages made by the famous navigator.

Ship's Interior
*A reconstructed, full-
size fragment of the
interior of La Niña,
one of the ships that
sailed with Columbus's
expedition, demon-
strates the living
conditions that sailors
endured while
crossing the oceans.*

Santa Maria
*Models of the three ships from
Columbus's fleet (Santa Maria, La Niña,
La Pinta), and navigation instruments,
illustrate the equipment available to
mariners in the early 16th century.*

Ground floor

Main entrance

Astrolabe
*One of the early naviga-
tional instruments, the
astrolabe was developed in
the 2nd century BC. It
was used to measure
the height of
heavenly bodies
above the horizon.
The collection here
includes a bronze
astrolabe from the first
half of the 16th century.*

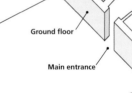

KEY

☐	Ecuadorian art
☐	Mexican culture
☐	Yanomami culture
☐	Marine charts and navigational instruments
☐	Columbus and his voyages
☐	Canary Islands and discovery of America
☐	Las Palmas de Gran Canaria
☐	Gran Canaria
☐	16th–20th century painting

GALLERY GUIDE
*The exhibits are arranged on three levels, in 12 rooms
surrounding two inner courtyards and in underground
chambers. The underground chambers contain treasures of
pre-Columbian art. The ground floor is given to Columbus's
expeditions, the development of cartography and the history of
the Canary Islands as the gateway to the New World. The first-
floor rooms present an overview of Las Palmas history, from
the 15th until the 19th century. There are also separate rooms
displaying items on loan from Madrid's Prado Museum.*

★ St Lucia
This painting by Guamart de Amberes is one of the museum's collection of works by 16th-century Dutch and Italian painters, some of which belong to the Prado Museum. They include paintings by Guido Reni, the Carracc brothers and Guercino.

First Floor

VISITORS' CHECKLIST

Colón 1. **Tel** *928 312 373, 928 312 384.*
Tel *928 331 156.*
◻ 9am–7pm Mon–Fri; 9am–3pm Sat–Sun. ● 22 May, 24 Dec, 31 Dec. ∅
www.grancanariacultura.com

★ External Portal
Casa de Colón features a magnificent portal crowned by a Tudor arch. This exquisite ornament combines plant and animal motifs, with two lions supporting the town's crests.

Courtyard
At the centre of the inner courtyard stands an old well. Centuries-old galleries and arcades, in typical Canary style, keep the rooms cool and shady.

Basement vaults

★ Pre-Columbian Art
An extensive collection of pre-Columbian artifacts of gold and other metals includes original items and replicas associated with the Spanish conquests in Central and South America.

STAR EXHIBITS

★ External Portal

★ Pre-Columbian Art

★ St Lucia

Jardín Botánico Canario, near Tarifa Alta

and growing in their natural environment are plants from all the islands in the archipelago. They include species of the native Canary palm, Canary pine and heathers. Also featured are plants from other regions including the Azores, Madeira and the Cape Verde Islands as well as two thousand cacti, from all corners of the world.

🌺 **Jardín Botánico Canario**
🔲 9am–6pm daily

Tafira Alta ❷

🏚 3,000. ℹ Jardín Canario. **Tel** 928 353 604. 🎊 San Francisco (Oct).

Set among the hills is the small town of Tafira Alta, famous for its beautiful residences surrounded by gardens. These colourful villas, featuring a variety of architectural forms and details, have maintained the original colonial atmosphere of the place. Many houses show the influence of Moorish or Bauhaus style. No wonder then, that Tarifa Alta is a favourite with Las Palmas's financial elite and with wealthy foreigners.

At the beginning of the 20th century, the British built several elegant hotels here, including **Los Frailes**. This was used as a meeting place by General Franco's supporters as they plotted to overthrow Spain's Republican government in 1936.

Environs

The Botanical Gardens, Jardín Botánico Canario Viera y Clavijo, situated on the outskirts of town, are named after José Viera y Clavijo (1731–1813), the author of the *Canary Islands Dictionary of Plants*. The gardens were created in 1952 by a Swede, Eric Sventenius (1910–73), who remained their director until his death. Set on terraces

◁ Las Palmas de Gran Canaria

Caldera de Bandama ❸

It is worth travelling the 6-km (4-mile) distance from Tafira, half of which is over a narrow mountain road, in order to reach the peak of the volcano Pico de Bandama. This relatively low mountain (570 m/1,866 ft) provides one of the best viewpoints on Gran Canaria. Mirador de Bandama offers a magnificent view over the whole of Las Palmas and the mountainous centre of the island. Below is the vast volcanic caldera of Bandama, 1,000 m (3,300 ft) in diameter and 200 m (650 ft) deep. It is named after a Dutch merchant, Daniel von Damme. In the 16th century, von Damme, together with his wife Juana Vera, who was born in Gran Canaria, grew

vines inside the crater. Today the area is overgrown with orange and fig trees and palms. Eucalyptus and agaves grow on the slopes, among shrubs and bushes.

A golf course, just south of Pico de Bandama, was set up by English residents of the island in 1891. It is the oldest golf course in Spain.

Santa Brígida ❹

🏚 17,500. 🚌 🚆 Sat–Sun.
🎊 Corpus Christi (Jun).

This prosperous old town lies on the slopes of a gully covered with cypress and tall palms. Its picturesque narrow streets are lined with eucalyptus trees and flower-filled balconies. As a result of its proximity to Las Palmas, Santa Brígida is often visited by the capital's inhabitants.

The slopes of the neighbouring mountain are clothed with vineyards producing Vino del Monte – the best red wine on the island. The terrace in front of **Santa Brígida Parish Church** provides a good view over the surrounding palm groves. This triple-nave, Neo-Gothic basilica was built in 1904 on the site of a chapel constructed in 1520 by Isabel Guerra, the granddaughter of Pedro Guerra – a conquistador and one of the conquerors of Gran Canaria. The chapel was subsequently replaced by a church built in 1580. This, in turn, was almost destroyed by fire in the late 19th century. The only part that escaped destruction was the tower, built in 1756.

Caldera de Bandama, almost 1 km (0.5 mile) in diameter

Annual Fiesta de la Virgen del Pino, Teror

Vega de San Mateo ❺

🏠 7,000. 🚌 Sat, Sun.
🎭 San Mateo (21 Sep).

This small town is situated in a fertile, green valley 13 miles (21 km) from Las Palmas. It is known for its large agricultural market, which is held every Sunday. As well as fruits, vegetables and numerous types of cheese, the local farmers also bring goats, pigs and cows for sale. San Mateo is equally known for its wickerwork baskets and for producing Canary Island knives, leather goods and woodwork. These and other local arts and crafts are often available at the weekend market.

On Calle Principal stands the church of San Mateo, a fine example of neo-Canary architecture. Above this two-nave building hangs a bell sent from Cuba by local emigrants. The church also houses a 17th-century statue of Saint Matthew – the town's patron saint.

Teror ❻

🏠 13,000. 🚌 🛈 Plaza de Sintes, 1.
Tel 928 630 075. 🚌 Sun.
🎭 Fiesta del Agua (last Sun in Jul), Virgen del Pino (8 Sep).

Since her first appearance among tree branches in 1481, Nuestra Señora del Pino (Our Lady of the Pines) has played an important role in the history and everyday life of

Gran Canaria. In 1914, Pope Pius XII proclaimed her the patron saint of the island. Teror, with its sanctuary, became the religious capital of the island. Every year, on 8 September, the town is visited by many pilgrims, who travel here from all over Gran Canaria.

Large historic houses line the town's main square, **Plaza de Nuestra Señora del Pino**. Some of these mansions date from the 16th century and have lavishly carved wooden and stone balconies.

The basilica of **Nuestra Señora del Pino**, completed in 1767, was the third church to be built on this site. Only the tower remains from the earlier church, and dates from

1708. Its octagonal shape and striking mix of Moorish and Baroque elements make the tower a distinctive landmark.

The main feature of the large, triple-nave interior is the vast, Baroque altar with its 15th-century, carved figure of the Virgin. The Virgen (known as both of the pine and of the snow) is the patron saint of the island and the reason for one of the biggest fiestas in the Canary Islands (see p25). Other attractions include the Treasure Room, which contains precious gifts, donated at past festivals, to celebrate the saint.

Not far from the church is **Plaza Doña María Teresa de Bolívar**, named after María Teresa, the wife of Simón Bolívar – a hero of South America's fight for independence.

Her family came from Teror, and the family crest adorns the square. The **Casa Museo de los Patrones de la Virgen**, built on the site of his former home, is a museum displaying old photographs, weapons and furniture, including the bed slept in by King Alfonso XIII during a 1906 visit.

Central part of the church façade in Teror

🏛 **Casa Museo de los Patrones de la Virgen**
Plaza Nuestra Señora del Pino, 8.
Tel 928 630 239. ☐ 11am–6:30pm Mon–Sat, 10:30am–2pm Sun.

Drawing room in Casa Museo de los Patrones de la Virgen in Teror

Arucas ❼

🚶 32,500. 🚌 ℹ️ Plaza de la
Constitución, 2. **Tel** 928 623 136.
🍴 Mon–Fri. 🎭 Corpus Christi (Jun).

When approaching Arucas, the first sight you see is the towers of the Neo-Gothic **Parish Church of San Juan**. The church, mistakenly called a "cathedral", was designed by Manual Vega March and built between 1909 and 1977. As well as the fine stained-glass windows and retable, the interior features the sculpture of Cristo Yacente (the Resting Christ), which is the work of a local sculptor, Manuel Rasmos.

The old **town hall** in Plaza de la Constitución, designed by José A. López de Echegarret, was built in 1875 and then rebuilt in 1932. On the opposite side of the square is the leafy **town park**, which boasts many species of rare tropical trees, including the soapbark tree (Quillaja saponaria).

Encircling the park, **Calle de la Heredad** features one of the town's most beautiful buildings, **Heredad de Aguas de Arucas y Firgas**, which was built in 1908 and now houses the Water Board. In the second half of the 19th century and the early years of the 20th century, the Board initiated the construction of an irrigation system and the town itself

Ceramic ornaments in Paseo de Gran Canaria, Firgas

acquired its present shape. The Canary Islands' largest **rum factory** was built in Arucas in 1884. The factory has a museum devoted to the history and distillation method of this drink. Near the factory entrance stands an early 18th-century chapel – **La Ermita de San Pedro**.

Environs
About 1.5 km (1 mile) north of Arucas is **Montaña de Arucas**. At the highest point of the town is a restaurant with a viewing platform, with views over town and the entire island.

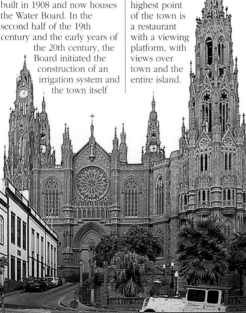
Neo-Gothic Parish Church of San Juan, Arucas

Firgas ❽

🚶 7,000. 🚌 🎭 San Luis (21 Jun).

Firgas is famous for its production of sparkling mineral water. The water is drawn from a spring some 5 km (3 miles) away, in Barranco de la Virgen, and 200,000 bottles a day are produced. Firgas water is very popular throughout the islands, where there is a shortage of fresh water.

A feature of Firgas, which celebrated its five hundredth anniversary in 1988, is the Paseo de Gran Canaria, where cascades of water flow along passages that were laid out in 1995. On either side of the passage, by the walls of surrounding houses, are benches whose backrests are decorated with landscapes or historic symbols of Gran Canaria. The white walls of the houses feature colourful town crests. The further section of the passage, above **Plaza de San Roque**, is filled with giant slabs with ceramic maps and views of the individual islands. These provide an unusual lesson in the geography of the Canary Islands. Still further along the passage there is a fine display of the flags of all the islands fluttering in the breeze.

The historic 15th-century **Molino de Gofio** and the 19th-century fountain were restored in 1988. The whole town is decorated with modern sculptures, including an amusing statue of a peasant with a pink cow.

Moya ❾

🏛 8,000. 🚌 🚤 Sun. 🎭 Virgen de la Candelaria (2 Feb), San Antonio (13 Jun).

Tucked away from the main tourist attractions, the road to this small town meanders through volcanic valleys, with countless turns and bends. The place is worth visiting for its vast, Neo-Romanesque church, dating from the first half of the 20th century. The church is imposing with two towers and a position at the edge of the **Barranco de Moya** precipice – a gully criss-crossed with wild crevasses.

Moya is the birthplace of Tomás Morales – a modernist Canary poet. The house in which he was born and lived was converted into a museum, **Casa-Museo Tomás Morales**, in 1976. There is a permanent exhibition dedicated to the poet which includes photographs, manuscripts and first editions of his works displayed in rooms decorated in period style. The museum also organizes exhibitions of contemporary art.

By the entrance to the nearby catacomb cemetery, typical of the Canary Islands, stands a large stone cross – a monument to the victims of the 1936 Spanish Civil War.

🏛 **Casa-Museo Tomás Morales**
Plaza de Tomás Morales.
Tel 928 620 217.
⬜ 9am–8pm Mon–Fri; 9am–2pm, 4–8pm Sat & Sun.

TOMÁS MORALES (1884–1921)

Tomás Morales is hailed as one of the Canary Islands' most outstanding poets. Although he completed medical studies at the University in 1909 and practised in Agaete and Las Palmas, his true passion was poetry. He started writing poems at the age of 15 and had his first works published in 1902. In 1908 his first book, *Poems of Glory, Love and Sea* appeared, and two years later Las Palmas Theatre staged his *Dinner at Simon's House* – a dramatic prose poem. His strong identification with his homeland is reflected in his work – a complex brew of feelings that combine a love of the sea, loneliness, warmth and eclecticism. His great poem *Ode to Atlantic*, celebrates man, ship and ocean.

Bust of Morales in front of the museum in Moya

Santa María de Guía de Gran Canaria ❿

🏛 14,000. 🚌 🎭 Fiesta del Queso de Flor (May), Nuestra Señora de Guía (15 Aug), La Rama de las Marías (3rd Sun in Sep).

The only noteworthy historic building in this town is the Church of **Santa María de Guía**, built on the site of a chapel erected in 1483–1509. Some parts of this triple-nave church date back to the 17th century; the façade was completed only in the middle of the following century.

Guía is the birthplace of José Luján Pérez (1756–1815), who was the most popular of the Canary Islands' sculptors during his lifetime. His works, such as the statue of Nuestra Señora de las Mercedes or St Sebastián, adorn the interior of the local church. However, Guía is best known for its cheese – *queso de flor*. It is made of cow's and goat's milk, with the flower of the blue thistle added. This gives the cheese its unusual flavour and allows it to remain moist even when stored for a long time.

Environs
Some 5 km (3 miles) east of Guía is **Cenobio de Valerón**, a group of about 300 caves set into a cliff at various levels. The caves were used for grain storage and for religious services. Guanche individuals were selected to spend several years in solitude in these caves, giving themselves to the service of the god Abor. Their prayers were to ensure the god's protection for the island's people.

🏛 **Cenobio de Valerón**
⬜ 10am–5pm Wed–Sun.

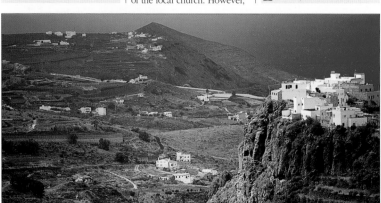

Breathtaking view of Barranco de Moya

How Rum is Made

Rum, a by-product of sugar production, is a drink normally associated with the Caribbean, where its most famous producers are Jamaica, Cuba, Haiti and Martinique. However, the legacy of the Canary Islands' sugar plantations *(see p32)* is a respected and thriving rum industry. The local rum is generally valued for its outstanding flavour and

Canary Islands rum served in a small glass

its warming and even medicinal properties. Its alcohol content can vary from 40 to 80 per cent. It is the main ingredient of another famous beverage, grog, which is 50 per cent rum, as well as of cocktails such as Daiquiri and Cuba Libre, which use rum. One of the Canary Islands' specialities is *ron miel* – a mead rum. Rum is also used in confectionery.

1 *Rum is made from sugar cane, which is processed in order to obtain sugar syrup and molasses – both are used in the later stages of production. As there are no big sugar-cane plantations on the islands, local rum is produced mainly from imported semi-finished products.*

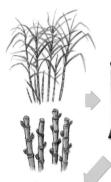

2 *Inside these large vessels, sugar juices or molasses undergo a fermentation process. Strong rums are produced by combining molasses with the scum collected from the boiling juices and the brew known as "dunder". The alcohol obtained by fermentation subsequently undergoes a distillation process.*

3 *To ensure a refined flavour, the rum is left to mature in traditional oak barrels – a process that can last anything between three and ten years. The room in which the barrels are stored must be maintained at a constant temperature and humidity.*

5 *The Canary Islands' rums are well known even outside of the archipelago. Particularly highly regarded is the rum from La Palma – the best brand is believed to be Ron de la Aldea. Also popular are mead rums, whose ingredients include palm juice. The resulting orange-coloured beverage is weaker than rum and its unique flavour resembles neither rum nor mead.*

4 *Bottling and labelling are the final stages of rum production. This is a fully automatic process, which takes place in perfectly sterile conditions, with no people present. The bottles are appropriately labelled, showing the brand and provenance of the product.*

Vast banana plantations around Gáldar

Gáldar ⑪

🏠 *22,000.* 🚌 🎉 *San Isidro (15 May), La Rama (20 Aug).*

At the foot of Pico de Gáldar volcano stands Gáldar – a sizeable town that was once the centre of Guanche civilization. There are no traces left of the ancient court of their ruler *(Guanarteme)* since, along with a small Spanish fort, it was destroyed to make way for the construction of **Santiago de los Caballeros Church**. This vast Neo-Classic church has three naves and was designed by Antonio José Eduardo. The construction works started in 1778 and were not completed until the mid-19th century.

Inside the church the *pila verde* – a green font brought from Andalusia in the late 15th century and, since the island's conquest, used for baptizing the local population. Other noteworthy features are the statues of Christ and the Virgin Mary – both the work of Luján Pérez.

On the square, opposite the town hall, grows the oldest dragon tree *(see p16)* in Gran Canaria, planted in 1719.

The star attraction of Gáldar is the **Cueva Pintada**. Discovered in 1873, the cave is decorated with rock paintings consisting of geometric patterns. Following conservation works, carried out between 1970 and 1974, the cave was closed in order to prevent the paintings from being destroyed by the increased humidity. A new archaeological park opened at the site in 2003. It features a museum, offering a virtual tour of the caves, a library and a restaurant. A replica of the cave can be seen at the Museo Canario in Las Palmas *(see p47).*

Environs

Just 2 km (1.5 miles) north of Gáldar is **Tumulo de la Guancha**. Discovered in 1936 during agricultural works, this Guanche cemetery dates from the late 11th century and consists of 30 round tombs, built of vast lava blocks. These were the burial places of members of the Andamanas royal family who ruled this part of the island.

At 6 km (4 miles) west, Sardina is at first glance an unremarkable fishing village. Nestled between high cliffs and a sandy beach, it tempts swimmers with its crystal-clear water and golden sands, as well as its excellent seafood.

Agaete ⑫

🏠 *5,700.* 🚌 🛈 *Antonio de Armas, 1.* **Tel** *928 898 002.* 🎉 *Bajada de las Ramas (4–7 Aug).*

Agaete lies on the northwest coast of the island, at the end of a steep ravine – **Barranco de Agaete**. Plantations of banana, papaya, avocado and mango flourish on the steep slopes. The small town of Agaete, with its narrow streets and whitewashed houses surrounded by lush greenery, has become popular with artists and art-lovers, who have converted local houses and garages into art galleries.

Punta Sardina lighthouse

Despite being an old town, which celebrated its 500-year anniversary in 1981, Agaete has few historic sites. The oldest is the parish church, which was built in the second half of the 19th century. There is also a charming, small botanical garden, **Huerto de las Flores**, which features more than 100 species of Canary and sub-tropical flora.

Environs

Some 2 km (1.5 miles) to the west is a small harbour, **Puerto de las Nieves**, with a terminal for ferries to Santa Cruz de Tenerife. This small, picturesque fishing village, nestling against tall cliffs, has become popular with tourists. Visitors are drawn by its craft shops, galleries and seafood restaurants, and apartment blocks have sprung up around the port.

Puerto de las Nieves' rich history can be seen in the opulent furnishings of the Ermita de las Nieves, a chapel, built in the 16th century. It contains a display of model sailing ships and a triptych devoted to the Virgen de las Nieves (Virgin of the Snows), painted by the Flemish artist Joos van Cleve (1485–1540). During the Fiesta de la Rama (Branch Festival) in August, the chapel's altar is carried in a procession to the nearby parish church in Agaete.

⚘ Huerto de las Flores

C/Huertes. ⏱ *10am–1pm, 4–7pm Mon–Sat.*

The whitewashed exterior of the Ermita de las Nieves

Cactualdea – cactus park in La Aldea de San Nicolás

La Aldea de San Nicolás ⓭

8,000. Bajada de la Rama (10 Sep), El Charco (11 Sep).

A fertile, green valley, criss-crossed with ravines, is the setting for this small town. It is surrounded by plantations of banana, orange, avocado, papaya and mango and the slopes are overgrown with cacti and bamboo. The only building worth visiting is the **San Nicolás Church**, built in 1972 along traditional lines, featuring sculptures by Luján Pérez. It was built on the site of an old chapel dating from the early 18th century.

A popular tourist attraction is **Cactualdea** – a park with thousands of cacti imported from Madagascar, Mexico, Bolivia and Guatemala; other plants include palms, dragon trees *(see p16)* and aloe. Other features of interest include a large amphitheatre, used for wrestling matches, and a Guanche Cave.

Environs
Some 9 km (6 miles) to the north is the **Mirador del Balcón** – a viewpoint poised on the edge of rugged cliffs, rising 500 m (1,650 ft) above the sea. It provides views over northeastern Gran Canaria.

Cactualdea
Tel *928 891 228. 10am–5pm daily.*

Puerto de Mogán ⓮

1,200. C/General Franco.
Tel *928 158 804. Fri.*
Virgen del Carmen (16 Jul).

Unlike the bustling resorts on the south of Gran Canaria, such as Playa del Inglés and Maspalomas, Puerto de Mogán is the ideal spot for visitors longing for some peace and

Gran Canaria Beaches

With its 236-km (146-mile) coastline, Gran Canaria has around 160 beaches, small and large. Unlike the northern beaches, which are rocky, the southern beaches are sandy. In some places, such as Playa del Inglés (popular with naturists, *see p187)* or Maspalomas, they stretch for miles and are lined with hotels, restaurants and clubs.

Taurito ② can boast the attractive beach around Mogán, on a par with Playa de Cura and Arguineguín.

Puerto de Mogán ①
Hidden among high cliffs, the sandy beach of this popular resort can barely accommodate all its guests.

Playa de los Amadores ③
This popular wide beach near Puerto Rico is fringed with beautiful palm trees and a wide, elegant promenade.

quiet. This picturesque town and yachting marina lie at the end of the green Mogán Valley, at the foot of a rocky plateau. The old and slightly scruffy fishing port and town lies adjacent to and behind the attractive, purpose-built marina and resort complex. The resort consists of a village-like complex of colourful, flower-decked apartments, prettily designed in Mediterranean style, lining narrow pedestrianized streets. The waterfront is lined with bars, shops and restaurants.

For swimming fans, there is a man-made rocky beach that shelters between the cliffs and is filled with several layers of sand that was imported from Africa.

There is a range of tourist trips available from here. A little, yellow submarine offers tourists the opportunity to get a glimpse of the rich under-water life of the Atlantic. Small replicas of old sailing ships ferry passengers to the beaches of Puerto Rico and Maspalomas several times a

Yellow submarine in Puerto de Mogán harbour

day. There are also deep-sea fishing trips to catch tuna and marlin. The renowned "Blue Marlin" angling competition is held here every July.

Environs
Around 8 km (5 miles) north of Puerto de Mogán, in a

fertile valley planted with such exotic crops as pawpaw and avocado, lies **Mogán**. This picturesque town is the capital of the district. There is a choice of good restaurants here, including Acayama on the edge of town, one of the best on the island.

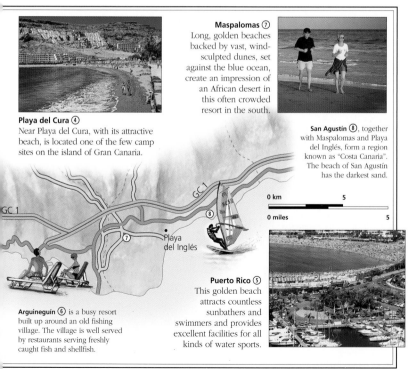

Playa del Cura ④
Near Playa del Cura, with its attractive beach, is located one of the few camp sites on the island of Gran Canaria.

Maspalomas ⑦
Long, golden beaches backed by vast, wind-sculpted dunes, set against the blue ocean, create an impression of an African desert in this often crowded resort in the south.

San Agustín ⑧, together with Maspalomas and Playa del Inglés, form a region known as "Costa Canaria". The beach of San Agustín has the darkest sand.

GC 1

GC 1

Playa del Inglés

0 km   5

0 miles   5

Arguineguín ⑥ is a busy resort built up around an old fishing village. The village is well served by restaurants serving freshly caught fish and shellfish.

Puerto Rico ⑤
This golden beach attracts countless sunbathers and swimmers and provides excellent facilities for all kinds of water sports.

Puerto Rico – one of Gran Canaria's most popular resorts

Puerto Rico ⑮

🏠 1,500. 🛈 Avda. de Mogán.
Tel 928 560 029.
🎉 María de Auxiliadora (May).

Puerto Rico lies on the coast, at the mouth of a large valley. This former fishing port has, in recent years, developed into a popular resort, thanks to its reputation as the sunniest place in Spain. Scores, if not hundreds, of hotels and apartments have been built on the terraces of the steeply descending slopes.

One of the best features of this town, which is swamped in greenery, is its small but picturesque beach, covered with sand imported from the Sahara. Other attractions include golf courses and a water park, featuring all kinds of amusements. Puerto Rico's numerous attractions range from watersports such as water-skiing, sailing, diving and windsurfing to leisure excursions such as glass-bottomed boats and open sea cruises for dolphin-watching. This helps to compensate for the fact that this is a rather over-built resort with remarkably limited amounts of sand for the numbers of visitors it receives.

Another very popular activity is sport-fishing for marlin, shark, eel and ray. Puerto Rico claims many world records in this area: the world's largest blue marlin, caught in 1997, weighed in at 488 kg (1,075 lb).

Maspalomas ⑯

🏠 36,000. 🛈 Avda. de España.
Tel 928 768 409. 📅 Wed, Sat.
🎉 San Bartolomé (24 Aug).

The biggest resort in Gran Canaria has more than 500 hotels, apartment blocks and chalets, capable of accommodating 300,000 guests at a time. The town is pulsating with life both day and night. Tourists flock here, attracted by miles of sandy beaches, as well as hundreds of restaurants, bars, discotheques and shops.

The resort is popular with surfers and windsurfers, as well as deep-sea fishing and diving enthusiasts. For those who enjoy aquatic fun and games, the resort also offers **Aquasur** – the biggest water-park on the island, with 29 slides. Another big attraction is **Holiday World** – an amusement park occupying 14,000 sq m (3.5 acres) and featuring

a traditional ferris wheel, 27 m (88 ft) high.

This large, modern resort, criss-crossed with numerous palm-lined boulevards, has an excellent golf course – the biggest on the island – while spiritual needs are served by the ecumenical church – **Templo Ecuménico**.

Although Maspalomas gives the impression of being a single entity, it is in fact a conglomeration of three separate resorts, reached by three different exits from the south-coast motorway.

The furthest east is **San Agustín**. This quiet, tourist town, full of greenery, with dark sand beaches, is aimed at an upmarket clientele, rather than at mass tourism. It has a number of luxurious hotels, exclusive clubs, a casino and scenic promenades.

In the middle of the Maspalomas coastline is **Playa del Inglés**. This is the most crowded and liveliest resort, with Yumbo, a multi-storey shopping/restaurant centre, in the middle of town.

To the south of Playa del Inglés are the **Dunas de Maspalomas** – a vast, 4-sq km (1.5-sq mile) expanse of dunes and now a national park with a salt-water lake and palm grove, which can only be explored on foot or by camel. The dunes provide a habitat for lizards, rabbits and naturists. (This is also an area used by cruising gay men.) The nearby lagoon provides numerous migrant birds with a stop en route between Europe and Africa.

The spectacular dunes of Maspalomas

Colourful parrots in Palmitos Parque

Environs

Some 10 km (6 miles) north of Maspalomas, set in a mountain valley, is **Palmitos Parque**. Amid its lush, tropical vegetation live 1,500 birds, including birds of paradise from New Guinea, miniature humming birds and toucans, with their colourful beaks. Bird shows involving trained parrots, eagles and falcons entertain visitors at intervals. Other attractions include the Casa de las Orquídeas, which houses around 1,000 orchids. The huge aquarium, with its vast tanks of water, has a large variety of fish from all over the world, including the Canary Islands' sea, Indian Ocean and South American waters. A further attraction of the park is the butterfly house – the largest of its kind in Europe. The park also boasts white-handed gibbons, whose natural habitats are the Malayan Peninsula and Burma, and who have been bred successfully here: the first time in captivity.

Just 6 km (4 miles) to the north is **Mundo Aborigen** – a reconstruction of an ancient Canary village. Set on a gentle slope, with a splendid view over the Barranco de Fataga, it consists of several crofts. Life-sized Guanche figures and recorded domestic animal noises give the setting some realism. A marked trail leads to a series of lifelike scenes including: a butcher gutting a goat; a doctor operating on a patient; wrestlers fighting in a small stadium. Nearby a farmer is shown sowing a field, while the local executioner can be

seen smashing a convict's head with a rock. A sentry, poised at the highest point above the village, keeps watch over the surrounding area.

Some 10 km (6 miles) northeast, at the end of a rocky valley, is the small theme park **Sioux City**, which represents a ragbag of familiar associations with American culture. At the entrance, next to a wooden cart containing models of the first settlers travelling west, we come across "Cadillac Café" with a genuine 1960s American car.

Visitors drinking in the saloon can enjoy dramatic interruptions from actors staging fights. Apart from such traditional fun there is also the "foam party" – a discotheque where participants throw foam at each other. The narrow streets of Sioux City provide the setting for scenes from westerns, including mock fistfights, gunfights and bank robberies. The air is filled with country and western music.

Statue of Indian at Sioux City

🐦 Palmitos Parque
Barranco de los Palmitos. *Tel 928 797 156.* ⏱ 10am–5pm daily. 🎫

🏛 Mundo Aborigen
Macizo de Amurga. *Tel 928 172 295.* ⏱ 9am–6pm daily. 🎫

🏛 Sioux City
Cañon del Águila. *Tel 928 762 573.* ⏱ 10am–5pm Tue–Sun. 🎫

San Bartolomé de Tirajana **❼**

🏠 34,500. 🚌 🎫 Carnival (Feb), Santiago (25 Jul).

Founded in the 16th century by the Spanish, this picturesque little town was once a shepherd settlement. Situated in the lush green valley of Tirajana, this district is known for its orchards of almonds, plums, peaches and cherries, which are used in the production of vodkas and liqueurs. The local speciality is cherry liqueur, *guindilla*.

The first chapel in San Bartolomé was built in the 16th century. In 1690, work started on its site to build a much grander, triple-nave parish church, which was not, in fact, consecrated until 1922. Its noteworthy features include the Mudéjar-style wooden vaults and carved statues of the saints. It is also worth visiting the old cemetery, set on a hill, where – contrary to the Spanish tradition – the dead were buried in the soil rather then being entombed in the cemetery wall.

Environs

Some 8 km (5 miles) to the south of San Bartolomé, in a beautiful setting of tall cliffs, palms and fruit trees, is **Fataga** – a mountain village with old houses and the 1880 church of San José. Next to the church are reservoirs – Embalse de Tirajana and Embalse de Fataga – both of which are excellent goals for walkers.

Children's water slide at the Aquasur water park, Maspalomas

Around Pico de las Nieves ⑱

An all-day tour through the mountains of Gran Canaria can start from any point. The diverse character of the island's landscape makes it an unforgettable experience. The scenic road follows a serpentine course as it climbs mountain slopes, and passes through enchanting villages and deep ravines. Lush sub-tropical vegetation, including exotic fruit trees and terraced fields, can be seen along the way. There are also numerous viewpoints en route that offer spectacular panoramas, even to the peak of Mount Teide on Tenerife. Some of the less accessible places can be reached by minor roads and tracks.

Artenara ⑦
One of the caves in this village houses a small chapel, another an unusual restaurant – Mesón de la Silla.

Caldera Pinos de Gáldar ⑥
On the road leading to Artenara, surrounded by the conifer forests of Pinos de Gáldar, stands a picturesque viewpoint. From here you can see the whole northern coast of the island.

Tejeda ⑧
This quiet little town, occupying a particularly scenic location on the mountain slopes, provides a good stopping place for lunch when touring the area.

Roque Bentayga ⑨
Along with nearby Roque Nublo, this basalt rock, rising to 1,412 m (4,632 ft) above sea level, was regarded as a holy place by the Guanches, who left rock inscriptions, granaries and ceremonial sites in this area.

LA ALDEA DE SAN NICOLÁS

GC 60

GC 60

MOGÁN

MASPALOMAS

0 km   2

0 miles   2

KEY

▬	Suggested route
▬	Scenic route
═	Other roads
✲	Viewpoint

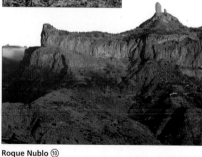

Roque Nublo ⑩
This 60-m (195-ft) tall basalt monolith tops a 1,700 m (5,578 ft) peak. Thought to have been held sacred by the Guanches, this finger of rock was formed by erosion, and is often shrouded in clouds.

Cruz de Tejeda ⑤

Carved in stone, this cross – from which the area takes its name – marks the central point of Gran Canaria. The view from this point on the mountain pass (altitude 1,450 m/4,757 ft) was described as a "petrified storm" by artist Miguel de Unamuno.

TIPS FOR TOURISTS

Starting point: San Bartolomé de Tirajana.
Length: 80 km (50 miles).
Stopping places: The best place to stop for lunch is the parador at Cruz de Tejeda, which has an excellent restaurant. There are also restaurants in Artenara and San Bartolomé de Tirajana.

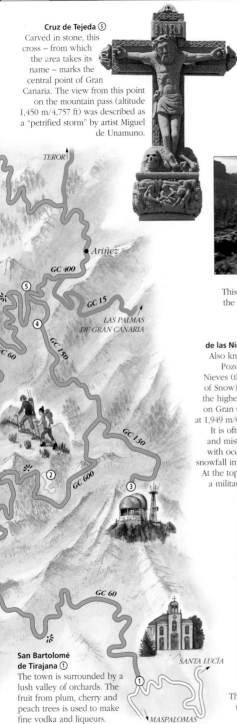

La Degollada de Becerra ④
This viewpoint offers a spectacular view to the west and of the Roque Bentayga peak.

Pico de las Nieves ③
Also known as Pozo de las Nieves (the Well of Snow), this is the highest peak on Gran Canaria at 1,949 m/6,394 ft. It is often cold and misty here, with occasional snowfall in winter. At the top stands a military radio station.

San Bartolomé de Tirajana ①
The town is surrounded by a lush valley of orchards. The fruit from plum, cherry and peach trees is used to make fine vodka and liqueurs.

Presa de los Hornos ②
The best view of the highest reservoir on the island can be seen near the summit of Roque Nublo (see p62).

Santa Lucía ⑲

🚌 🎇 *Fiesta de Ansite (29 Apr),*
Santa Lucía (13 Dec).

Located in the high country,
this tiny village stands 700 m
(2,300 ft) above sea level, in
the upper reaches of the
fertile palm valley of Santa
Lucía de Tirajana. Standing on
top of the hill is the **Church of
Santa Lucía**, which was built
in 1898 on the site of a former
17th-century chapel.

Various archaeological
finds, unearthed on the slopes
of the surrounding hills and
dating from the time of the
Guanches, can now be seen
in the local **Museo del
Castillo de la Fortaleza**.
This ethnography/archaeology
museum is housed in a
recently built pseudo-castle
with turrets and battlements.
The museum also features a
reconstructed bedroom,
typical of those in a 17th-
century Canary home, and
displays of pottery (including
a 3rd-century amphora), fish,
leather goods, basket-work,
skeletons and other exhibits.

Environs
A scenic road leads 5 km (3
miles) south to the viewpoint
of Mirador de Guriete, with its
spectacular views of the area.

🏛 **Museo del Castillo
de la Fortaleza**
Tel 928 798 310. ○ 11am–4pm
daily. 🌐 **www**.mygrancanaria.com

Agüimes ⑳

🏚 *6,000.* 🚗 🚌 🎇 *Nuestra
Señora del Rosario (15 Oct).*

The old part of this small
town, with its narrow streets
and beautiful houses, is
overshadowed by the two
huge towers of **San
Sebastián Church**, standing in
the Plaza del Rosario. The
basilica has three naves and
a barrel vault, and was constructed between 1796 and
1808. Along with the
cathedral in Las Palmas de
Gran Canaria, this is one of
the best examples of the
Canary Islands' Neo-Classical

Picturesque narrow streets of Agüimes

architecture. The vast dome
lends an oriental touch to the
building. The statues of saints
inside the church are the
work of a Canary sculptor –
Luján Perez (1756–1815).

Another attraction of
Agüimes is the **Parque de
los Cocodrilos**. This mini-zoo
puts on shows of trained
crocodiles and parrots.

The town comes to life
every September during the
Encuentro Internacional Tres
Continentes, an international
festival of theatre. Groups
from Europe, Africa and South
America come to participate
in this lively event.

🐊 **Parque de los Cocodrilos**
Ctra. de los Corralillos. **Tel** 928 784
725. ○ 10am–6pm Sun–Fri. 🌐

Ingenio ㉑

🏚 *12,000.* 🚌 🎇 *Virgen de la
Candelaria (2 Feb); Bajada del Macho
(2nd Sat in Oct).*

Situated in the eastern region,
near Barranco Guayadeque,
this small town is one of the
oldest on Gran Canaria. It
owes its name to the local
sugar-cane industry that
flourished here in the 17th
century (*ingenio* means sugar
mill). Later, the region turned
towards rum production but
now it is a largely agricultural
area, its main crop being

tomatoes. Ingenio is,
however, best known
for its embroidery.
There is a School of
Embroidery housed in
the **Museo de Piedras
y Artesanía** – a white,
bougainvillea-covered
building with deco-
rative turrets. The
museum also houses a
collection of rocks and
minerals, agricultural
tools, pottery and
basketwork.

The imposing
**Church of Nuestra
Señora de la
Candelaria** looms over
an attractive square,
bordered by pretty
houses with wooden
balconies.

Environs
On the slope of a mountain,
half-way along the road
between Ingenio and Telde,
is an archaeological site
discovered in the 19th century.
It consists of four caves,
including **Cuatro Puertas**,
with four openings (hence the
name), which used to be the
home of Telde rulers, or the
site of sacrifices. The other
caves, which face the sea,
were used by the Guanches
to bury the embalmed bodies
of their dead.

🏛 **Museo de Piedras
y Artesanía**
Camino Real de Gando, 1.
Tel 928 781 124. ○ 9am–6pm
daily. 🌐

**Entrance to Museo de Piedras y
Artesanía in Ingenio**

Green and white painted houses in Plaza de San Juan – the main square in Telde

Barranco de Guayadeque ㉒

2 km (1.5 miles) north of Ingenio.

A scenic, winding road runs 7 km (4 miles) along the bottom of the Guayadeque Canyon, whose name in the Guanche language means "place of the flowing waters". The stream flowing along the canyon supplies water to the neighbouring towns of Ingenio and Agüimes.

Guayadeque is overgrown with cacti, agaves, palms and Canary pines, in addition to about 80 species native to the Canary Islands. In spring, the parched, rough terrain of the canyon is softened by blossoming almond trees.

This region is one of the most important prehistoric burial grounds, where the dead, often wrapped in animal skins, were interred in inaccessible caves. Many of these graves were plundered in the 19th century by the local population, who sold the mummies to the Museo Canario in Las Palmas. Local caves were also used by the Guanches as dwelling places, food stores and as sites used for fertility rituals.

Barranco de Guayadeque is popular with modern-day people who, following in the footsteps of the Guanches, have made their homes in the caves. This small troglodyte population has a chapel carved into the rock to meet their spiritual needs, while more earthly delights are provided by cave bars serving the strong local wine, bread and Temisas olives in green mojo sauce.

Guayadeque is also popular for Sunday picnics. The road running along the canyon ends at Montañade las Tierras restaurant. Further on, the route is impassable for cars and ends up with a narrow footpath. During the summer, the sun's rays on the rocks dazzle spectators. In winter, the place can be cold, and clouds often cover the high ridges of the canyon.

Peaks shrouded in clouds above Barranco de Guayadeque

Telde ㉓

🏠 19,000. 🚌 🎆 San Juan (24 Jun).

During pre-colonial times, Telde was the seat of the local king of the Guanches. Following the conquest of the island, it became known as a port for loading sugar cane.

Towards the end of the 15th century, the Spanish built a small chapel here. In 1519, work commenced on the site to build the present **Church of San Juan Bautista**. The highlights of this large basilica are the Mannerist altar and a Flemish triptych dating from the first half of the 16th century.

From **Plaza de San Juan**, in which the church stands, runs **Inés Cemida**, a street connecting San Juan with another historic part of town – San Francisco. Here, the two-storey buildings are are similarly painted in white and green. The narrow streets are lined with houses adorned with balconies of wrought iron and timber.

FERNANDO DE LEON Y CASTILLO (1842–1918)

León y Castillo, an engineer and diplomat born in Telde, played an important role in the regeneration of Gran Canaria. It is to him that the island owes the development of the Las Palmas harbour, gaining the island equal status with Tenerife. Opposed to Tenerife's domination, he was an advocate of the archipelago's division into two provinces. In 1881, he became Minister of Foreign Affairs, and also served as Spanish ambassador to France. In recognition, he was award-ed the title of Marqués del Muni.

Bust of León y Castillo, in Telde

FUERTEVENTURA

F uerteventura is blessed by sun and sand in equal measure. Much of its interior, consisting of arid dunes and rocky mountain ridges, is reminiscent of the western Sahara, which lies only 100 km (62 miles) to the east. Most of the island's tourists stick to the coast where the fine sandy beaches are irresistible to sun worshippers, and strong winds provide ideal conditions for surfing.

With a distance of 97 km (60 miles) between Punta de la Tinosa, in the north, and Punta de Jandía, in the south, Fuerteventura is the longest and the second largest of the Canary Islands. Yet despite its size, it is one of the most sparsely populated, and its 87,000 or so inhabitants are outnumbered by the many goats that scratch a meal from the island's dry scrub.

Goats – both a symbol of the island and part of its landscape

An island known as Forte Ventura first appeared on a map drawn by the cartographer Angelino Dulceta in 1339. Between 1402–05 it was taken by conquistadors, led by Jean de Béthencourt and Gadifer de la Salle. The village that grew up around the camp of Jean de Béthencourt, Santa María de Betancuria, subsequently became the island's capital. Territorial expansion in the mid-17th century extended to the region of El Cotillo and included the seat of the former kingdom of Maxorata. Volcanic eruptions and sand carried from the Sahara desert, as well as frequent droughts during the 18th and 19th centuries, caused the collapse of Fuerteventura's agriculture, once called the granary of the Canaries, and today most of the island's revenue comes from tourism.

The climate is harsher here than on the other islands thanks in part to a cooler prevailing wind called *gota fría*. The annual temperature stays more or less constant at around 19° C (66° F).

The arid climate and deforestation are responsible for the limited vegetation found here. An almost total absence of rain means that drinking water must be obtained either by desalination or shipped over from the mainland.

Miles of unspoiled golden beaches south of Corralejo

◁ The steep shores of the gulf near Ajuy

Exploring Fuerteventura

Fuerteventura was discovered by tourists later than the other islands in the region and as a consequence the local tourist industry is still in its infancy. The number of visitors is increasing, however, as news gradually spreads of the island's scenic landscape, and the peace and quiet to be found here. The vast stretches of white beach are a particular draw to sun worshippers – the more accessible ones are found in the northern part of the island, near Corralejo, the wilder ones around Cofete. The shores of Jandía provide perfect conditions for surfing and windsurfing, while rich underwater life is a tempting attraction for divers. Fuerteventura is also an excellent area for walking and cycling. Those interested in history will find many interesting places to visit, including Betancuria and Pájara.

LOCATOR MAP

Mountain view on the road from Pájara to La Pared

SIGHTS AT A GLANCE

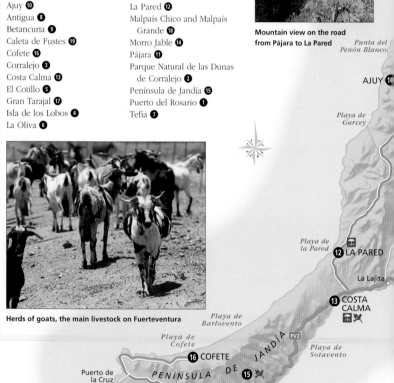

Herds of goats, the main livestock on Fuerteventura

Punta de la Tinosa

El Río

ISLA DE LOS LOBOS 4

CORRALEJO 3

Punta la Barra

Playas de Corralejo

EL COTILLO 5

Lajares

PARQUE NATURAL DE LAS DUNAS DE CORRALEJO 2

Montaña Roja 312m

Montaña de Escantraga 529m

FV1

LA OLIVA 6

Punta Paso Chico

FV10

Tindaya

Monumento a Miguel de Unamuno

Punta de la Tiñosa

as Los olinos

Tetir

FV10

TEFÍA 7

PUERTO DEL ROSARIO 1

Casillas del Ángel

Playa Blanca

FV20

La Ampuyenta

FV30

Playa de las Caletillas

BETANCURIA 9

Triquivijate

FV2

ANTIGUA 8

Pico de ncuria 725m

CALETA DE FUSTES 19

Vega de Río Palmas

FV20

Tiscamanita

MALPAÍS CHICO & MALPAÍS GRANDE

Casas de las Salinas

PÁJARA

Tuineje

18

FV50

FV2

Casas de Pozo Negro

Punta Gorda

Tesejerague

FV20

FV2

Playa de los James

GRAN TARAJAL 17

Las Playitas

arajalejo

```
0 km        5
|===========|
0 miles     5
```

The lush garden of Casa de Santa María, in Betancuria

GETTING THERE

Fuerteventura has direct air links with Lanzarote, Gran Canaria and Tenerife, and connects via Tenerife to the western islands. There are also flights from mainland Spanish cities as well as a number of European centres. Regular ferry links connect Puerto del Rosario with Arrecife (Lanzarote) and Las Palmas de Gran Canaria, and Corralejo with Playa Blanca (Lanzarote). A hydrofoil runs from Morro Jable to Las Palmas de Gran Canaria. The local transport is limited.

SEE ALSO

• *Where to Stay* pp158–60.

• *Where to Eat* p174.

KEY

▬▬	Motorway
▬	Major road
▬▬▬	Minor road
▬	Scenic route
△	Summit

Scenic approach road leading to the centre of La Pared

Drawing room of Casa Museo de Unamuno, Puerto del Rosario

Puerto del Rosario **❶**

🏃 31,000. 🛫 🚌 ⛴
ℹ️ C/1Mayo, 37, 928 530 844.
🎭 Nuestra Señora del Rosario (7 Oct).

Puerto del Rosario, the current administrative centre of Fuerteventura, was established in 1797 as a port for locally produced soda and grain. The port began to grow in the mid-19th century and by 1860 had become the capital of the island. Until 1957, the town, whose name means Port of Roses, was Puerto de Cabras – Port of Goats – in reference to the watering hole in the nearby canyon.

Today the port has a thriving cargo and passenger harbour, with ferries sailing to Gran Canaria and Lanzarote. It also has a yachting marina. Not far from the town – which is the largest on Fuerteventura and inhabited by more than half of the island's population – is an international airport.

Another feature of Puerto del Rosario is the huge barracks of the Spanish Foreign Legion. In 1975, when the Spaniards finally left the western Sahara, 3,000 legionnaires were transferred here – numbers have since dwindled and there are now fewer than 1,000.

While in Puerto del Rosario, it is worth taking time to visit the church of **Nuestra Señora del Rosario**, with its classical façade. Standing opposite it is **Casa Museo de Unamuno**, which will interest lovers of

Spanish literature, as it was the home of the writer and philosopher Miguel de Unamuno during his exile. Part of the house is furnished with period pieces including the original desk used by the writer, as well as a collection of personal objects and documents. It represents a typical interior from his times.

🏛 **Casa Museo de Unamuno**
C/del Rosario 11. **Tel** 928 862 376.
⏰ 9am–2pm Mon–Fri.

Environs
Just 12 km (7 miles) to the north is a small village, **Cassilas del Angel**, with pretty houses. The beautiful church of Santa Ana (Saint Anne), dates from 1781 and has a black, volcanic-stone façade.

Parque Natural de las Dunas **❷**

In the northeast corner of the island is the Parque Natural de las Dunas de Corralejo, which stretches south right up to the base of the Montaña Roja volcano (312 m/1,023 ft).

Goats picking at the scrub in the Parque Natural de las Dunas

Occupying 27 sq km (10 sq miles), this wide belt of seemingly endless, shifting sands encroaches on the road between Puerto del Rosario and Corralejo and descends to the ocean.

Reminiscent of the Sahara desert, the Parque Natural de las Dunas de Corralejo is almost totally devoid of any vestiges of civilization. Even when the tourist season is at its height there is plenty of solitude and open space to be found here (don't forget to take a hat). The only signs of life are the stone walls built as windbreaks on the sandy hills. The area was declared a National Park in 1987.

Sand-sculpture of a dragon on a beach, Corralejo

Corralejo **❸**

🏃 12,500. ⛴ ℹ️ Plaza Pública de Corralejo, 928 866 235. 🛒 Mon, Tue, Thu, Fri. 🎭 Carnival (Mar), Nuestra Señora del Carmen (16 Jul).

This northernmost town of Fuerteventura has a passenger harbour, with ferries sailing several times a day to Playa Blanca in Lanzarote. Small cruising boats also take tourists to the neighbouring island of Los Lobos. Weather-beaten fishing boats moored at the quayside and several fish restaurants add a touch of charm to this old fishing village.

Over the past decade Corralejo has become one of Fuerteventura's most important vacation centres, along with the Jandía peninsula. Visitors come here not so much for the town but for its setting, with striking views of Lanzarote and Los Lobos and the wonderful beaches to the south of the centre. Excellent conditions for surfing and windsurfing are another

Jet-skis and sailing school in Corralejo harbour

attraction. Thanks to a year-round stiff breeze, the El Río strait between Corralejo and Lanzarote is an ideal place for water sports. The clear water teems with a rich variety of fish. Angling, diving and glass-bottomed boat trips are very popular.

The only interesting sight in town is its modern church in **Plaza de la Iglesia**. The town's main attraction is sand-sculpting – on a small beach by the harbour, giant dragons and camels can be conjured up before your eyes.

Isla de los Lobos ❹

This small volcanic island, occupying only 4.4 sq km (1.7 sq miles) is situated in the El Río strait, between Fuerteventura and Lanzarote. It can be reached by small cruising boat from Corralejo or

---

MIGUEL DE UNAMUNO (1864–1936)

Miguel de Unamuno, the "Philosopher from Salamanca", played a major part in the rebirth of Spanish literature and in the intellectual life of Spain in the early 20th century.

He was the rector of Salamanca University from 1900. Having spoken out against the dictatorship of Primo de Rivera he was forced into exile in the Canary Islands for a few months. His opposition to Franco led to his being put under house arrest. In his work, he advocated the view that philosophy should express the tragedy of the human dilemma. Declaring himself a defender of "pure Spanishness", his *Spanish Travels and Scenes* (1922) is a testament to the author's love for his homeland.

Miguel de Unamuno, outspoken and defiant

---

by glass-bottomed motor-yacht. The island of Los Lobos is very young, little more than 6,000–8,000 years old, and owes its name to the seals – *lobos marinos* – which once made their home on its sandy shores.

According to the history books, the French adventurer de la Salle dropped anchor by the island of Los Lobos in 1402. He and his crew were saved from starvation by seal meat. In the early 15th century, Jean de Béthencourt built a hermitage on the island. Later on, the island served as a base for pirates raiding the neighbouring islands of the archipelago. It was also a centre of the slave trade.

The island was inhabited by its only residents – the lighthouse keeper and his

family – until 1968. It has remained uninhabited. Thanks to the fact that the island remained uninhabited for so long, it has retained its original ecosystem. The natural botanical garden on the slopes of the Montaña Lobos is used as a resting place by migrating birds.

The whole of the island of Los Lobos is a nature reserve. The sandy coves offer ideal conditions for swimming and relaxing, while angling is limited to a few allocated spots. There is a good marked walking trail around the island; it starts and ends in Casas del Puertito – a small hamlet with a harbour. There is no accommodation on the island, but day visitors can enjoy peace, tranquility and great views of Fuerteventura.

Isla de los Lobos, a fine destination for picnics, swimming and hiking trips

Fishing harbour in El Cotillo, with the mighty Fortaleza del Tostón guarding its entrance

El Cotillo ❺

🚌 ℹ️ 928 866 235. 🎉 *Nuestra Señora del Buen Viaje (3rd Sun in Aug).*

The early days of this small fishing town are associated with the Guanches. This was once the seat of the tribal chiefs of Maxorata – the ancient kingdom that encompassed the northern part of Fuerteventura.

The round fortified tower – **Fortaleza del Tostón** – dates from more recent times. A small fort, it was built in 1797 as a defence against British and Arab pirates. Thanks to restoration work it is now well preserved. Approached via stone steps with a drawbridge, this is a two-storey structure. Originally the upper floor housed a water tank, while the lower level was used as soldiers' quarters.

The small harbour features a **giant rock** rising out of the water. Although picturesque, it is hard for fishermen to navigate during rough weather. El Cotillo also offers scenic coves and sandy beaches.

La Oliva ❻

🎉 2,300. 🚌 ℹ️ 928 866 235. 🎉 *Nuestra Señora de la Candelaria (2 Feb), Nuestra Señora del Rosario (Oct).*

Situated at the northern end of Fuerteventura, La Oliva is one of the prettiest villages on the island and a popular excursion destination. It stands in the shadow of Montaña de Escantraga (529 m/1730 ft). The first European settlers arrived here in the early 14th century. In 1709, the newly established military governor of the island (the "Colonel") selected La Oliva as his seat. The town soon became the military capital of the island and, along with Betancuria, a centre of Fuerteventura's political life.

The military headquar-

Sculpture, Centro de Arte Canario

ters were at the **Casa de los Coroneles**. The "House of Colonels", built in the 18th century, is a large austere edifice featuring two low towers at the corners and numerous windows: it is said to have one window for each day of the year though this is inaccurate. The nearby **Casa del Capellán** (Chaplain's House) is a modest single-storey building with an ornately decorated portal and window frames.

In the town centre stands the **Iglesia de Nuestra Señora de la Candelaria**. The white walls of this attractive church, which dates from 1711, stand in stark contrast to its square belfry, built of black volcanic stone and visible from miles away. The interior of the church houses numerous fine features, including a Mudéjar ceiling, a large painting of The Last Judgement, a Baroque altar painting and various other sculptures and paintings by the 18th century artist Juan de Miranda. The **Museo del Grano** – with an exhibition on grain production in an early 19th-century granary, is worth a visit.

🏛 **Museo del Grano La Cilla**
Tel 928 868 729. ⏰ 10am–6pm Tue–Sat. ⬤ *Sun, Mon.* 🚫

The triple-naved Iglesia de Nuestra Señora de la Candelaria, La Oliva

For hotels and restaurants in this region see pp158–60 and p174

Tefía ❼

🏛 230.

This village, which lies on the road from La Oliva to Betancuria, has an interesting open-air museum – the **Ecomuseo de la Alcogida** – featuring seven reconstructed houses typical of traditional Fuerteventura architecture. The exhibition illustrates the former life of the islanders, their occupations relating to farming and crafts, and also explains the process of the houses' reconstruction.

Reconstructed farm buildings in the Ecomuseo de la Alcogida, Tefía

🏛 **Ecomuseo de la Alcogida**
Tel 928 175 434.
⬜ 10am–6pm Tue–Sat.

Environs
Some 12 km (7 miles) northeast is the small town of **Tetir**. It's worth visiting for its traditional houses with balconies and the local church, Santo Domingo de Guzmán (1745). The square in front of the church features a bust of Juán Rodriguez y Gonzáles (1825–93), the founder of the Banco de Canarias, who was born here.

A further 8 km (5 miles) north, on the slopes of **Montaña Quemada**, stands a monument to Miguel de Unamuno. Reaching over 2 m (7 ft) in height, it was carved in 1970 by Juan Borges Lineres.

Antigua ❽

🚌 🎇 *Nuestra Señora de Pino (8 Sep).*

Antigua, in the centre of Fuerteventura at the foot of the mountains, is – true to its name – one of the oldest towns on the island. It was established in 1485 by the settlers arriving from Andalusia and Normandy, who began cultivating the soil and breeding animals. Many windmills erected at the time were used to irrigate the fields. In 1812, Antigua was granted municipal rights and from 1835 it was the capital of the island.

Its more interesting features include the small, single-nave church of **Nuestra Señora de**

Antigua (1785), which has wooden vaults and a high altar incorporating folk motifs.

The **Centro de Artesanía Molinos de Antigua**, situated on the town's outskirts and surrounded by a low wall, is a museum village, built under the supervision of César Manrique, which includes a craft centre, a reconstructed

Façade of the late 18th-century church, Antigua

windmill, and a gallery and exhibition halls devoted to ethnography and archaeology.

🏛 **Centro de Artesanía Molinos de Antigua**
Tel 928 878 041. ⬜ 10am–6pm Tue–Sat. 🈺

Environs
Travel 8 km (5 miles) to the north for **La Ampuyenta**, a small village with a 17th-century chapel, San Pedro de Alcántara. This picturesque sanctuary is surrounded by a fortification erected by Norman settlers.

Some 9 km (6 miles) south is the village of **Tiscamanita**, with the 17th-century chapel of San Marcos. At the **Centro de Interpretación de los Molinos**, visitors can learn about the island's many windmills.

🏛 **Centro de Interpretación de los Molinos**
Tel 928 164 275. ⬜ 10am–6pm Tue–Sat. 🈺

JEAN DE BÉTHENCOURT (C.1360–1422)

On 1 May 1402, Jean de Béthencourt, together with Gadifer de la Salle, set sail from La Rochelle in France, at the head of a small expedition intent on conquering the Canary Islands. He left some of his men on Lanzarote and sailed to Spain to seek support. He returned not only with ships, soldiers and money, but also with a title – he was now the lord of four of the islands: Fuerteventura, Lanzarote, El Hierro and La Gomera. The furious de la Salle immediately returned to France. Béthencourt, having handed over the power to his nephew, Maciot de Béthencourt, also returned to France in 1406. He died at his castle in Normandy in 1422.

Jean de Béthencourt, Norman conqueror

Betancuria's lush vegetation, a contrast to the stark mountains beyond

Betancuria 🌀

🏃 600. 🚌 ℹ️ C/Amador
Rodríguez, 6, 928 878 092.
📅 San Buenaventura (14 Jul).

Nestling in a volcanic crater sheltered from the winds, Betancuria lies in the central region of the island, where the rugged peaks of extinct volcanoes punctuate the wide, fertile valleys. Practically all of this area is within the Parque Natural de Betancuria. The highest peak, Pico de Betancuria, offers a splendid vantage point.

The town was founded in 1404 and was given its full name, Villa de Santa María de Betancuria, by Jean de Béthencourt. The Norman made the town the island's capital and it remained so until 1834. Betancuria's inland position was intended to protect it against pirate raids. However, in 1593, the Berber pirate Xabán de Arráez pillaged it mercilessly, destroying virtually every building and taking 600 of its inhabitants captive.

Today, Betancuria is the prettiest village on Fuerteventura. At its centre stands the **Iglesia de Santa María**. The first church built on this site in 1404 was elevated to the status of a cathedral and bishopric by Pope Martin III in 1425, but no bishop ever arrived to take up the post. In 1593, the church was burned by Arráez; it was rebuilt in 1620. Noteworthy features of its interior include the Baroque altar, the original stone floor set in a wooden frame, the carved stalls and the coffered

ceiling. The space behind the choir contains a vast painting, *Nava de La Iglesia*, depicting the church as a ship, painted by Nicolas Medina in 1730.

On the northern outskirts of the village is the Franciscan abbey of **San Buenaventura** – the oldest abbey on the island. Its roof collapsed in the mid-19th century and what remains today are merely scenic ruins. Next to the abbey stands **Pozo del Diablo** – Devil's Pit. According to legend, Satan was chained to this rock and forced to carry stones used in the building of the abbey.

Betancuria has two small museums. The **Museo de Arte Sacro**, established in a former parish house, has a collection of sacred art and photographs showing almost every church on the Canary Islands. The **Museo Arqueológico** has a collection dating from the time of the Guanches, as well as antique items of everyday use. Visitors to the restored 16th-century town house of Casa

de Santa Maria can pick up souvenirs in the craft shop.

🏛 **Museo de Arte Sacro**
Alcalde Carmelo Silvera, s/n. 🕐
11am–4pm Mon–Fri, 11am–
2pm Sat.

🏛 **Museo Arqueológico**
Roberto Roldán, 12–14. **Tel** 928
878 241. 🕐 10am–6pm Tue–Sat.

Environs
Some 2 km (1 mile) north of Betancuria, Mirador de Morro Velosa offers a fine view over the island's dramatic lunar-like landscape.

Ajuy 🔟

30 km (19 miles) southwest of Betancuria.

Ajuy perches on the shores of a small bay and is surrounded by steep cliffs. Jean de Béthencourt, accompanied by Gadifer de la Salle, landed here in 1402 and embarked on the conquest of the island. For many years the bay served as a harbour for settlers arriving in Betancuria.

Today Ajuy is a quiet fishing village. The fishing season lasts from May until October and during this time the simple beach-side restaurants serve up the day's catch. Numerous caves, such as the Arco de Jurao, can be explored.

With its rocky seabed, vast underwater caves and shoals of darting fish, Ajuy is a paradise for scuba divers.

Waves battering the steep cliffs around Ajuy

Old irrigation equipment, Pájara

Pájara ⓫

🏠 🎎 *Virgen del Carmen (16 Jul).*

To the south of Betancuria lies the small town of Pájara, linked with the island's capital by a scenic road. This is one of the oldest settlements on Fuerteventura. It was founded by fishermen and goatherders who settled here in the 16th century.

Historic attractions include the church of **Nuestra Señora de la Regla**. Built in 1684, the church is worth seeing for its Latin American influences. The stone reliefs above the main portal depict stylized images of fish, lions, birds and snakes devouring their own tails. The origin of these motifs, said to be inspired by Aztec art, is unknown. The church's interior features two wooden altars, including a smiling figure of the Madonna and Child, and one of Our Lady of Sorrows (Nuestra Señora de los Dolores), the patron saint of the island.

Environs
Some 11 km (7 miles) northeast lies **Vega de Río Palmas**. Here, perched among high rocks is the hermitage of Nuestra Señora de la Peña which features another image of Our Lady of Sorrows. Each year on the third Sunday in May a feast is held here in her honour. The church (1666) contains statues of saints, believed to have been brought here by Béthencourt for the first church built in Betancuria.

Portal of the church in Pájara

La Pared ⓬

About 21 km (13 miles) south of Pájara.

This small tourist town has undergone a fair degree of development and includes an elegant hotel. It is worth visiting both for its historical associations and for its landscape.

Before the Spanish conquest, a land wall running around here *(la pared)* marked the boundary between two rival Guanche kingdoms: Maxorata and Jandía. Much of the wall may have been dismantled to use as building material; today no trace of it remains.

La Pared has the most extensive dunes to be found anywhere in Fuerteventura and separates the Jandía peninsula from the remaining part of the island. It also forms a natural border between two beaches of completely different sand colour. The southern Playa del Vejo Rey has golden sand. To the north, Playa de la Pared consists of black sand.

A trek of several hours along some interesting

volcanic formations leads to a ravine at the foot of the Risco del Pasco mountain, where it joins the road leading to Morro Jable.

Costa Calma ⓭

Costa Calma is an upmarket modern resort distinguished by its tasteful architecture. It lies at the northern end of Playa del Sotavento, which is the longest and most scenic beach on the island, with excellent conditions for windsurfing.

The first private homes appeared here in the late 1960s and the first hotel was built in 1977. The rapid growth of Costa Calma contributed to the construction of an asphalt road connecting Puerto del Rosario with Morro Jable. The building of a seawater desalination plant followed in 1986. Large-scale construction works began in the mid-1990s to provide tourist facilities, including hotels, restaurants and shops.

Environs
The small village of **La Lajita** lies 6 km (4 miles) north. Visitors come here for the **Zoo Parque de los Camellos**, home to 200 species of exotic birds and mammals from around the world. A local garden centre sells specimens of tropical and subtropical flora, as well as native plants. Other attractions include half-hour camel rides and parrot shows.

🐫 **Zoo Parque de los Camellos**
Tel 928 161 135. ⏰ 9am–6pm daily. 🖥 www.lajitaoasis.com

An eerie lunar landscape, the mountainous region north of La Pared

Virtually uninhabited northern coast, the Península de Jandía

Morro Jable

🏠 6,000. 🚌 ⛴

Set amid long sandy beaches, on the southern end of Fuerteventura, Morro Jable is an old fishing village with narrow streets and lively taverns, which serve dishes of freshly caught seafood. Once a sleepy little place, the village has grown in recent years to become the biggest resort on the island.

The modern part of town is geared for tourists and includes countless hotels and apartments, shopping malls, restaurants and bars. Hydrofoils and ferries sail from the local harbour to Las Palmas on Gran Canaria, while the marina is full of yachts. Morro Jable is also a good starting point for hikes on the Península de Jandía.

Península de Jandía ⑮

The Jandía Peninsula is surrounded by miles of scenic beaches with fine white sand. The longest beaches with the highest waves to be found on the island, they are particularly attractive to surfers, while the secluded beach of Barlovento, on the northwestern shore, is popular with scuba divers.

The area around Puerto de la Cruz, near Punta de Jandía – the southwestern headland

of the island with rocky shores and a solitary lighthouse – has in recent years become a Mecca for caravanning holiday-makers. In this remote region, it is possible to escape from most of the noise and bustle of mass tourism.

A considerable part of the peninsula, with its rugged hills, is a conservation area and forms part of the **Parque Natural de Jandía**. Covering 140 sq km (55 sq miles), it features many species native to the island. In the remote mountain valleys, it is still possible to see wild goats and donkeys.

During World War II, this was a closed area and belonged to the German industrialist Gustav Winter. Rumour has it that he ran a secret submarine base in southwest Fuerteventura during the war and stories about spies and buried Nazi treasure persist to this day.

Cofete ⑯

🏠 20.

Judging by the surroundings of this small, windswept village, Fuerteventura appears to be a desert island. Only a roughly surfaced road connects it with Morro Jable. At the height of Playa de Juan Gómez, the road forks: one road leads to the southwestern end of the island; the other winds up at Cofete. Cofete is the end of the line and marks the starting point for hiking trails along the ridge of Gran Valle and the pass between the peaks of Pico de Zarza and Fraile.

Beyond the village, perched below the Degollada de Cofete, is Gustav Winter's imposing villa. Cofete features the only restaurant found on the northern shore. A 2-km (1-mile) trail leads to the coast, and the Playa de Cofete, and further on, to Barlovento.

Gustav Winter's villa, on land given to him by General Franco

Windmills

Windmills of all types, driven by the steady trade winds, form an important element of the Canary Islands' landscape. Introduced in the 17th century, they came to replace the horse-driven mills – *tahonas*. The oldest type of windmill is the *molino*. Built of local stone, plastered in white, with a round body and conical roof, the *molino* has four to six sails. The 19th century saw the arrival of a second type of windmill – the *molina*. This differed from the previous design in the way its structure was exposed. Modern turbines were later introduced for use in desalination plants. In recent years an increasing number of wind farms have been popping up all over the island. These are used for generating electricity.

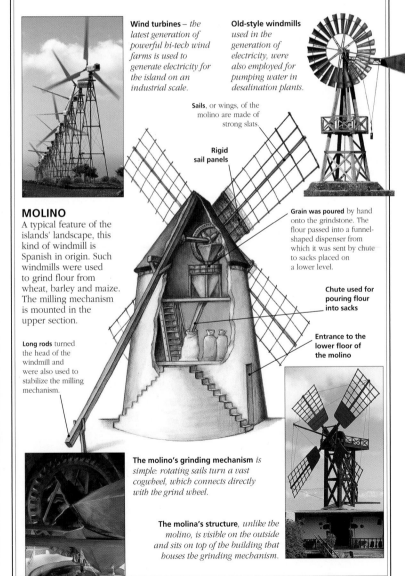

Wind turbines – *the latest generation of powerful hi-tech wind farms is used to generate electricity for the island on an industrial scale.*

Old-style windmills *used in the generation of electricity, were also employed for pumping water in desalination plants.*

Sails, or wings, of the molino are made of strong slats.

Rigid sail panels

MOLINO

A typical feature of the islands' landscape, this kind of windmill is Spanish in origin. Such windmills were used to grind flour from wheat, barley and maize. The milling mechanism is mounted in the upper section.

Grain was poured by hand onto the grindstone. The flour passed into a funnel-shaped dispenser from which it was sent by chute to sacks placed on a lower level.

Chute used for pouring flour into sacks

Entrance to the lower floor of the molino

Long rods turned the head of the windmill and were also used to stabilize the milling mechanism.

The molino's grinding mechanism *is simple: rotating sails turn a vast cogwheel, which connects directly with the grind wheel.*

The molina's structure, *unlike the molino, is visible on the outside and sits on top of the building that houses the grinding mechanism.*

Gran Tarajal ⑰

📧 🛈 *928 162 723.* ☑ *Fiesta de San Diego de Alcalá (13 Nov).*

This fair-sized town, the second largest on Fuerteventura, and an important trade centre, is free of much of the gloss typical of modern resorts. Due to its great strategic importance a fort was built here at the time of the island's invasion by Jean de Béthencourt.

From the early 20th century, the local port played a more important role than that of the island's capital and even now it is used for shipping merchandise from the Península de Jandía including tomatoes, fish and cattle. For those who enjoy swimming, Gran Tarajal has a safe but drab beach consisting of grey sand.

Apart from the single-nave church of **Nuestra Señora de la Candelaria**, built in 1900, which can be found in the

Waterfront at the harbour, Las Playitas near Gran Tarajal

town centre, there are virtually no historical sights.

Environs
A detour 8 km (5 miles) to the east leads to a small fishing village – **Las Playitas**. The peaceful atmosphere contrasts with that of the crowded resorts. Instead of vast hotels and apartments, guests are invited to stay in old fishermen's cottages clad with bougainvillaea and peppers, and boasting fantastic sea views. Local bars and restaurants serve fresh fish daily. Near the harbour is a small stony beach. Some 6 km (4 miles) to the north is **Punta de la Entallada**. This is the point of Fuerteventura closest to Africa and is reached by a narrow, winding road. On top of 300-metre (1,000-ft) tall cliffs is a lighthouse. Built in 1950, it resembles a fortress. The site offers a splendid view across the mountainous part of the island and the Atlantic.

Malpaís Chico and Malpaís Grande ⑱

The inhospitable Regions of Malpaís Chico and Malpaís Grande bear witness to the island's volcanic past, and occupy the central-eastern

---

Fuerteventura's Beaches

Fuerteventura, one of the least populated of the Canary Islands relative to its size, features the archipelago's most beautiful beaches, which stretch for miles. The loveliest of these are on the Península de Jandía, where sunseekers will readily find peace and quiet. There are almost 150 of these remote beaches, of which some are popular with nudists (*see p187*).

Cofete ②
It takes a determined effort to reach this remote and windswept beach of white sand near the village of Cofete.

Puerto de la Luz ③
This tiny fishing hamlet, situated on the southwestern tip of the island, is extremely remote. Popular with windsurfers, it has just one local restaurant, which serves fresh seafood.

Playa de las Pilas ④
is a small but pretty beach in a natural and unspoilt setting. The calm sea and gentle winds attract many visitors.

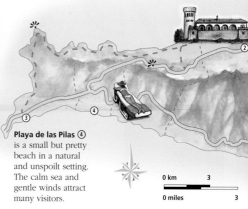

0 km 3
0 miles 3

part of Fuerteventura. It would be pointless to look for any traces of human activity here.

Don't look for any roads either. The bleak landscape is traversed by two hiking trails. One leads around Malpaís Chico, which was formed by lava flowing from the Caldera de Gaíra. The other, leading to Malpaís Grande, passes through the national park, declared a conservation zone in view of its unique geological features. Wildlife is scarce; one of the few creatures to inhabit this desert area is the Egyptian vulture.

Caleta de Fustes ⑲

🏃 2,600. 🚌 🛈 Caleta Dorada, El Castillo, 928 163 576. ⚓ Nuestra Señora del Carmen (16 Jul).

Caleta de Fustes is one of the island's main vacation centres. Though not the most attractive resort, it is a quiet place. Located in the middle of the eastern coast, it is convenient for the airport. It features sprawling, low-built apartments, built around a horseshoe bay with a safe, sandy beach. The resort is an excellent choice for visitors with small children.

At its centre is **Pueblo Majorero** – a modern, village-like complex of shops, bars and restaurants. One of the bungalow estates, the Barceló Club El Castillo, is built round the old **El Castillo** watchtower near the harbour. Built in 1741, it bears witness to the strategic importance of this place during the 18th century.

Tourist attractions include a good range of facilities for water sports including diving and windsurfing, and the island's first golf course.

El Castillo, the watchtower in Caleta de Fustes

Playa de Barlovento ① is a remote beach popular with scuba divers, and can only be reached by off-road vehicles.

Costa Calma ⑦ is a fast-developing resort. The local beach borders Playa de Sotavento.

FV 2

Playa de Sotavento ⑥
The 22-km (14-mile) belt of beaches is nicknamed "Rhapsody in Blue" due to the combination of wonderful beaches and azure, crystal-clear water.

Morro Jable ⑤
Located on the southern end of the Sotavento beaches, Morro Jable has a promenade running along the municipal beach with restaurants, bars and cafés.

LANZAROTE

This is volcano country. Known as the Isla del Fuego, or Fire Island, most of Lanzarote's 795 sq km (300 sq miles) is covered with solidified lava in tones of black, pink, purple and ochre, and peppered with nearly 300 volcanic peaks. Many tourists stick to the coast, especially the northern shores. Others prefer to head inland to trek through Lanzarote's breathtaking lunar landscape.

Much of the local architecture is in harmony with the island's unique landscape. The inhabitants continue to build in the traditional style and, as a result of strict planning controls, Lanzarote is almost totally free of high-rise buildings. This trend has been influenced by the artistic concepts of the late architect and artist César Manrique regarding the development of the island. In 1993, to support the local population in their efforts to preserve the natural landscape, UNESCO declared Lanzarote a Biosphere Reserve.

The island's name probably derives from the distorted name of the Genoese sailor Lanzarotto (or Lancelotto) Malocello, who first arrived here in 1312. In 1402, the island was conquered by Jean de Béthencourt.

The proximity of the African coast made the island prone to attacks by Algerian and Moroccan pirates, who often plundered the then capital, Teguise. In the 16th and 17th centuries, the island was also raided by English and French pirates. These attacks, combined with years of droughts and catastrophic volcanic eruptions, led at one time to the almost total depopulation of the island.

In the absence of any natural resources, the main occupations of the inhabitants were agriculture and fishing. Large plantations of prickly pear and vineyards still flourish. Other crops include tomatoes and sweet potato. In recent years, tourism has become the dominant industry, generating 80 per cent of the island's revenue. The development of agriculture and tourism has resulted in a severe water shortage. Until recently, drinking water was shipped in. Then, in 1964, the first desalination plant was opened and today almost every large estate has its own unit.

Timanfaya National Park logo

Camel caravan in Parque Nacional de Timanfaya

◁ Typical vineyards in La Gería

Exploring Lanzarote

Although Lanzarote is almost totally devoid of
vegetation, many tourists, enchanted by the
shapes and colours of its unique volcanic
landscape, regard the island as the most
picturesque in the archipelago. Camels, used in
agriculture and tourism, are an intrinsic element
of the landscape. Visitors also come here for the
beaches. Lanzarote's northern shores are good
for surfing; the waves are especially good at La
Santa. The strange architectural designs of César
Manrique, which merge with the natural
landscape, are another of the island's attractions.

LOCATOR MAP

SIGHTS AT A GLANCE

Fountain and church in the main
square, San Bartolomé

Mosaic in Tahiche's César Manrique Fundación

GETTING THERE

Lanzarote has air links with the other islands of
the archipelago and with mainland Spain.
Regular charter flights also bring in visitors from
all over Europe. Frequent ferries connect
Lanzarote with nearby Fuerteventura and Gran
Canaria. The capital and other main towns have
reasonable public transport. Not all places on the
island are so well served, however. Many places,
even those that are particularly attractive to
tourists, cannot be reached by bus and it is
advisable to make use of organized coach tours
or to hire a car. Though the main roads are well-
surfaced, some remote beaches require an
all-terrain vehicle.

Playa Papagayo near Playa Blanca

SEE ALSO

Roque del Este

Montaña Clara

Playa de las Conchas

Playa Lambra

ISLA GRACIOSA 9

Caleta del Sebo

Playa de la Cantería

8 ÓRZOLA

MIRADOR DEL RÍO 10

MALPAÍS DE LA CORONA 7

△ Monte Corona 609m

LZ1

GUINATE 11

CUEVA DE LOS VERDES 6

Máguez

5 **JAMEOS DEL AGUA**

HARÍA 12

○ Punta de Mujeres

Arrieta

Playa de Famara

LA CALETA DE FAMARA 14

Mirador de Haría

La Isleta

La Santa

Famara

Mala

L767

LZ10

4 **GUATIZA**

Tinajo

LZ1

TIAGUA 15

TEGUISE 13

LZ20

Tao

LZ30

Caldera Blanca 449m

Mozago

3 **TAHICHE**

Z67

Monumento al Campesino

△ Pico Partido 517m

Madasche

16 **SAN BARTOLOMÉ**

LZ1

LZ20

2 **COSTA TEGUISE**

L730

23 **LA GERIA**

Argana

Macher

Tias

1 **ARRECIFE**

LZ22

L22

L740

Playa Honda

Punta Montañosa

24

PUERTO DEL CARMEN

Playa Blanca

aya uemada

KEY

━━━ Motorway

━━━ Major road

━━━ Minor road

──── Scenic route

△ Summit

0 km 5

0 miles 5

Picturesque house on the ocean front, Arrieta

Charco de San Ginés, in Arrecife, with its small, picturesque fishermen's cottages

Arrecife **❶**

🏃 *43,000.* ✈ *6 km (4 miles) west of Arrecife.* 🚌 ℹ *Calle Blas Cabrera Felipe, 3, 928 811 762.* ⚓ *Sat.* 🎭 *Carnival (Feb), San Ginés (Aug).*

Arrecife has genuine Spanish character. With modern houses and a palm-lined promenade, it has been the capital of Lanzarote since 1852, as well as the island's main seaport and commercial centre. It is not as picturesque as the rest of the island, but there are some interesting sights and no high-rise apartment blocks; instead the one-storey houses are built in the traditional style. The attractive main shopping street, Castillo y Leon, has goods at much cheaper prices than at the major tourist resorts, and a number of cafés and restaurants.

The first harbour, protected by small islands and reefs, existed here as early as the 15th century. Two forts, the **Castillo de San Gabriel** (1574–99) and **Castillo de San José** (1771) were built to protect the island from seaborne raiders and have survived to this day.

The castle of St Gabriel, situated on a small island, is reached by a long drawbridge – Puente de las Bolas, or "Balls Bridge". Destroyed during a pirate attack in 1586, the castle

was restored by Italian engineer Leonardo Torriani. It used to house an archaeological museum and can still be admired from the outside.

The San José fortress, restored by Manrique, was turned into a modern art gallery in 1979. Four rooms of the **Museo Internacional de Arte Contemporáneo** are used for temporary exhibitions of the great masters, including Pablo Picasso, Joan Miró, Oscar Domingue or Manrique himself. Recitals of chamber and modern music are held in the concert hall. Manrique designed the spacious and stylish gallery as well as the castle restaurant.

Also worth visiting are the **Casa Augustín de la Hoz**, now a club, and **Casa de Los Arroyos**, dating back to 1749 and featuring a courtyard

with wooden galleries and a well at its centre. This is now the home of the **Centro Cientifíco Cultural**, housing a permanent exhibition devoted to the outstanding physicist Blas Cabrera Felipe (1878–1945), who was born in Arrecife and whose bronze statue stands on the square by Paseo Marítimo.

Quite different in character is the area around **Charco de San Ginés**, with its pretty fishermen's cottages overlooking a small lake that connects to the sea. The **Iglesia de San Ginés**, completed in 1665, is dedicated to the patron saint of Arrecife. This triple-naved church with timber vaults features late-Baroque statues of San Ginés and the Virgen del Rosario, which were brought from Cuba.

🏛 **Museo Internacional de Arte Contemporáneo**
Castillo de San José, Carretera de Naos. **Tel** *928 598 500.* ◯ *11am–9pm daily.* 📷

Costa Teguise **❷**

🏃 *4,500.* 🚌 ℹ *Avenida de las Islas, 928 592 542.*

This is the third largest resort on the island, after Puerto del Carmen and Playa Blanca. Just 9 km (6 miles) northeast of Arrecife, it is fairly new and dates back to 1977, when the five-star Gran Melia Salinas hotel was built here with the assistance of César Manrique.

Arrecife's Iglesia de San Ginés

This large resort with low-rise holiday developments of white bungalows has a golf course, a marina and a shopping centre. It also has some pleasant sandy beaches. The largest and most scenic of these is Playa de las Cucharas. Smart and modern, Costa Teguise once attracted an elite clientele (King Juan Carlos of Spain has a private villa here) though it is today fairly similar to other resorts on the island.

Constant breezes mean that the place is popular with windsurfers. Those preferring safer water sports can enjoy the water park located just outside town.

Monument at Playa de las Cucharas, Costa Teguise

Tahiche ❸

5 km (3 miles) north of Arrecife.

Just outside the town, on the lava fields created by the 1730–36 volcanic eruptions, stands **Taro de Tahiche**. This house was built in 1968 by César Manrique, who lived here until 1988. Four years later he donated Taro de Tahiche to the **Fundación César Manrique**. Founded by himself and a circle of his friends, this organization aims to promote architecture that is in harmony with the natural environment.

In keeping with this aim, Manrique built his house amid the island's characteristic blue-black lava flows. The cubic forms above ground draw on the traditional style of the island, though the space is opened out with contemporary touches such as large windows and wide terraces. Below ground, the design becomes more startling still. The lower floor features five volcanic "bubbles" – interconnected by tunnels. These vast compartments, 5 m (16 ft) in diameter, were formed by solidifying lava. Each of the "bubbles" has its own basalt staircase leading from the lower floor to the upper level. In one of the rooms, the upper and lower spaces are linked by a fig tree, which rises from the lower floor and into the drawing room above.

The house, which became the embodiment of the artist's dream to live near and in harmony with nature, now houses a modern art museum which has examples of Manrique's own works and project designs, plus other modern art, including works of art by Pablo Picasso, Antonio Tapiès, Joan Miró, and Jesús Soto.

Taro de Tahiche, Manrique's former home

The broad terraces and garden are an essential part of the house. Situated within the garden, near the café, is a giant mural made in 1992 by Manrique, using volcanic rock and ceramic tiles.

🏛 **Fundación César Manrique**
Taro de Tahiche. **Tel** *928 843 138.*
⏱ *Nov–Jun: 10am–6pm Mon–Sat, 10am–3pm Sun; Jul– Oct: 10am–7pm daily.*

CESAR MANRIQUE (1919–1992)

César Manrique – painter, sculptor, architect, town-planner and art restorer – was born in Arrecife. Having completed his army service in 1937–39, he devoted himself to art. His abstract paintings were exhibited across Europe as well as in Japan and the United States, and he won international acclaim. In 1968, he returned to Lanzarote and brought his talent to bear on the task of protecting the natural environment against the uncontrolled development of the island for tourism. Manrique's efforts paid off and rules were introduced for developers dictating the height, style and colour of buildings. In addition, Manrique's own designs incorporating volcanic forms helped to create many architectural masterpieces on all the Canary Islands. Manrique died in a car accident in 1992 but he left his mark on Lanzarote, both in terms of his bold designs and in the restrained way traditional island life has adapted to tourism.

César Manrique, against the backdrop of immense lava fields

Giant metal cactus at the entrance to Guatiza's Jardín de Cactus

Guatiza ❹

🏛 820. 17 km (11 miles) northeast of Arrecife.

The small town of Guatiza, situated north of Lanzarote and featuring the lovely 19th-century chapel of **Santa Margarita**, is surrounded by vast plantations of prickly pear. The plant is host to the cochineal insect – a source of vermilion or crimson dye.

Situated at the very centre of the cactus fields, on the outskirts of Guatiza, is the **Jardín de Cactus**, designed by César Manrique. At the entrance to the garden, established in 1987–92, stands an 8-m (26-ft) tall metal statue of a cactus. The large garden, which has a good restaurant, was built in an enormous pit, originally dug by the villagers who were excavating volcanic ash to fertilize their fields.

The Jardín de Cactus is arranged in the form of a giant amphitheatre, dominated by a white windmill. Growing on the terraces are about 10,000 specimens, representing over 1,000 varieties of cactus.

🌵 **Jardín de Cactus**
Tel *928 529 397.*
⏰ *10am–5:45pm daily.* 📷

Jameos del Agua ❺

Carretera de Orzola. 🚌 ***Tel*** *928 848 020.* ⏰ *9:30am–7pm Tue; 9:30am–2am Fri & Sat.* 📷

In the late 1960s, César Manrique turned these natural caves, formed within a lava flow, into a complex of entertainment venues.

Situated in the northeastern part of the island, just a short walk from the sea, the caverns are well worth visiting. A staircase leads down to an underground restaurant and, further on, to a giant cave, 62 m (203 ft) long, 19 m (62 ft) wide and 21 m (70 ft) high.

The cave features a salt lake, connected to the ocean (look out for the unique blind species of crab). The bed is below sea level and the water level rises and falls with the tide.

Above the caves is Jameo Grande. This picturesque, irregularly-shaped swimming pool is surrounded by artistically arranged tropical flora. Jameo Grande opens to an underground auditorium, seating 600. This unique setting is famous for its outstanding acoustics. Apart from the natural features in the caves, another point of interest is the exhibition on volcanoes.

At night one of the caves is used as a nightclub – a striking setting for a dancefloor.

A palm beside the pool in one of Jameos del Agua's sunken craters

Cueva de los Verdes ❻

26 km (16 miles) north of Arrecife. ***Tel*** *928 173 220.* ⏰ *10am–6pm daily.* 📷 🎫

Cueva de los Verdes is a 7-km (4-mile) long underground volcanic tunnel, and was created by the eruption of the nearby Monte Corona, about 5,000 years ago. One of the world's longest volcanic tunnels, it is formed from a tube of solidified lava. The cave's name has nothing to do with its green colour. It derives from the name of a shepherd family, the Verdes (Greens), who inhabited it in the 18th

Exploring the Cueva de los Verdes

and 19th centuries. From the 17th century onwards, the cave was used by the local population as a shelter from pirates and slave traders.

In 1964, artificial lighting was installed and 2 km (1 mile) of the cave was opened to visitors. The tour takes about 50 minutes. One of the caves included in the tour features a small lake. Although only 20 cm (8 inches) deep, the stone vaults reflected in the water make it appear far deeper. Another cave has been converted to a concert hall.

Lichen growing on the volcanic debris in Malpaís de la Corona

Malpaís de la Corona ❼

These volcanic badlands bear testimony to the extreme volcanic activities that shook the northernmost point of the island some 5,000 years ago. This wild terrain, strewn with volcanic rock and slowly being colonized by sparse vegetation, occupies 30 sq km (12 sq miles) between the village of Orzola and the headland of Punta de Mujeres, near Arietta.

On the western end of Malpaís, visible from far and wide, stands the mighty Monte Corona volcano. This measures 1,100 m (3,600 ft) in diameter at its base, and 450 m (1,500 ft) at its top section. Standing 609 m (2,000 ft) high, the eruptions of this volcano produced the wide belt of strange lava formations (the Malpaís de la Corona), which include the Cueva de los Verdes and Jameos del Agua.

Orzola ❽

 100.

This fishing village, lying at the northern tip of Lanzarote, is a haven of peace. It is known mainly for its excellent seafood restaurants, which stretch along the coastal seafront.

Orzola is also famous for the picturesque **Playa de la Cantería**, situated to the west. This beach is not suitable for bathing, however, as strong sea currents create unfavourable conditions.

A frequent motorboat service provides links with the neighbouring island of **Graciosa**. From here, you can travel by fishing boat as far as the islands of **Montaña Clara** and **Alegranza**.

You won't be allowed to explore, however, as these two small and uninhabited islands form part of the national park, which was founded in 1986, and are off-limits to visitors.

Isla Graciosa, seen from Mirador de Guinate

Isla Graciosa ❾

 650.

The smallest inhabited island of the archipelago has an area of just 27 sq km (10 sq miles). Separated from Lanzarote by the straits of El Río, it was dubbed the "gracious island" by Jean de Béthencourt and fully meets the expectations of visitors looking for a quiet rest.

An ideal place for scuba divers, anglers, hikers or anyone wishing to escape the brasher elements of tourism, Isla Graciosa plays to its strengths and offers a slow pace and a minimum of amenities. The island is fringed by long beaches of golden sand dunes.

The most beautiful of these is **Playa de las Conchas**, stretching over many kilometres of the northern shore. It is regarded as one of the most picturesque of all the beaches of the archipelago and provides a good view of the uninhabited smaller islands: **Montaña Clara, Roque del Este** and **Alegranza**.

There are no hotels on Graciosa, but the village of **Caleta del Sebo**, linked by a ferry service to Orzola, has a few pensions and restaurants.

Orzola, on the northern end of Malpaís de la Corona

Mirador del Río 🔟

Tel *928 173 536.* ⬜ *10am–6pm daily.* 🅿️

The most famous viewpoint on Lanzarote is situated at the northernmost point of the island, 479 m (1,630 ft) above sea level. This spot, hidden among rocks, provides a breathtaking view over the high cliffs of the northern shore. Clearly visible is the island of **Graciosa** and, beyond it, **Montaña Clara** and **Alegranza**.

In 1898, when Spain was at war with the United States over Cuba, a gun emplacement was built here, guarding the straits of El Río, which separate Lanzarote from Graciosa.

In 1973, the former gun emplacement was transformed by César Manrique to provide a belvedere and visitors have been coming here ever since. Built into the rock, with an enormous window stretching the length of the room, is a minimalist bar and restaurant. Its stone walls are painted white. The only significant decorations inside are the huge mobiles by César Manrique. Their function is not merely decorative; they are also meant to dampen noise, because of the poor acoustics of the place.

Sign at the Mirador del Río

Haría's town square with its restored, whitewashed houses

Guinate 🔟

🏞️ *50.* 🚍

Situated at the foot of the Monte Corona volcano, Guinate is a small village that is popular with bird lovers.

The **Guinate Tropical Park**, spread out on terraces, features water cascades, ponds and fine gardens. Here you can see some 1,300 exotic birds, representing about 300 species, as well as many small apes. The famous shows featuring trained birds are a big hit with children (look out for the scooter-riding parrots!).

🦜 **Guinate Tropical Park**
Tel *928 835 500.* ⬜ *10am–5pm daily.* 🅿️ www.guinatepark.com

Environs
Just outside the village, the **Mirador la Graciosa** provides fine views over Graciosa, Alegranza and Montaña Clara.

Haría 🔟

🏞️ *1,100.* 🚍 ℹ️ *Plaza de la Constitución, 928 835 251.* 📅 *San Juan (23 Jun), San Pedro (29 Jun).*

Cubic, whitewashed houses, reminiscent of North African architecture, along with numerous palms, give this picturesque village an almost Middle-Eastern flavour. The

scenic valley in which Haría is situated, known as the "valley of a thousand palms", was once home to far more of these trees. Many of them were burned during a pirate attack in 1856.

The shady, tree-lined **Plaza León y Castillo** is surrounded by restored historic houses. At one end of the square stands the church of **Nuestra Señora de la Encarnación**.

Environs
Not far south of Haría is the **Mirador de Haría**. A winding road leads to the mountain pass, providing a fine view over the village, the surrounding volcanoes, the high cliffs, and Arietta.

Teguise 🔟

🏞️ *1,500.* 🚍 ℹ️ *C/ General Franco, 1, 928 845 072.* 📅 *Sun.* 📅 *Nuestra Señora del Carmen (16 Jul), Virgen de las Nieves (5 Aug).*

Teguise is one of the oldest towns on Lanzarote. It was founded in 1418 by Maciot – nephew and successor of Jean de Béthencourt – who, it is said, lived here with Princess Teguise, the daughter of the Guanche king, Guadarfía.

Spacious squares and well-kept cobbled streets lined with beautifully restored houses are testimony to Teguise's former glory. A good time to visit is on Sundays, when there is a

Tourists enjoying the wonderful view from the Mirador del Río

flourishing handicrafts market and folk dancing.

For centuries the town was one of the largest and richest on the island. Until 1852, it was its capital city. The fame and the wealth of Teguise, bearing the proud name of La Villa Real de Teguise (the Royal City of Teguise), attracted pirates who raided it repeatedly. The Callejón de la Sangre ("street of blood") owes its name to the worst of these raids and commemorates the victims of the massacre that took place in 1596.

The eclectic church of **Nuestra Señora de Guadalupe** stands in the town square. Since its construction in the mid-15th century, it has been rebuilt many times. The interior furnishing is Neo-Gothic and features a statue of the Virgin Mary of Guadalupe. On the opposite side of the square stands the **Palacio Spínola**. This beautiful residence, with its small patio and a well, was built in 1730–80. The reconstruction work, supervised by César Manrique, has restored the palace interiors to their former glory. Now the Palacio Spínola fulfils a double function as a museum and as the official residence of the Canary Islands' government.

Also of interest are two conventual churches. The 16th-century **Convento de**

Castillo de Santa Bárbara, high above Teguise

Miraflores was used as a burial site for the most prominent citizens of Lanzarote, and is now a venue for cultural events. Inside the 17th-century **Convento de Santo Domingo** is the original main altar. Now the abbey houses a modern art gallery – the Centro Arte. Towering over the town is the **Castillo de Santa Bárbara**. The castle was built in the early 16th century on top of the 452-m (1,480-ft) high Guanapay peak, and provides a view over almost the entire island. Within the castle is the **Museo del Emigrante Canario**, which tells the story of emigrants to South and Central America.

Lion from Teguise Palace

🏛 **Palacio Spínola**
Plaza de San Miguel. *Tel 928 845 181.* ⏱ 9am–3pm Mon–Fri, 9am–2pm Sat–Sun. 📷

🏛 **Museo del Emigrante Canario**
Volcán de Guanapay. *Tel 928 845 001.* ⏱ 10am–6pm Mon–Fri, 10am–4pm Sat–Sun. 📷

La Caleta de Famara ⑭

🚶 650. 35 km (22 miles) north of Arrecife. 🚌

A small fishing village, with only a handful of restaurants, attracts visitors to **Playa de Famara**, one of the most beautiful beaches on Lanzarote. **Urbanización Famara**, situated to the north, is a cluster of holiday chalets.

The beautiful 3-km (2-mile) long sandy beach stretches along the base of tall cliffs formed during the most recent volcanic eruption in 1824. Behind the beach, which provides a wonderful view over **Isla Graciosa**, runs a long band of dunes. The heavy swell produces some splendid waves and makes this a popular surfing beach, though the strong currents can be dangerous.

The village also attracts quite a few painters. In view of its rich flora and fine scenery this whole area, including the cliffs and the Famara massif, has been declared a conservation area.

Playa de Famara, one of Lanzarote's most beautiful beaches

Windmill and camel at the Museo Agrícola El Patio, Tiagua

Tiagua ⑮

🏘 300. 🚌

This modest town offers visitors an insight into local history and tradition.

The **Museo Agrícola El Patio** provides a glimpse of past agricultural practices. The complex was opened in 1994 on the site of a farm dating back to 1845 when a group of impoverished farmers began to cultivate the fertile land. A century later, it was the biggest and best-run estate on the island.

As well as a number of well-preserved windmills, the indoor exhibitions feature displays of folk costumes, agricultural tools, a loom, some fine examples of plaitwork, and a collection of original photographs.

🏛 **Museo Agrícola El Patio**
Tel 928 529 134. ⬜ *10am–5pm Mon–Fri, 10am–2pm Sat.* 🖼

San Bartolomé ⑯

🏘 5,000. 🚌
📷 San Bartolomé (15 Aug).

Known to the Guanches as Ajei, San Bartolomé has some fine examples of traditional Canary architecture, including the 18th-century **Casa Pedromo**, with its beautiful courtyard and tiny chapel of Nuestra Señora del Pino. Today it houses the **Museo**

Etnográfico Tanit. Various exhibits, such as musical instruments, agricultural tools, furniture and wine production equipment, illustrate the island's economic history. In the town centre is a large, stylish square, containing the parish church of **San Bartolomé** (1789).

🏛 **Museo Etnográfico Tanit**
C/ Constitucíon, 1. Tel 928 520 655. ⬜ *10am–2pm Mon–Sat.* 🖼

Environs

A short way north, towards Mozaga, stands the **Monumento al Campesino** (Peasant's Monument). This 15-m (50-ft) tall construction was designed by César Manrique, and built in 1968 by Jesús Soto. Made of old water containers once used on fishing boats, the

Manrique's homage to peasant life

monument is devoted, in Manrique's own words, "to the nameless farmers, whose hard work helped to create the island's unique landscape".

The nearby **Casa-Museo del Campesino** houses a cluster of workshops devoted to various crafts, illustrating former rural life on Lanzarote. Its restaurant is a good place for lunch.

🏛 **Casa-Museo del Campesino**
⬜ *10am–6pm daily.*

Parque Nacional de Timanfaya ⑰

See pp92–3

Yaiza ⑱

🏘 650. 🚌 ℹ️ *Departamento de Turismo, 928 518 150.* 📷 *San Marcial (Jun), Nuestra Señora de los Remedios (1st week in Sep).*

Nestling at the foot of the Montañas del Fuego, Yaiza is regarded, along with Haría, as one of the most picturesque small towns on the island. In the 19th century, rich merchants settled here and to this day some houses with palm-shaded façades bear evidence of this former wealth. The parish church of **Nuestra Señora de los Remedios** dates from the 18th century. This triple-naved church was built on the site of

One of the former residences in Yaiza, now a hotel

Los Hervideros, south of El Golfo

a former chapel dating back to 1699 and has a number of fine 18th-century paintings.

The Baroque vault decorations, incorporating folk elements, give the church its unique atmosphere. Numerous shops along the main street sell embroidery, pottery and other items.

Environs
Just 2 km (1 mile) east of Yaiza, **Uga** is the departure point for camel trips across the volcanic landscape.

El Golfo ⑲

🏛 110. 7 km (4 miles) northwest of Yaiza.

The sleepy village of El Golfo is home to a small crater lagoon, **Lago Verde**, which was created by the an underwater volcano. Its emerald-green colour is due to the sea algae that thrive in it. El Golfo's restaurants make it popular with tourists while the presence of olivine (an olive-green semi-precious stone) attracts geologists and jewellery makers to the area.

Taking the path from the village, you get the best view of the lake, which is surrounded by dramatic, volcanic rocks resembling a petrified wave, and separated from the ocean by a narrow strip of black volcanic sand.

Environs
South of El Golfo are **Los Hervideros** ("the kettles"). As the name suggests, the waves "boil" inside the vast caves of the 15-m (50-ft) high cliffs.

Salinas de Janubio ⑳

9 km (6 miles) north of Playa Blanca.

The greenish waters of a natural lagoon are employed to produce salt. Long used to preserve fish, the salt is still extracted by the traditional method of evaporation.

The sea-salt plant is believed to be the largest operating on the archipelago and currently produces about 2,000 tons of salt per annum. Years ago, the water was pumped into the lagoon by windpower; today the pumps are electrically driven.

Most of the local salt is still bought by fishermen, with a small portion sold as table salt. Each year, during the Corpus Christi festival, the local inhabitants use tons of dyed salt to create magnificent decorations for the streets and squares of the island's capital.

Sunset over the checkerboard salt pans of Salinas de Janubio

Playa Blanca ㉑

🏛 500. 🚌 🚢 ℹ️ Muelle de Playa Blanca, 928 518 150. 🏖 Wed. 🎉 Nuestra Señora del Carmen (Jul).

A former fishing village, Playa Blanca has become one of the largest resorts on the island in recent years, with regular ferry links to nearby Fuerteventura. Yet despite its numerous restaurants, bars and shops, the village remains relatively quiet and is a popular destination for family holidays.

It has several beaches. One of the best is the small beach situated near the centre, which has clear water and wonderful views over the neighbouring islands of Fuerteventura and Los Lobos. The **Playas de Papagayo** beaches, situated 4 km (2 miles) south of Playa Blanca, are also popular with visitors.

Castillo de las Coloradas, one of Playa Blanca's former defences

Environs
The **Castillo de las Coloradas**, in Punta del Águila, is a watchtower dating from 1741–8. Between here and Punta de Papagayo is a string of scenic coves with sandy beaches: **Playa de las Mujeres**, **El Pozo** and **Papagayo**. Their fine sand and warm, clear waters attract an ever-increasing number of visitors.

This area is a part of the **Los Ajaches** nature reserve, created in 1994, which includes a bird protection zone. There is an entrance charge and the only access from Playa Blanca is by a minor road. Nearby, on the very edge of a cliff, are the remains of the island's first Norman settlement, **San Marcial del Rubicón**, founded in 1402 by Jean de Béthencourt.

Parque Nacional de Timanfaya 🔟

Between 1730 and 1736 the Montañas del Fuego – or Fire Mountains – belched forth smoke and molten lava, burying entire villages, and turning the island's fertile lowlands into a sea of solidified lava, grey volcanic rock and copper-coloured sand. Today, the lava remains are Lanzarote's greatest attraction. Situated to the southwest, they have become the heart of the national park, established in 1974, and include the 517-m (1,700-ft) Pico Partido. For the time being, the area is quite safe, though the lava still bubbles away under the surface and a whiff of sulphur hangs in the air.

Park Logo
This mischievous little devil, designed by César Manrique, marks the boundaries of the national park.

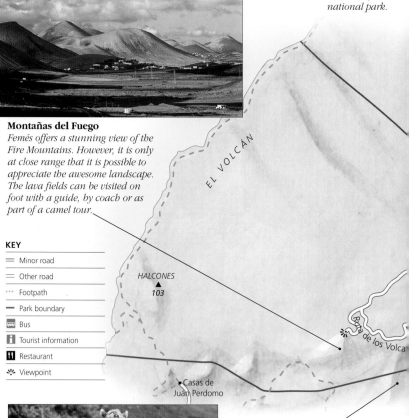

Montañas del Fuego
Femés offers a stunning view of the Fire Mountains. However, it is only at close range that it is possible to appreciate the awesome landscape. The lava fields can be visited on foot with a guide, by coach or as part of a camel tour.

EL VOLCÁN

HALCONES
▲
103

Boca de los Volcanes

● Casas de
Juan Perdomo

KEY

═	Minor road
═	Other road
···	Footpath
▬	Park boundary
🚌	Bus
ℹ	Tourist information
🍴	Restaurant
✹	Viewpoint

Echadero de los Camellos
This dromedary station includes a small exhibition illustrating the use of camels by humans. Camelback tours last half an hour and take in the outer reaches of the park.

Fire in a Crater
*Dry pieces of lichen, thrown into a shallow rock
hollow, begin to burn quickly, demonstrating the
continuing volcanic activity of this area.*

VISITORS' CHECKLIST

**Centro de Visitantes
Interpretación**, *Mancha Blanca.*
🚹 *C/Languneta, 64. Tinajo,
928 840 238, 928 840 240.*
Fax 928 840 251.
🕐 *10am–6pm daily.*
♿ ✔ 🅿 🍴

Geyser
*Water poured into
underground pipes turns
to steam within seconds.
Islote de Hilario has the
highest underground
temperature in the park,
reaching 600° C (1,112° F)
at a depth of 12 m (40 ft).*

CALDERA BLANCA
▲
149

TINAJO

CALDERA ROJA
427

LZ-67

CALDERA DE
LOS CUERVOS
502

PICO PARTIDO
517

YAIZA

0 km   1

0 miles   1

★ Volcanic Grill
*Taking advantage of the 300° C (572° F) temperatures,
the volcanic grill is used to cook meat and fish at the El
Diablo restaurant, designed by César Manrique (1970).*

★ Ruta de los Volcanes
*This is the most interesting part of the national park open
to visitors. However, there is a wide variety of different
landscapes and volcanic formations elsewhere in the park.*

STAR SIGHTS

★ Ruta de los Volcanes

★ Volcanic Grill

Femés ②

🏃 230. 🎏 San Marcial (7 Jul).

Overlooked by the 608-m (2,000-ft) high volcanic peak of Atalaya de Femés, this village once boasted one of the island's oldest religious buildings – the **Ermita San Marcial del Rubicón** cathedral, devoted to the patron saint of the island and destroyed in the 16th century by pirates. The present church, built on the site in 1733, is devoted to the same saint. Its white-painted walls are decorated with models of sailing ships, testimony to the seafaring heritage of the Canary Islands. Unfortunately, the church is open only during services.

In the centre of Femés, by the side of the road, is a fine viewpoint, which provides a scenic panorama of Montaña Roja and the ocean. The opposite side of town overlooks the panorama of Montañas del Fuego.

Ermita San Marcial del Rubicón, in Femés

La Geria ㉓

Northeast of Uga.

Stretching on both sides of the road from Masdache to Uga, the valley of La Geria is the main vine-growing area on Lanzarote. Set within this black cinder landscape that once featured only the occasional palm tree, the vineyards look as if they have been transplanted wholesale from another planet. They occupy 52 sq km (20 sq miles) and have been declared a protected area. The valley, right up to the volcanic slopes, is dotted with small hollows, sheltered from the drying wind by low, semicircular walls. Each hollow *(gería)* is covered with volcanic cinder that absorbs dew at night and maintains the required humidity. Each contains a single vine. There are over 10,000 such hollows here.

The grapes are used to produce the very sweet and

Lanzarote's Beaches

Lanzarote's 250-km (150-mile) long shoreline offers only 30 km (20 miles) of sandy beaches, some of which are popular with nudists *(see p187)*. In contrast to the long beaches of Fuerteventura, these are usually fairly small and consist of golden or white sand. Particularly beautiful beaches are found north of Arrecife.

Puerto del Carmen ③ has several easily accessible but built-up beaches. The main ones are Playa Blanca and Playa de los Pocillos, both over a kilometre (half a mile) long with golden sand.

Playas de Papagayo ①
A dirt track leads to several lovely sandy beaches, situated in a picturesque cove at the foot of a high cliff, on the southern shore of the island. The journey is rewarded by the sheer beauty of the area.

aromatic Malvasía – an excellent quality wine for which Lanzarote is famous. Malvasía, as well as other brands of local wine, can be purchased cheaply in one of the many local *bodegas* (wine-shops). All visitors coming to *bodegas* may sample the wine before buying.

The vineyards tend to be small. El Grifo, situated at the northern end of La Geria, is a good example. Its outbuildings house a wine museum – **Museo del Vino de Lanzarote** – arranged in an old *bodega* dating from 1775. Apart from the old equipment used in the production and storage of wine, the museum has a library with more than 1,000 books, plus several 17th- and 18th-century manuscripts devoted to winemaking.

Museo del Vino de Lanzarote
Tel 928 524 951.
10:30am–6pm daily.
www.elgrifo.com

Puerto del Carmen ㉔

2,700. *Avda. de las Playas, 928 513 351.* *Nuestra Señora del Carmen (Aug).*

In recent years this fishing village has become one of the island's top resorts. Visitors come for the beaches along the Avenida de las Playas, which are regarded as some of the island's most beautiful.

In Puerto del Carmen, which is densely filled with hotels, pensions and white villas, there is no shortage of shops, nightclubs, banks and restaurants. Numerous agencies encourage visitors to sample the local attractions, such as windsurfing, diving, fishing and trips by catamaran to Fuerteventura and Lobos.

Environs

Just 9 km (6 miles) north, **Puerto Calero** has the island's loveliest marina. It also offers boat rides to the Papagayo beaches and submarine trips for glimpses of the rich life beneath the Atlantic waves.

The harbour district, the oldest part of Puerto del Carmen

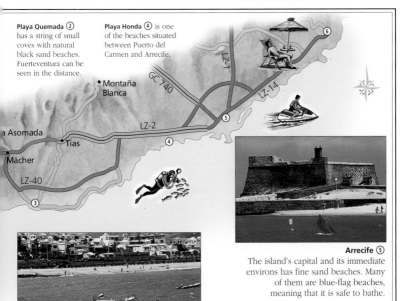

Playa Quemada ② has a string of small coves with natural black sand beaches. Fuerteventura can be seen in the distance.

Playa Honda ④ is one of the beaches situated between Puerto del Carmen and Arrecife.

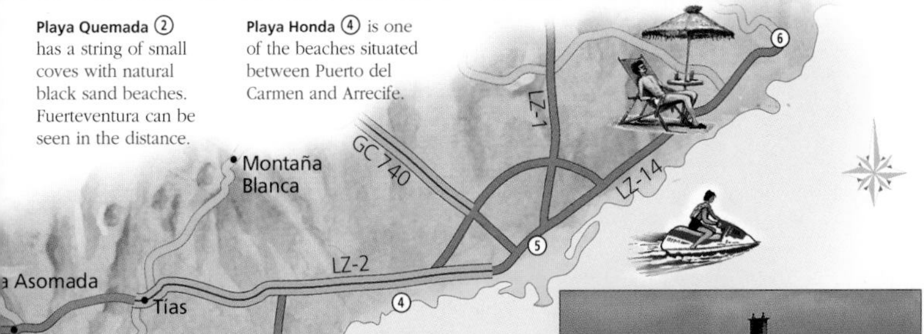
Montaña Blanca
GC 740
LZ-1
LZ-14
LZ-2
a Asomada
Tías
Mácher
LZ-40
③
④
⑤
⑥

Arrecife ⑤
The island's capital and its immediate environs has fine sand beaches. Many of them are blue-flag beaches, meaning that it is safe to bathe.

Costa Teguise ⑥
The sandy beach of Las Cucharas is not only ideal for sunbathing, but also provides opportunities to take windsurfing lessons and go on diving expeditions to a nearby shipwreck.

TENERIFE

In the language of the Guanches the name Tenerife meant "white mountain". This referred to the looming Pico del Teide – Spain's tallest peak. The 3,718-m (12,195-ft) volcano is at the heart of the island and forms part of the national park, attracting many thousands of visitors every year. Depending on the season, its summit is enveloped in clouds, sulphur or a good dusting of snow.

Covering an area of 2,354 sq km (908 sq miles), Tenerife is the largest of the archipelago's islands. Situated between La Gomera and Gran Canaria, 300 km (186 miles) from Africa, it has about 850,000 inhabitants. The northern areas are the most densely populated, in particular around Santa Cruz – the island and provincial capital.

Balcony adorning a house in La Orotava

Pico del Teide divides the island into two distinct climate zones. Sheltered by the crater, the northwestern area is humid, covered in lush tropical vegetation, and supports evergreen vineyards. The southern part is hot, rocky and arid. Because of this, Tenerife, like Gran Canaria, is often referred to as a "miniature continent".

By far the most important element of the island's economy is tourism.

Its beginnings go back to the late 19th century when the first tourists arrived in search of blue skies, sun and clean air. The first hotel – the Grand Hotel Taoro in Puerto de la Cruz – was built in 1892 and was then one of the largest hotels in Spain.

However, the real boom in tourism began in the late 1960s. At first, tourists came mainly to the fertile, northern region of the island. Soon, however, tourism reached the south and, before long, its rocky shores were covered with many truck-loads of sand imported from the Sahara. Investment was stepped up with the addition of smart hotels and a dash of greenery. The gamble paid off and today most of the visitors to Tenerife prefer the southern resorts, such as Playa de las Américas and Los Cristianos.

The seafront boulevard, Playa de las Américas

◁ Pico del Teide, the symbol of Tenerife, visible from almost everywhere on the island

Exploring Tenerife

Attracted by the mild climate and an average coastal temperature of 21° C (68° F), Tenerife attracts thousands of tourists. Most visitors stay in large resorts where they have the opportunity to indulge in a variety of sports. The rocky, volcanic terrain of the national park, with its rivers of solidified lava, is fantastic for walking and there are still some relatively remote villages within the region of the Anaga Mountains. In February and March, the island explodes in a riot of colour for the carnival, which in terms of its exuberance ranks alongside that of Rio de Janeiro.

LOCATOR MAP

Masca, one of the most beautiful villages on Tenerife

GETTING THERE

The island of Tenerife has two airports: Reina Sofía in the south and Los Rodeos in the north. Both airports are able to receive international and charter flights. Ferries from Tenerife sail to all the islands of the archipelago and to Cadiz. TITSA lines provide bus transport, although not everywhere on the island has bus links. In this case, visitors should make the most of organized coach tours or hire a car.

Punta del Hidalgo

Chamorga
Faro de Anaga

Punta del Hidalgo   Taganana

BAJAMAR **4**

TF12   *El Bailadero*

3

Tegueste   **ANAGA MOUNTAINS**

TF13

San Andrés

2 LA LAGUNA

CORONTE **5**   TF5   TF24

auzal   Taco

La Esperanza

La Matanza   **1** SANTA CRUZ DE TENERIFE

La Victoria

TF1   Santa María del Mar

OROTAVA   Tabaiba

Arafo   Las Caletillas

19 CANDELARIA

GÜIMAR **20**

ña Astrophysical servatory   Puerto de Güimar

Fasnia

TF28

Arico

mo de Arico

TF1

San Miguel de Tajao

El Médano, a favourite destination for windsurfers

SEE ALSO

- *Where to Stay* pp162–4.
- *Where to Eat* pp176–9.

KEY

▬▬	Motorway
▬	Major road
═	Minor road
▬	Scenic route
△	Summit

Golden sand beaches of Playa de las Américas

SIGHTS AT A GLANCE

Santa Cruz de Tenerife ❶

Santa Cruz de Tenerife took its name from the Holy Cross of the conquistadors, which Alonso Fernández de Lugo erected after landing on Añaza beach in 1494. During the 16th century, this former fishing village became an important port for land-locked La Laguna. Since 1723, the town has been the administrative centre of Tenerife, and was the capital of the entire archipelago from 1822–1927. Today, the economic life of Santa Cruz is dominated by its deep-water harbour, which can accommodate luxury liners, tankers arriving from Venezuela and the Middle East, and container ships loaded with bananas and tomatoes ready for export.

The imposing bell tower of Nuestra Señora de la Concepción

Exploring Santa Cruz de Tenerife

Though it does not have many historic sights, the capital of Tenerife has many attractions. The town's unique atmosphere is provided by the 19th-century, colonial-style architecture. Visitors come for the plentiful shopping opportunities, the museums and art galleries, the musical repertoire of the Tenerife Auditorium, the annual classical music festival and, above all, the carnival.

🏛 Museo de la Naturaleza y el Hombre

C/Fuente Morales, s/n.
Tel 922 535 816. ⬜ 9am–7pm Tue–Sun. ⬤ 1 Jan, 24–25 Dec. ▨
The natural history museum occupies a Classical building that was once a military hospital. The exhibition is a colourful multimedia show dedicated to the geology, archaeology, and flora and fauna of the Canary Islands.
In addition to the ever-popular mummies and skulls

of the Guanches, it also displays a small collection of artifacts (including pottery, African carvings and pre-Columbian art) as well as fossils from around the world.

🔒 Iglesia de Nuestra Señora de la Concepción

C/Domínguez Alfonso.
Though this church was built in 1498, its present appearance is the result of reconstruction work carried out in the second half of the 18th century. Its richly furnished interior features paintings and sculptures, including the magnificent main altar by José Luján Peréz.
The church serves as a pantheon and houses mementoes of the island's history, including a silver cross (Santa Cruz) of the conquistadors and British flags captured during Nelson's attack on the city in 1797.

Madonna at Plaza de la Candelaria

🚇 Plaza de España

The circular Plaza de España is in the town centre near the harbour. The giant monument standing in the middle of the square – **Monumento de los Caídos** – featuring bronze figures, is the work of Enrique César Zadivar and commemorates the victims of the 1936–39 civil war.
The vast building on the south side of the square is the Cabildo Insular and was designed by José Enrique Marrero. An example of the Fascist architecture of the 1930s, it houses Tenerife's council building and Santa Cruz's main tourist office.

🚇 Plaza de la Candelaria

Plaza de la Candelaria is a popular local meeting place and promenade. Laid out in 1701, it adjoins Plaza de España on the west. Its official name is Plaza de la Constitución. The monument standing at its centre – **El Triunfo de la Candelaria** – depicts the patron saint of the island. Carved in white Carrara marble and unveiled in 1787, it is the work of the Italian master, Antonio Canova. Another landmark on the square is the **Palacio de Carta** (1742). Formerly the Prefecture, it now contains a branch of the Banco Español de Crédito. It is worth seeking out for its fine example of a traditional Canary patio.

Plaza de España, a good orientation point when exploring the town

Calle Castillo, the main shopping street, also good for handicrafts

🏪 Calle Castillo

Many visitors come to Santa Cruz with the sole purpose of spending a few hours in the little shops in and around Calle Castillo – the main pedestrianized shopping precinct.

Except during the siesta, which takes place between 1–4:30pm, bargains are to be had in the local shops lining this attractive narrow street, whether they be electronic goods, watches or designer-label clothes. Several large handicraft centres sell embroidery, wickerwork and pottery.

🔒 Iglesia San Francisco
C/Villalba.

Opposite the Museo de Bellas Artes stands the monumental Franciscan abbey founded around 1680. It was restored and extended in the 18th century and acquired an additional chapel named Capilla de la Orden Tercera.

Inside the abbey church there is a fine 17th-century wooden altar and pulpit with beautifully painted decorations. The chapel became the parish church in 1869.

🏛 Museo de Bellas Artes
C/José Murphy, 12. **Tel** 922 244 358.
◯ 10am–8pm Tue–Fri, 10am–3pm Sat & Sun. 🎟

Founded in 1898, the Museo's prize possessions are its exhibits from the Prado, including works by Old Masters, such as Jan Brueghel and José de Ribera, as well as works by anonymous Spanish painters from the 17th and 18th centuries. In addition to collections of coins and armour, there is an exhibition of Canary art, with many paintings depicting local events and

Baroque portal of the Iglesia San Francisco

landscapes, such as *Santa Cruz Harbour* or *Landscape around Laguna,* by Valentín Sanza y Carta (1849–98).

🎨 TEA (Tenerife Arts Centre)

Avenida de San Sebastián, 10. **Tel** 922 849 057 ◯ 10am–8pm daily.
This innovative building showcases both temporary and permanent contemporary photography, painting and sculpture exhibitions.

🏪 Mercado de Nuestra Señora de África

Avenida de San Sebastián ◯ 9am–3pm Mon–Sat.
This market-hall was built in 1943 in the style of North African architecture. Fruit, vegetables, flowers, fresh fish, poultry, cheeses, herbs and spices are sold here.

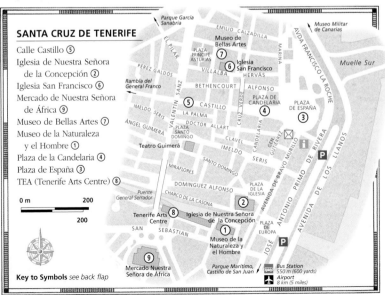

SANTA CRUZ DE TENERIFE

0 m   200

200

Key to Symbols *see back flap*

The palm-shaded Plaza del 25 de Julio

♣ Parque Marítimo

Designed by the famous
Canary architect and artist
César Manrique (see p85), the
construction of the park
began in 1995. The capital
has thus acquired an
innovative recreation area
with two giant swimming
pools, a children's paddling
pool, and a beach. Work is
currently under way to build
an adjacent **"Palmetum"** – a
park displaying all the world's
species of palm trees.

♠ Castillo de San Juan

Situated on the waterfront,
the protective fort of Castillo
de San Juan was built in 1643.
One of its functions was to
guard the safety of the port,
once famous for the trade in
African slaves that was carried
out on the Los Llanos wharf.

The nearby small chapel of
Nuestra Señora de Regle
dates from the same period.
Now both these buildings are
overshadowed by the colossal
edifice of the **Auditorio
de Tenerife**, which is to
become the island's leading
performing arts venue.

♨ Rambla del General Franco

This is one of the most
elegant streets in Santa Cruz.
With its smart houses,
numerous restaurants and
cafés, it sweeps in a semicircle through most of the
town. At its northern end, at
the junction with Avenida de
Francisco La Roche, stands an
enormous monument to
General Franco. Its wide
central reservation separates

two busy traffic lanes. Planted
with tall palms and laurel
trees, it is a veritable "art
boulevard". Modern
sculptures are set amid the
trees, which are illuminated
at night and bear plaques
with the names of famous
artists from around the world,
including Michelangelo,
Vermeer, Piranesi, Warhol
and Pollock. Every Sunday,
a lively antiques fair takes
place here.

Lush, green avenue in Parque
García Sanabria

♨ Plaza del 25 de Julio

The 25th of July Plaza is a
green oasis at the centre of
the crowded, buzzing city. Its
charm is enhanced by the
central fountains and

landscaped areas of trees and
shrubs. The place, popular
with the inhabitants of Santa
Cruz, has a circle of original
benches made of stone
imported from Seville. Note
the backrests decorated with
ceramic tiles featuring old
advertisements.

♣ Parque García Sanabria

Established in the 1920s, this
attractive and peaceful park
was named after the mayor
of Santa Cruz. The park is
full of lush tropical plants and
has a wonderful collection of
trees. It has since been
improved by the addition of
a fountain and a number of
modern sculptures. Besides
being a good place to cool
off, the park provides a brief
lesson in Tenerife's history.
The backrests of three benches
depict the arrival of the
conquistadors, the daily life of
the Guanches and their defeat
at the battle of Acentejo.

🏛 Museo Militar de Canarias

C/San Isidro, 2. **Tel** 922 843 500.
◻ 10am–2pm Tue–Sat. 🎫
Founded in 1988, the
museum occupies the former
premises of the Curatel de
Almeida, a fortress dating
back to 1884. The exhibition
features ancient weapons of
the Canary Islands, 17th-
century Spanish militaria,
and weapons dating from the
19th century.

Banners, uniforms and the
personal belongings of many
famous soldiers form a major
part of the exhibition. A
separate section is devoted to
the July 1797 battle against
the British fleet under Nelson.
The most famous exhibit – El
Tigre – is a cannon that fired
the grapeshot that tore
into Nelson's arm during
the attack on Santa Cruz.

Henry Moore sculpture in Rambla del General Franco

La Laguna ❷

🏛 130,000. 🚌 ℹ C/Carrera, 1,
922 601 106. 🏛 daily.
🎉 San Benito Abad (1st Sun in Jul),
Santísimo Cristo (7–15 Sep).

Officially named Ciudad de
San Cristóbal de la Laguna, La
Laguna is Tenerife's second
largest town. Situated in the
middle of the fertile valley of
Aguerre, it owes its name to
the lagoon on whose shores
it stood, which was drained
in 1837.

Founded in 1496 by the
conquistador Alonso
Fernández de Lugo, the town
was the original residence of
the Adelantados – the island's
military governors. Until 1723,
La Laguna was capital of the
island but moving the capital
to Santa Cruz has done
nothing to hinder
the town's
development.

La Laguna is a
university town
and its academic
traditions go back
to the first half of
the 18th century.
**San Fernando
University**, still in
existence, opened
its doors for the first time in
1817. Since 1818, the town
has been a bishopric.

Despite its dynamic
development (with some of
the suburbs virtually merging
with Santa Cruz), the old
town's layout has maintained
its traditional form with
a network of narrow streets
and alleys following a
chequerboard pattern. The
district includes several
noteworthy houses that have
wooden balconies and lavish
portals crowned with crests.
They include **Casa del
Corregidor** and **Casa de la
Alhondiga** (both dating from
the 16th century), the 17th-
century **Casa Alvaro
Bragamonte** and the 18th-
century **Casa Mesa** and **Casa
de los Capitanes**.

The meticulously restored
Casa Lercaro, built in 1593 by
Genoese merchants, now
houses the **Museo de Historia
de Tenerife**. Opened in 1993,
it presents the history of the
island from the times of the

Spanish conquest through to
the 20th century. The
collection includes old
documents, tools and 16th-
century paintings. Among the
collection's highlights are
some of the oldest maps of
the archipelago.

Nearby is another
noteworthy building – the
Palacio Episcopal. The
bishop's palace features a
beautiful stone façade dating
from 1681. Of equal interest
are some 19th-century
buildings, such as the **Casino
de la Laguna** (1899)
whose creators drew on
French designs, and the
ayuntamiento – the town
hall of 1829 that houses the
banner under which de Lugo
fought during his conquest
of Tenerife *(see p32)*.

The present town hall, with
its interior frescoes
illustrating the
island's history,
stands in **Plaza de
Adelantado**. The
adjacent church of
San Miguel (1507)
was founded by de
Lugo himself. Also
in the tree-shaded
square is the
**Convento de
Santa Catalina**, with its
original cloisters, and the
Palacio de Nava – a good
example of Spanish colonial
architecture. Behind the
square is a large market hall,
where fruit, cheese and
flowers are sold.

St Christopher, La
Laguna's patron saint

Patio of the Palacio Episcopal

**Portal of Iglesia de Nuestra Señora
de la Concepción**

To the east of Plaza de
Adelantado stands the
Cathedral (1904–15). The
building features a twin-
towered façade dating from
1825. The main feature of the
interior is the magnificent
retable (or alterpiece) at the
back of the altar, dating from
the first half of the 18th
century. Behind the main
altar stands the simple tomb
of Alonso de Lugo.

In Plaza de la Concepción
stands the **Iglesia de Nuestra
Señora de la Concepción**
(1502) – an example of the
architectural style dating from
the time of the conquest.
This triple-naved Gothic-
Renaissance church features
a magnificent reconstructed
wooden vault. Each
year, in August,
thousands of pilgrims
flock to the **Santuario
del Cristo** – a small
church at the northern
end of La Laguna's old
quarter – to pay homage
to a statue of Christ
carved in the late 15th
century. This fine Gothic
sculpture by an
unknown artist was
brought to Tenerife
in 1520, by Alonso
de Lugo.

🏛 **Museo de Historia
de Tenerife**
C/San Agustín, 22. **Tel** 922
825 949. ◯ 9am–7pm
Tue–Sun. ◯ 1 & 6 Jan,
24–25 & 31 Dec. 🎟

Anaga Mountains ❸

A picturesque range of volcanic peaks, the Anaga Mountains are lush and green thanks to a cool, wet climate. Narrow tracks lead through craggy, inaccessible valleys, and wind among steep rock faces and dense forests. For walkers, the effort required to deal with arduous paths is amply rewarded by the breathtaking views of the rocky coast below, and by the chance to see a wide variety of birds and plants.

Cliffs ⑩
These tall, rugged cliffs, which run west of Taganana, thrust their way into an often rough ocean, creating picturesque nooks and inlets. They are difficult to reach, and are best admired from the deck of a cruising boat.

Taganana ⑨
This enchanting village lies at the foot of the mountains, amid palm trees. The access road runs in the shadow of the Roque de las Animas – the Ghost Rock.

Road to La Laguna ⑪
Known as the gate to the Anaga Mountains, the road to La Laguna runs from Mirador Pico del Inglés, through the Las Mercedes plateau.

FLORA OF THE ANAGA MOUNTAINS

The lush, evergreen vegetation of this remote region, including forests of laurel and juniper trees, and heather, ferns and herbs gives the air its spicy scent. This area is deservedly popular with nature lovers. Dense bushes shelter the twisting roads from the wind, but are difficult to trek through when straying from a trail or path. Although the weather is not very warm, the humid air encourages the growth of vegetation.

Heather and ferns on the roadside near Chinobre

Santa Cruz de Tenerife ①
The capital of Tenerife, in the northeastern part of the island is the start of the two motorways – del Norte and del Sur.

LA LAGUNA

Valle Seco

0 km   1

0 miles   1

Roque de las Bodegas ⑧

The bay and the rocky beach is a favourite place for surfers. Further to the east are Almaciga and Benijo, two fishing villages poised on top of the cliffs, which have a handful of restaurants.

Faro de Anaga ⑦

From Chamorga – one of the loveliest villages on Tenerife – a steep path, 2 km (1 mile) long, runs eastwards to the Anaga lighthouse, which stands on a high peak.

Chinobre ⑥

The road leading from the El Bailadero Pass to Chinobre is where, according to folk legend, witches used to hold their Sabbaths. Thirteen kilometers (8 miles) to the west, at the foot of the Taborno summit, is the Mirador Pico del Inglés.

Igueste de San Andrés ④

The inhabitants of this quiet village at the mouth of a ravine grow mangoes, avocados and bananas. The plantations stretch all the way to the ocean.

Barranco de las Hubertas ⑤

The road from San Andrés to El Bailadero runs along the bottom of a ravine. On both sides are isolated farms standing in the cool shade of palm trees and mountain valley terraces, planted with crops.

San Andrés ②

This former fishing village is now a resort. It has narrow, shady streets and is justly famous for its handful of little seafood restaurants.

Playa de las Teresitas ③

The fine sand for this 2-km (1-mile) long beach was imported from the Sahara. Lined with palm trees, which lend the place an exotic character, the beach is a favourite spot with people from Santa Cruz.

KEY

▬ Suggested route

═ Other road

∙∙∙ Footpath

☼ Viewpoint

Around the rocky swimming pools in Bajamar

Bajamar **❹**

 1,800. 🚌

The inhabitants of Bajamar once made their living from fishing and cultivating sugar cane. In recent years it has become popular as a resort and is a well-known tourist centre for Tenerife's northern coast. The high coastal cliffs and the soaring peaks of **Monte de las Mercedes** provide a scenic backdrop for the numerous hotels and bungalows. The main road is lined with restaurants and cafés. Visitors who like bathing will enjoy the large complex of sea-water swimming pools.

Environs
Some 4 km (2 miles) to the northeast is **Punta del Hidalgo** – a headland offering a fine view of the rocky coast and banana plantations. Strong winds create excellent conditions for windsurfing though the currents make it dangerous for novices. Punta del Hidalgo is a starting point for a marked hiking trail to the cave dwellings at Chinamada.

Tacoronte **❺**

🏙 *3,500.* 🚌 🕌 *Sat, Sun.*
🎎 *Cristo de los Dolores (1st Sun after 15 Sep).*

A coastal village, set 450 m (1,476 ft) above sea level, Tacoronte and its environs are famous for their excellent wines. When in the area, you should visit one of the many wineries to sample some of the fine local vintages.

Tacoronte has two churches: the **Iglesia del Cristo de los Dolores** features a revered 17th-century statue of Christ, which during the harvest festival is carried through the streets of the town. Also noteworthy are the Baroque woodcarvings decorating the interior. The **Iglesia de Santa Catalina** (1664) has a fine wooden vault and rich interior furnishings.

Environs
Famed for its wine, **El Sauzal** is a short way to the south. Its main attraction is La Casa del Vino La Baranda – a complex in a renovated country house, which comprises a wine museum, wine-tasting hall, bar and store, as well as an excellent restaurant.

La Orotava **❻**

See pp108–11.

Puerto de la Cruz **❼**

See pp112–13.

Loro Parque **❽**

See pp114–15.

Los Realejos **❾**

🏙 *17,000.* 🚌
🎎 *San Sebastián (22 Jan).*

A sprawling town overlooked by the peak of the Tigaiga Mountain, and criss-crossed with a network of steep and winding streets, Los Realejos consists of two parts: Realejo Bajo (the lower town) and Realejo Alto (the upper town).

The town played an important part in Tenerife's history. It was here that the last free chieftains of the Guanches surrendered to the Spanish invaders in 1496.

In the upper part of Los Realejos stands the **Iglesia de Santiago Apóstol** (1498). The oldest church on the island, it has a beautiful mudéjar (Spanish-Moorish) wooden vault. At the entrance to the town, from the direction of Puerto de la Cruz, stands a **romantic castle**, built in 1862. This square structure, with four almost round towers at its corners, is set in a beautifully tended garden. Unlike other fortresses on the Canary Islands, built during

Tacoronte, situated on the coast and surrounded by vineyards

Los Realejos castle, among its garden and tall palms

the 16th and 17th centuries on the ocean coast for defence, the Los Realejos castle was never used for military purposes.

Icod de los Vinos ⑩

🏠 8,000. 🛈 922 869 600. 🚌
🎪 San Antonio Abad (22 Jan), San Marcos (Mar), Fiestas del Cristo del Drago (1st Sun after 17 Sep).

As its name suggests, this small town is in the heart of a fertile wine-growing region.

However, tourists visit Icod mainly in order to see the legendary symbol of the islands – the **Drago Milenario**. Reputed to be over 1,000 years old, this dragon tree is probably half that age. The biggest specimen in the archipelago, it is best seen from the Plaza de la Iglesia.

The triple-naved church of **San Marcos** was built in the 15th and 16th centuries. Its interior features a beautiful coffered ceiling and a silver high alter. Other interesting items include the painting of Santa Ana, attributed to Bartolomé Murillo, and a fine marble font (1696).

One of the chapels houses the **Museo de Arte Sacro**. The jewel of its collection is an enormous filigree silver cross. Made in Cuba in 1663–8, by Jeronimo de Espellosa y Vallabridge, it is 2.45 m (8 ft) high. Weighing 48.3 kg (106 lb), this gleaming filigree

Huge dragon tree, in Icod de Vinos

silver cross is thought to be the largest ever made.

At **Mariposario del Drago**, close to the dragon tree, you can learn about the life cycle of butterflies. This covered attraction has many tropical butterflies, which flutter freely among jungle vegetation and water gardens.

🏛 **Museo de Arte Sacro**
Iglesia San Marco. **Tel** 922 810 695. ⬜ 9:30am–6pm. ● Sun.

🏛 **Mariposario del Drago**
Avenida de Canarias, s/n. **Tel** 922 815 167. ⬜ 9am–6pm daily. 🖼

Garachico ⑪

🏠 2,500. 🚌
🎪 San Sebastián (20 Jan), Romeria de San Roque (16 Aug).

Established in the 16th century by Genoese merchants, Garachico, on the north coast of Tenerife is a jewel of a town, with several historic buildings and traditional-style houses providing a rare sense of architectural unity.

Garachico was once the most important port on the island (later developing into a centre of sugar production) until the eruption of the Volcán Negro in 1706 put an end to its prosperity. Lava buried whole districts and most of

the harbour, with only a handful of houses escaping destruction, together with the **Castillo de San Miguel** (1575), which guards Garachico Bay. The only portion of the former **Santa Ana** church to escape is the 16th-century façade. The restored interior has a Baroque font and a crucifix attributed to Martín de Andujar.

Other relics of the town's former glory include the **Palacio de Los Condes de la Gomera** (Palace of the Counts of Gomera), standing in Plaza de la Libertad, and several former convents, including the 17th-century **Santo Domingo**, now a modern art museum, and **San Francisco Nuestra Señora de los Angeles**. A section of this 18th-century convent is occupied by a modest museum – **Casa de la Cultura**. Also in the Plaza de la Libertad is a **monument** to **Simón Bolívar**, liberator of South America. Leading from the square, **Estaba de Porte** is lined with houses that have fine wooden balconies.

Every winter, Garachico is battered by Atlantic gales. The huge waves are truly spectacular, especially when the water level drops to reveal the vast **Roque de Garachico**.

🏛 **Museo de Arte Contemporáneo**
Plaza de Santo Domingo. **Tel** 922 830 000. ⬜ 10am–1pm, 3–6pm Mon–Sat, 10am–1pm Sun. 🖼

Entrance to Castillo de San Miguel, Garachico

La Orotava

Decorative gargoyle

Prior to the conquest of the island, the town of La Orotava, situated on Tiede's northern slopes, belonged to Taoro – the richest of the Guanche kingdoms on Tenerife. Soon after the Spanish conquest, settlers from Andalusia populated the Orotava valley and the first churches and residences appeared in the 16th century. The beauty of their wooden decorations is reminiscent of the Arabian palaces of Southern Spain. After gaining its independence from La Laguna in 1648, La Orotava began to develop rapidly and, today, it is one of the loveliest towns in the entire archipelago.

Exploring La Orotava

La Orotava is one of the best-preserved old towns on Tenerife. Its steep, narrow, cobbled streets captivate most visitors as do the enchanting 17th- and 18th-century townhouses. Their wooden, exquisitely carved balconies, fashioned from dark wood, represent the quintessence of Canary architecture.

Most of the interesting buildings are found in the compact old town. Excellent signposting makes it easy to find all of the sights.

🔒 Iglesia de la Concepción

Plaza Casañas. ◐ *daily.*
The Iglesia de la Concepción, or Church of the Immaculate Conception, located in Plaza Casañas, presents a unique atmosphere. The magnificent interior, with its

wooden sculptures created by several local artists, including Fernando Estévez and José Luján Pérez, is only enhanced by the recordings of Mozart's music, which are played here almost all day. The original church, built in the 16th century, was destroyed by earthquakes in 1704 and 1705. The present triple-naved church is the result of restoration work carried out between 1768 and 1788 by two architects – Diego Nicolás and Ventury Rodríguez – who together produced this fine example of Canary Baroque architecture, which takes much of its inspiration from the sacral buildings of Latin America. In 1948, the church was listed as a national monument.

🏛 Calle Carrera Escultor Estévez

The town's defining feature is the chain of streets, including Doctor Domingo González Garcia, San Francisco and Calle Carrera Escultor Estévez, which run in a semicircle through the old part of La Orotava. Lined with charming houses built mostly

Carrera Escultor Estévez, the main street in La Orotava

in the second half of the 19th century, the streets wind up the hill toward Plaza del General Franco. The tourist office at No. 2 Calle Carrera Escultor Estévez can supply free town maps indicating the must-see sights along this street. One interesting stopping-off point is El Pueblo Guanche – an ethnographic museum occupying a renovated townhouse. The museum has a shop selling handicrafts and food products and also a restaurant.

🏛 Plaza del Ayuntamiento

During Corpus Christi, this pleasant square, which is situated at the very heart of the old town and towered over by its Neo-Classical town hall, becomes the focus of religious celebrations. At this time, the paving stones of the tree-lined square are covered with unusual, colourful "carpets", created from volcanic ash, soil and sand. Visitors can take home images of these fleeting works of art because they are recorded on colourful post-cards that can be found on sale throughout the town all year round.

The imposing façade of the Iglesia de la Concepción

For hotels and restaurants in this region see pp162–4 and pp176–9

The tree-lined Plaza de la Constitución

🏛 Palacio Municipal

The town's administration centre is the *ayuntamiento* – the late Neo-Classical town hall, built in 1871–91, which has a modest façade virtually free of decoration. Its vault is painted with the heraldic arms of other towns on Tenerife, and with wall carvings depicting allegorical figures, which represent agriculture, history, morality and the law. Its patio once featured the oldest and largest dragon tree in the Canary Islands, which was destroyed during a storm in 1868.

🌿 Hijuela del Botánico

C/Tomás Pérez.

⬭ daily from dawn till dusk.

La Orotava's botanical garden was established in 1923 using shoots and cuttings taken from the Jardín Botánico in Puerto de la Cruz, which is famous throughout the Canary Islands. This process gave the garden its name, Hijuela del Botánico, meaning "daughter of the botanical garden". Today, the relatively small garden is blooming and features over 3,000 species of tropical and subtropical plants.

🏛 Plaza de la Constitución

This is a good place to sit down and admire La Orotava from the comfort of one of the bars and cafés, which come to life in the evenings. The Plaza, a relic of the old town's merchant past, has a tree-lined terrace, offering fine views over the buildings below. The multicoloured roof tiles and slender church towers combine to produce a memorable panorama of the town and valley that is reminiscent of Florence.

🏛 Iglesia de San Agustín

The north side of the Plaza de la Constitución is occupied by the church and abbey of St Augustine. Dating from the 17th century, this building features a beautiful façade with a Renaissance-Baroque portal. The church has many fine historic remains and a panelled ceiling, while the former abbey is now a school of music.

Decorations on the Iglesia de San Agustín

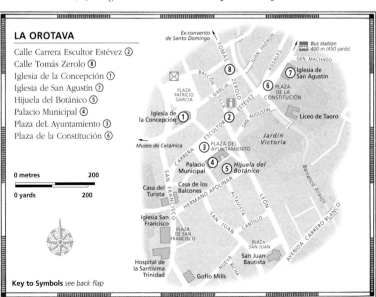

LA OROTAVA

Calle Carrera Escultor Estévez ②
Calle Tomás Zerolo ⑧
Iglesia de la Concepción ①
Iglesia de San Agustín ⑦
Hijuela del Botánico ⑤
Palacio Municipal ④
Plaza del Ayuntamiento ③
Plaza de la Constitución ⑥

Ex-convento de Santo Domingo

Bus station 400 m (450 yards)

GEN. MACHADO

⑦ Iglesia de San Agustín

PLAZA PATRICIO GARCIA

⑧

⑥ PLAZA DE LA CONSTITUCIÓN

Iglesia de la Concepción ①

②

Liceo de Taoro

Museo de Cerámica

③ PLAZA DEL AYUNTAMIENTO

Jardín Victoria

0 metres 200

0 yards 200

Palacio Municipal ④ ⑤ Hijuela del Botánico

Casa del Turista

Casa de los Balcones

Iglesia San Francisco

PLAZA DE SAN FRANCISCO

PLAZA SAN JUAN

San Juan Bautista

Hospital de la Santísima Trinidad

Gofio Mills

Key to Symbols see back flap

🏛 Calle Tomás Zerolo

Almost every street or alley in La Orotava offers some historic interest. Calle Tomás Zerolo, which passes through the lower part of the old town, is no exception. It features the **Convento de Santo Domingo**, which has a small museum of Latin American handicrafts, and, opposite it, the **Casa Torrehermosa** – a colonial-style house built in the 17th century for the Hermosa family. Today, this residence houses the Impresa Insular de Artesanía – a small workshop and museum devoted to local handicrafts.

Wooden galleries around the patio of the Casa de los Balcones

🏛 Casa de los Balcones

C/San Francisco, 3–4. **Tel** 922 330 629. ☐ 8:30am–6:30pm daily. **www**.casa-balcones.com

The "House of Balconies", also known as the Casa de Fonseca, is a major landmark of La Orotava. Its light-coloured façade is adorned with a heavy, carved door, smart windows and long teak balconies. The palm-shaded patio, brimming over with greenery, is surrounded by the first- and second-floor galleries, which rest on slender wooden columns.

The house, built in 1632–70, has its own small museum of Canary art and handicrafts. Here, visitors can view and buy local products, including embroidery, lace, pottery, regional costumes and other souvenirs (don't miss the miniature balconies of La Orotava!).

🏛 Casa del Turista

Calle San Francisco, 4. **Tel** 922 330 629. ☐ 9am–7pm Mon–Fri, 8:30am–5pm Sat.

Standing on the opposite side of the road to the Casa de los Balcones is the Casa del Turista, also known as the Casa de Molina. This is a magnificent Canary townhouse once belonging to a wealthy family. It was known collectively (with the 17th-century Casa Mesa and the Casa de los Lercaro) as the Doce Casas or "twelve houses". The house is built in a style similar to that of Casa de los Balcones, but is older, dating from 1509. It also offers the chance to view and purchase local handicrafts. Its prize exhibit is a religious scene made from coloured volcanic sand. This type of decoration, for which the town is famous, is made during Corpus Christi. The terraces at the back of the house provide a fine view over the Orotava valley.

Stone portal of Casa del Turista

🔒 Iglesia San Francisco

C/San Francisco.

The church of San Francisco, with its Baroque portal and rather plain interior, stands in the palm-shaded Plaza de San Francisco and serves as the hospital chapel.

The church stands next to the **Hospital de la Santísima Trinidad** (Hospital of the Holy Trinity), which has occupied the 18th-century Convento de San Lorenzo since 1884. The interior is closed to visitors. Note the revolving drum on the door where foundling babies were placed to be cared for by the nuns.

🏛 Gofio Mills

C/Doctor Domingo González García.

In the south, Calle San Francisco becomes Calle Doctor Domingo González García. The street features a number of 17th- and 18th-century mills that once produced *gofio* (a roasted mixture of wheat, maize or barley). One of these mills is still working. Here, visitors can see the entire process of flour production, as well as buy the end product. One room has a display showing the production process prior to the introduction of electrical machinery.

🔒 Iglesia San Juan Bautista

C/San Juan Bautista

The single-nave church of St John the Baptist was built in the 18th century. Its modest façade, with a monumental belfry, does nothing to hint at the magnificence of its interior. Thanks to the beautiful *artesonado* – the wooden coffered ceiling – and the opulent interior decorations featuring sculptures by Luján Peréz and Fernando Estévez, the church is regarded as one of the most precious historic sites in La Orotava. The fine altars deserve special attention.

In front of the church is a bust of the Venezuelan President, Rómulo Betancourt (1909–81).

The simple façade of Iglesia San Juan Bautista

🏛 Museo de Cerámica – Casa de Tafuriaste

C/León, 3. **Tel** 922 333 396.
🕐 10am–6pm Mon–Sat, 10am–2pm Sun. 📷

The island's passion for ceramics reached its peak even before the advent of the European conquerors, and remains alive to this day, particularly among the local population of La Orotava. The primitive designs, which are based on old Guanche forms, are popular with many tourists, as are items representing a more modern style of pottery.

Orotava's Museo de Cerámica was founded to cater for this interest. The museum is housed in the Casa de Tafuriaste – a much-restored Canary townhouse from the 17th century, which is about 2 km (1 mile) west from La Orotava's old town on the La Luz-Las Candias road.

On the museum's first floor, there is a fine display of antique ceramics.

Modern pottery from Casa de Tafuriaste

The collection includes nearly 1,000 vessels from the Canary Islands and Spain. Down on the ground floor there is a pottery workshop, where visitors can see demonstrations of how modern jugs and bowls are made.

The gift shop sells a wide variety of these items to take home as souvenirs.

🏛 Liceo de Taoro

C/San Augustín. 📷

Above the Plaza de la Constitución stands the charming, eclectic building of the former grammar school, with a well-maintained 100-year-old garden. These days, it houses a club with elegant reception rooms, a bar (which is open to non-members), games room and a library.

🌿 Jardín Victoria

Plaza de la Constitución.
🕐 8am–9pm daily. 📷

Bordering the Liceo de Taoro is the 19th-century Jardín Victoria – full of beautiful flowers and palm trees, arranged on terraces along a shallow ravine with a stream running at the bottom. The main architectural feature of this garden is the mausoleum of **Diego Ponte del Castillo**, made of Carrara marble.

🔒 Ex-convento Santo Domingo

C/Tomás Zerolo, 34.

On the outskirts of La Orotava's old town stands a 17th–18th-century Dominican convent, which has a triple-naved church featuring a magnificent polychromatic wooden coffered ceiling. The remaining rooms of the former convent are arranged around a patio with lovely balconies resting on wooden columns. These rooms are occupied by the compact **Museo de Artesanía Iberoamericana**, which opened in 1991. This ethnographic museum has an interesting exhibition of handicrafts from Spain and Latin America. The collection includes traditional musical instruments (look out for the Canary *timple* – a kind of ukelele), pottery, textiles, wickerwork and some fine locally produced furniture.

🏛 Museo de Artesanía Iberoamericana

Tel 922 323 376. 🕐 9am–5pm Mon–Fri, 9am–2pm Sat. 📷

Jardín Victoria, situated in a ravine

Environs

The **Mirador de Humboldt** is 5 km (3 miles) northeast. This splendid viewpoint overlooks the entire Orotava valley and is named after the geographer, traveller and naturalist, Alexander von Humboldt, who visited Tenerife in 1799.

Some 30 km (19 miles) south, along a scenic road that crosses the Orotava valley, stands the **Izaña Astrophysical Observatory**. The observatory is near the entrance to the Parque Nacional del Teide, and occupies a picturesque spot 2,200 m (7,210 ft) above sea level, close to the top of the Izaña mountain.

CORPUS CHRISTI

Apart from Epiphany, Corpus Christi is the most celebrated religious festivals in the Canary Islands. The most extravagant festivities on Tenerife are held in La Orotava and La Laguna, which try to outdo each other in the splendour of the occasion. The streets of the town are lined with magnificent floral decorations, and the Plaza del General Franco is adorned with pictures and "carpets" made of volcanic sands, which can take months to prepare.

Preparing a floral picture from volcanic sand

Puerto de la Cruz ●

Rising up from the sea front, Puerto de la Cruz was the principal port of the island after the destruction of Garachico. By the late 19th century, it had already become a resort and a popular destination for upmarket British visitors and remains so to this day. The hotels tower above banana plantations, shopping arcades, casinos, restaurants, cafés and nightclubs, as well as numerous historic sites. An artificial lagoon and warm, clear water attracts over 100,000 visitors each year to the area.

Portal of the Iglesia de Nuestra Señora de la Peña de Francia

🔒 Iglesia de Nuestra Señora de la Peña de Francia

The triple-naved cathedral was built in 1684–97. Its tall tower was added in the late 19th century.

In the dark interior of the church the eye is drawn to Baroque sculptures – the work of the local artist Fernando Estévez, and José Luján Pérez, a well-known island artist. No less precious are the paintings by Luís de la Cruz. The cathedral's organ was brought from London in 1814.

A bust of Augustín de Bétancourt (1758–1824), founder of the Engineering College in Madrid, stands in front of the church.

🏚 Calle Quintana

The street leads to Punta del Viento, a terrace poised on the edge of the ocean and affording a fine view over the rocky coast and **Lago Martiánez**. Branching off eastwards is **Calle de San Telmo**, a seaside promenade with stone seats and numerous bars. The **Monopol Hotel** – one of the oldest hotels in Puerto de la Cruz – stands in Calle Quintana.

🏚 Plaza de Europa

Hugging the shoreline, this square was laid out in 1992, but is based on 18th- and 19th-century European-style town planning. Its features include the **town hall** (1973) and the **Casa de Miranda** (1730), a fine old town house, which now accommodates a restaurant specializing in local fare.

🏚 Casa de la Real Aduana

Calle de las Lonjas. **Tel** 922 378 103.
⬜ Mon–Sat.
This was built in 1620 for Juan Antonio Lutzardo de Francha and is the oldest house in town. After the destruction of Garachico it became the seat of the governor and from 1706 to 1833 served as the customs house. The building was restored in the 1970s and now houses a cultural centre and a shop selling local crafts. The tourist information office is here too.

Town crest at Plaza de Europa

🏚 Puerto Pesquero

The history of this picturesque fishing harbour, situated on a small, stony beach, goes back to the 18th century, when the town was the main exporter of the island's agricultural produce. Today you can buy freshly caught fish direct from the fishermen.

🔒 Iglesia de San Francisco

C/San Juan.
The Church of St Francis is built around the Ermita de San Juan, which was constructed in 1599. One of the oldest buildings in Puerto de la Cruz, it is decorated with sculptures and paintings, from the 16th century up to modern times.

Today, this modest building serves as an ecumenical church, and holds services for all Christian denominations in the town.

🏚 Plaza del Charco de los Camerones

Many of the town's most historic buildings are found in Plaza del Charco, a square shaded by palm and laurel trees, which were brought in 1852 from Cuba. The centre of the square is occupied by a huge yam plant within a fountain. The plaza is a pleasant place to sit and watch the world go by, particularly on Sundays, when locals promenade in their Sunday finery.

🏛 Museo Arqueológico

C/El Lomo, 9A. **Tel** 922 371 465.
⬜ 10am–1pm & 5–9pm Tue–Sat, 10am–1pm Sun. 📷
This small museum, opened in 1991, is devoted to the history and cultural heritage of the Canary Islands. Its exhibits include a collection

View of the entrance to Puerto Pesquero fishing harbour

Lush banana plantations south of Parque Taoro

of Gaunche products and the mummified remains of the island's original inhabitants.

♠ Castillo de San Felipe

This small 17th-century fort once guarded the harbour entrance against attacks from pirates and the ships of Spain's two maritime rivals: France and England. Now the fort, situated in the western part of town, often serves as a venue for temporary exhibitions. To the west of the fort is the **Playa Jardín** – the town's longest beach.

♣ Parque Taoro

This majestic park is an enchanting spot and a good place to escape the bustle of town. The park has cascades, waterfalls, streams crossed with bridges, small ponds and viewing terraces. At the centre of the park lies the **Jardín Risco Bello Acuático** – a tropical water garden that is home to many varieties of fish, as well as ducks and swans.

⛲ Lago Martiánez

Playa Martiánez. **Tel** 922 385 955.
◯ 10am–6pm daily. ◖ May. 🖊
This artificial lagoon, designed by César Manrique, was built in 1969. Conjuring up a subtropical paradise, it consists of a complex of seawater swimming pools and gurgling fountains, which contrast with the surrounding lava field. There is also an ultra-smart casino here.

Playa Jardín, a popular beach with tourists

VISITORS' CHECKLIST

🚶 40,000. 🚌 ℹ️ C/Las Lonjas, s/n, 922 386 000. 🛒 Tue, Thu, Sat. 🎭 Fiesta del Carmen (16 Jul).

♣ Jardín Botánico

C/Retama, 2. **Tel** 922 389 484.
◯ 9am–7pm daily. 🖊
The local botanical garden is one of the oldest in the world. It was established in 1788 at the request of Carlos III of Spain, by Alonso de Nova Gimón.

Today, the lush garden is crammed with over 1,000 species of plants and trees from the Canary Islands, as well as flora from all over the world.

PUERTO DE LA CRUZ

Calle Quintana ②
Casa de la Real Aduana ④
Iglesia de San Francisco ⑥
Iglesia de Nuestra Señora
  de la Peña de Francia ①
Plaza de Europa ③
Plaza del Charco de
  los Camerones ⑦
Puerto Pesquero ⑤

Casa de la Real Aduana
PLAZA DE EUROPA
Puerto Pesquero ⑤
Lago Martiánez
Ayuntamiento
Ermita San Telmo
MEQUINEZ
SANTO DOMINGO
Iglesia de San Francisco
Iglesia de Nuestra Señora de la Peña de Francia
PLAZA DE LAS VEGAS
LOMO
Museo Arqueológico
QUINTANA
SAN TELMO
SAN FELIPE
Castillo de San Felipe
PLAZA DEL CHARCO DE LOS CAMERONES
SOTELO
LA HOYA
PEREZ
ZAMORA
NIEVES RAVELO
BLANCO
SAN JUAN
AUGUSTIN DE BETHENCOURT
MIRANDA
PUERTO VIEJO
A VERDAD
DR INGRAM
IRIARTE
COLOGAN
ESQUIVEL
ZAMORA
IRIARTE
AVE. DEL GENERALISIMO
Bus station
200 m (220 yards)
VALOIS
VALOIS
BLANCO
CARRETERA DEL NORTE
Parque Taoro
CARRETERA DEL TAORO
Jardín Botánico

0 metres   200
0 yards   200

Key to Symbols see back flap

Loro Parque **8**

From the day it opened in 1972, this tropical plant complex has been hugely popular and has been visited by over 11 million tourists. The huge area contains many animals and birds, magnificent orchids and dragon trees. It offers numerous tourist attractions, including shows of performing seals, parrots, dolphins and the largest facility for orcas in the world. The entrance to the park leads through an authentic Thai village. Built in 1993, it consists of six buildings which were built in Thailand and shipped in sections to Tenerife, where they were reassembled by Thai craftsmen.

★ Dolphinarium
This is Loro Parque's biggest draw and can accommodate 1,800 spectators at a time to watch the show in what is claimed to be Europe's largest dolphinarium.

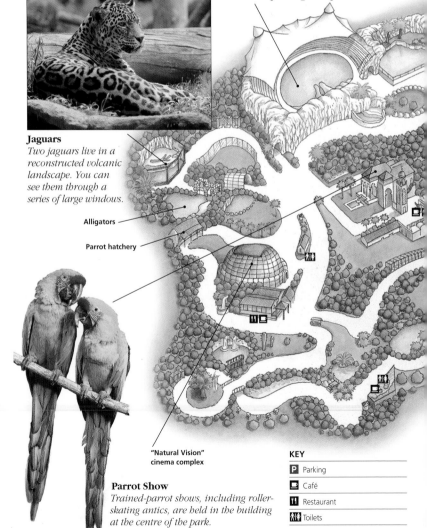

Jaguars
Two jaguars live in a reconstructed volcanic landscape. You can see them through a series of large windows.

Alligators

Parrot hatchery

"Natural Vision" cinema complex

Parrot Show
Trained-parrot shows, including roller-skating antics, are held in the building at the centre of the park.

KEY

🅿 Parking

🏠 Café

🍴 Restaurant

🚻 Toilets

★ Penguin House
With frost-covered rocks and a water temperature of 8° C (46° F), the Penguin House recreates a natural habitat, enabling the inhabitants to forget that they are living on Tenerife.

VISITORS' CHECKLIST

Puerto de la Cruz, C/San Felipe.
Tel. 922 373 841.
⏰ 8:30am–5pm daily. 🅿️ ♿
www.loroparque.com
Free transport by tram from Playa Martiánez (every 20 min).

Tower of Fish
A school of fish swim inside an illuminated glass cylinder, more than 8 m (26 ft) tall, which stands next to the Penguin House.

Entrance

Amphitheatre and trained seal shows

```
0 m        50
0 yards     50
```

Gorillas
A sizeable number of gorillas live out their days in relative freedom in the park, in an area of 3,500 sq m (4,200 sq yards).

★ Shark Aquarium
Several species of shark can be viewed in the aquarium. A specially designed glass-tunnel walkway allows visitors to watch sharks swimming directly overhead.

STAR ATTRACTIONS

★ Dolphinarium

★ Penguin House

★ Shark Aquarium

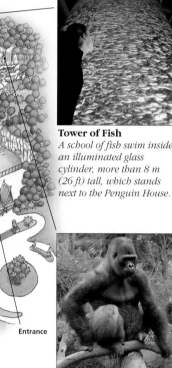

Masca ⑫

🏃 150. 🚌

Masca, with its scenic position at an altitude of 600 m (2,000 ft), is a popular destination for day trips from many of the big resorts. Just above the small village is a terrace, which offers an impressive outlook, especially at sunset, towards Mount Teide on one side, and the Atlantic on the other.

Masca was once a refuge for pirates and accessible only by mule. Even today, it can only be reached via a steep, winding road. Though narrow, the road is a feat of modern engineering and uses small lay-bys along the roadside to allow vehicles to pass each other. The incredible views as the road winds through the mountains are reason enough to visit.

The village is charming and consists of a handful of old, red-tiled, stone houses clinging to the sides of the gorge, and surrounded by lush palm trees. Roadside vendors offer prickly pears and oranges to passers-by.

Crops are grown in small fields on terraces, which descend towards the Barranco de Masca ravine. The villagers also keep bees that gather nectar from the surrounding flowering meadows. The village is an excellent starting point for hikers. One of the best routes leads along the Masca ravine, to the seashore. A fit mountain walker should be able to get there and

The green square of Plaza de la Iglesia in Los Silos

back again in under four hours. Take care, however, as the return hike is steep and fairly arduous.

Environs

Past the village, the road leads north through the Macizo de Teno massif, towards the coastal flatland. Some 10 km (6 miles) along the route is the scenic village of **El Palmar**. The nearby **Montaña de Talavera** has had chunks cut out of it to provide soil for the banana plantations.

Another 4 km (2 miles) further on is **Buenavista**, the island's westernmost village, which has a small fishing harbour and a pebble beach.

A short way eastwards in the midst of banana plantations, **Los Silos** is a quiet little town with a compact 19th-century layout. In the town centre is a typical tree-shaded square, with a coffee pavilion. The shady square is idyllic and has traditional Canary houses with wooden balconies.

Santiago del Teide ⑬

🏃 500. 🚌 ℹ️ *Paseo Maritimo, Playa de la Arena, 922 860 348.*

Should you visit Santiago del Teide in February, when the countless almond trees are in bloom with pink and white blossom, you will see it is particularly lovely. The small town is surrounded by vineyards and cornfields, and nestles among the foothills of the Teno massif. La Gomera can be seen in the distance.

The pride of the town is the Baroque parish church of **San Fernando**. The small town is surrounded by was built in the mid-16th century and stands at the end of the main street. Its asymmetric façade is adorned with a wooden, grill-shaded balcony. A tall belfry has been added at the northern end of the church. The small, Moorish-looking domes give the building its distinctive look.

Look out for the strange figure in front of one of the side altars: it represents Christ on horseback, wearing a black Spanish hat and carrying a sword.

Environs

Branching off from the southern approach road to the village is a path to **Camino de la Virgen de Lourdes**. The path, dedicated to the Virgin Mary of Lourdes and with a shrine and an ornamental bridge, leads along the slope of the mountain to a grotto decorated with flowers.

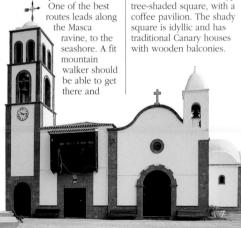

The façade of San Fernando with its wooden balcony, Santiago del Teide

For hotels and restaurants in this region see pp162–4 and pp176–9

Los Gigantes and Puerto de Santiago ⑭

The giant cliffs, known as the **Acantilados de los Gigantes** ("Cliffs of the Giants"), form the ridge of the Teno massif. Some 10 km (6 miles) long, this steep cliff-face plunges 500 m (1,600 ft) into the ocean. The dark rocks are best seen by boat. Trips often leave from Puerto Deportivo and usually travel further north to include a wonderful view over the **Barranco de Masca**.

Situated beneath the cliffs, the small town of **Los Gigantes** is a typical Canary holiday resort, the biggest on the northwest coast of Tenerife, with apartment complexes sprawling over the slopes. Its yachting marina has diving clubs and offers angling trips.

The town itself, with its concentrated development, gives the impression of being overcrowded. Only narrow alleys separate small hotels and apartment blocks.

A seaside boulevard connects Los Gigantes with nearby **Puerto de Santiago**, which has long been a resort, although on a smaller scale. The main attraction here is the dark volcanic-sand beaches, including the most popular of them, **Playa de la Arena**, situated to the south. Most of the fishermen here have traded in their rods and nets and take tourists out for boat trips instead.

Boulevards along the beach in Playa de las Américas

Playa de las Américas and Los Cristianos ⑮

🏙 20,000. 🚌 ⛴ 🛈 C/General Franco, 922 730 133. 🎪 Fiesta del Carmen (beg. of Sep).

You would not think so to look at it now but Los Cristianos was once a sleepy fishing village. Today, it is a year-round provider of fun and sun with artificial beaches, sprawling hotel-apartments, and countless bars, discos and souvenir shops. Many people embrace the noise and kitsch good humour of the place and Los Cristianos is one of the most popular resorts in the archipelago. It extends into the virtually identical Playa de las Américas, which merges in its turn with **Costa Adeje** a little further up the coastline.

A promenade, running alongside the crowded beaches and the harbour wall, has shops, restaurants and bars. In Las Américas the promenade turns into a palm-shaded boulevard several miles long, which runs above numerous sheltered beaches. The most exclusive among them is the **Playa del Duque**. Ferries and hydrofoils make regular trips from Los Cristianos' port to La Gomera and El Hierro.

Environs
A short way northeast, **Parque Ecológico Las Águilas** has displays of condors in flight, evening variety shows and a floodlit pool full of crocodiles. Some 7 km (4 miles) north, and a two-hour walk from the town of Adeje, is the **Barranco del Infierno**, a wild gorge with an impressive waterfall.

Harbour in Puerto de Santiago, against the steep cliffs of Los Gigantes

Parque Nacional del Teide ⑯

Some 3 million years ago volcanic subsidence left behind the 16-km (10-mile) Las Cañadas depression with the island's emblematic volcano, Teide, at its centre. In 1954 the area was turned into one of the largest national parks in Spain. Marked paths guide visitors round the best of this awesome wilderness of ash beds, lava streams and mineral tinted rocks. The refurbished parador, next to the road leading along the plateau, is the only hotel in the park. The same road leads to the lower cable-car station and the El Portillo visitor centre.

Pico Viejo
The crater of this volcanic cone, which last erupted in the 18th century, measures 800 m (2,624 ft) in diameter.

Los Roques de García
Close to the parador is a much photographed set of strangely shaped rocks, rising some 150 m (500 ft) above the crater floor.

Boca de Tauce
This lookout provides a stunning view of the gulleys and slopes of the national park.

Llano de Ucanca
This treeless plain contains the rocks of Los Azulejos. Their blue-green glitter is due to the copper deposits within them.

PICO DEL TEIDE

The most recent eruption of Mount Teide occurred in 1798. At 3,718 m (12,195 ft), it is the highest mountain in Spain. Today, you can only visit its peak if you have a permit (ask at the Oficina del Parque Nacional for details). The viewing platform in La Fortaleza, reached by a footpath leading from the top cable-car station, affords (on a clear day) an incredible view of the entire archipelago, stretching hundreds of miles.

Early map showing Teide as the world's highest mountain

KEY

▬	Major road
▭	Minor road
═	Other road
···	Footpath
▬	Park boundary
·-..	Seasonal river
P	Parking
H	Tourist information
✣	Viewpoint
H	Restaurant

SANTIAGO DEL TEIDE

PICO VIEJO ▲ 3134

PIC• DEL TEID•

371•

TF 36

MONTAÑA GANGARRO ▲ 2191

TF 21

GRANADILLA DE ABONA

0 km   2
0 miles   2

Izaña Astrophysical Observatory
At the entrance to the park, the observatory gives astronomers the chance to make the most of the island's clear skies.

VISITORS' CHECKLIST

🚌 342 (Playa de las Americas)
348 (Puerto de la Cruz). ℹ Oficina del Parque Nacional, C/Emilio
Calzadilla, 5–4a, Santa Cruz de
Tenerife, 922 290 129. ◯ 9am–
2pm Mon–Fri. ♿ cable-car only.

Refugio de Altavista
This modest shelter is located along the trail leading to Pico del Teide, at an altitude of 3,270 m (10,726 ft).

LA OROTAVA

P ℹ El Portillo

LA LAGUNA

TF 24

TF 21

MONTAÑA
BLANCA
▲
2760

MONTAÑA
RAJADA
▲
2509

P

Cable-car
Built in 1971, the cable-car takes only eight minutes to whisk tourists to within 200 m (656 ft) of Teide's summit.

🍴 ℹ P

Las Cañadas
The seven cañadas (sandy plateaux) are the result of the collapse of ancient craters. Only a few species of plant can grow in this dusty, arid wasteland.

Echium wildpretii (tajinaste)
This striking plant, a kind of viper's bugloss, has bright red stalks. It can grow up to 2m (6 ft) high and is one of the symbols of Tenerife.

Roque Cinchado
One of the Roques de García, the Cinchado is this strange shape because it is wearing away faster at the bottom than the top.

Vilaflor

🏛 *1,800.* 🚌

With an elevation of 1,400 m (4,600 ft), Vilaflor is the highest village in the Canaries. In the 19th century the village became famous for its lacework. Close to the

The giant "Pino Gordo" just outside Vilaflor

village, which is surrounded by pine forests, is "Pino Gordo", a pine tree over 40 m (130 ft) tall. In the plaza at the top of the village is the **Iglesia de San Pedro** (1550), which has a statue of the church's patron saint.

Environs
Hikers can set out from Vilaflor for the so-called **Paisaje Lunar** ("Lunar Landscape"), a curious rock formation made of weathered cones of sandstone.

El Médano ⑱

🏛 *1,500.* 🚏 *Plaza del Médano, 922 176 002.* 🚌 🎭 *San Antonio de Padua (14 Jun).*

El Médano, a former fishing village, is now famous for its bay, fringed by long, sandy beaches. These stretch south to the **Punta Roja**, towered over by the **Montaña Roja** volcano (now a nature reserve). The strong winds (known as *alisios*) make the

place very popular with windsurfers (international competitions are held here). The winds are also utilized in the **Parque Eólico de Granadilla** – a wind farm, supplying electricity to over 3,000 homes.

Environs
Some 5 km (3 miles) to the northwest, at the end of the runways of Reina Sofía Airport, is the **Cueva del Hermano Pedro** – a cave converted into a sanctuary, dedicated to Father Peter, the first Canary saint (1626–67).

Candelaria ⑲

🏛 *14,500.* 🚌 🚃 🚏 *Avenida de la Constitución 7, 922 032 230.* 🛒 *Sat, Sun.* 🎭 *Nuestra Señora de la Candelaria (15 Aug).*

Candelaria is famous for its religious sanctuary, the most important in the archipelago. Once each year in August, crowds of pilgrims come to the **Basílica de Nuestra**

Tenerife's Beaches

With the possible exception of Las Teresitas, near Santa Cruz, the beaches of Tenerife are not nearly as scenic as those of Fuerteventura, though they are nevertheless popular with tourists. Numerous diving packages are on offer to visitors, from courses aimed at beginners to expeditions into the depths of the ocean. Reliable winds make the place popular with windsurfers and conditions are also good for many other watersports, from paragliding to waterskiing.

Playa San Blas ④ is situated near Los Abrigos. From here a modern road leads to Golf del Sur, the biggest golf course on Tenerife and one of the finest on the Canary Islands.

Los Abrigos ⑤ is a fishing village next to a quiet, rocky beach, and is known for its many excellent fish restaurants.

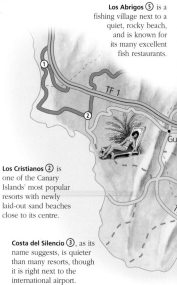

Los Cristianos ② is one of the Canary Islands' most popular resorts with newly laid-out sand beaches close to its centre.

Playa de las Américas ①
The local volcanic beaches of black and grey sand have been covered with light imported sand, to make them more attractive to visitors.

Costa del Silencio ③, as its name suggests, is quieter than many resorts, though it is right next to the international airport.

Señora de Candelaria to pray to the Black Madonna – the patron saint of the Canary Islands.

According to legend, in 1390 two fishermen from a Guanche tribe found a miraculous statue that had been washed up on the beach (it was probably a figurehead from a shipwreck). The tribe placed it in one of the coastal caves as an object of veneration and there it remained until 1826, when it was swept away during a violent storm. The basilica itself was built in 1958 on the site of an earlier 16th-century church. The present statue of the Madonna is the work of Fernando Estévez (1827). It has been placed inside a niche above the main altar. The wall around the niche has paintings by Jose Aguiar and Manuel Martín Gonzáles. The church's main entrance features

a vast painting of the Black Madonna by Dimas Coello (1986).

The basilica adjoins the 17th-century church of **Santa Ana**. Both churches stand along the northwest frontage of **Plaza de la Patrona de Canaria**, a huge square that includes nine bronze statues depicting the legendary Guanche rulers, known as the *Menceyes*.

Imposing façade of the basilica, Candelaria

Güimar ⑳

🏠 15,500. 🚈 🛳 San Pedro (29 Jun).

The largest town in southeast Tenerife, Güimar has an eclectic mix of 19th-century houses. On a small square in the town centre stands the 18th-century church of **San Pedro Apóstol**.

Statue of a Guanche chieftain, Candelaria

The town is famous for the **pyramids** made from uncut stone that were unearthed in the suburb of Chacona in the 1990s. The anthropologist Thor Heyerdahl and the ship owner Fred Olsen persuaded the authorities to seal off the area and founded the **Parque Etnográfico** museum.

🏛 **Parque Etnográfico Pirámides de Güimar**
C/Chacona, s/n. **Tel** 922 514 510. ⏰ 9:30am–6pm daily. ⬤ 1 Jan & 25 Dec. 🖳 **www.** piramidesdeguimar.net

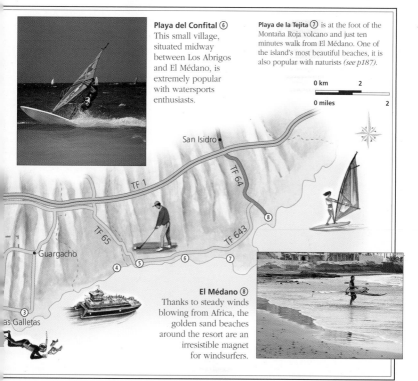

Playa del Confital ⑥
This small village, situated midway between Los Abrigos and El Médano, is extremely popular with watersports enthusiasts.

Playa de la Tejita ⑦ is at the foot of the Montaña Roja volcano and just ten minutes walk from El Médano. One of the island's most beautiful beaches, it is also popular with naturists (*see p187*).

0 km 2
0 miles 2

San Isidro

TF 1
TF 64
TF 65
TF 643

Guargacho

③ Galletas
④ ⑤ ⑥ ⑦ ⑧

El Médano ⑧
Thanks to steady winds blowing from Africa, the golden sand beaches around the resort are an irresistible magnet for windsurfers.

LA GOMERA

*L*a Gomera, the Isla Redonda or Round Island, is the "alternative" Canary Island. A mere 378 sq km (146 sq miles), it has little tourism infrastructure and only small pebble-and-sand beaches. Many visitors treat it as a day trip. Some, however, come for this very absence of commercialism, drawn by the mountainous countryside and an ancient laurel forest that is perfect for hiking.

Despite the poor soil and the hilly conditions, the inhabitants of La Gomera, who lived on the island during the Guanche era as well as those who arrived after the Spanish conquest, made a living as farmers. Fields were set on terraces cut into the slopes of ravines. Crops included potatoes, tomatoes, bananas and grapes. To this day many of the local people are engaged in farming and the island has maintained its agricultural character.

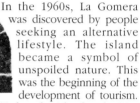

Cacti decorating an island windowsill

The isolation of the island, its inaccessibility and the difficulties in cultivating the fertile land all contributed to its poverty and often caused many of the Gomerans to leave for South America (though quite a few are returning now). Signs of emigration are still visible in the form of numerous deserted villages.

In the 1960s, La Gomera was discovered by people seeking an alternative lifestyle. The island became a symbol of unspoiled nature. This was the beginning of the development of tourism. Today, the island authorities try to maintain a balance between the traditional economy and the proceeds of tourism, and strive to protect the historic landscape from the trappings of civilization that threaten it.

One of the outstanding features of La Gomera that attracts many visitors each year is the Garajonay national park. This is one of the world's oldest natural forests and provides an excellent area for walking. Equally interesting are the local customs. Some of them, including a unique whistle language, have survived since the times of the Guanches.

Harbour entrance in San Sebastián de La Gomera

◁ Green terraces of cultivated fields, on the slopes of the Valle Gran Rey

Exploring La Gomera

Most visitors come to La Gomera on day trips, arriving from nearby Tenerife. This small island, though somewhat short of historical sites, such as those on Gran Canaria or Tenerife, is extremely attractive in terms of its landscape. Deep ravines, rocky summits, mist-shrouded laurel forests and valley slopes descending in terraces all compensate for the lack of long, sandy beaches. Rich in unspoilt areas and seemingly untainted by tourism, the island is an excellent place for hiking. With no industry, motorways and few large hotels, La Gomera is a haven of peace and suits those wishing to escape the bustle of the larger resorts.

LOCATOR MAP

ATLANTIC OCEAN

SANTA CRUZ DE TENERIFE

LAS PALMAS DE GRAN CANARIA

SIGHTS AT A GLANCE

Agulo ❸
Alajeró ❽
El Cercado ❻
Hermigua ❷
Parque Nacional de Garajonay pp130–31 ❼
Playa de Santiago ❾
San Sebastián de La Gomera ❶
Valle Gran Rey ❺
Vallehermoso ❹

Punta de los Roques

Los Órganos

Playa de Vallehermoso

Las Rosas

VALLEHERMOSO ❹
△ Roque Cano 650m

Punta del Viento

Macayo

Meriga

Playa de Alojera
Epina

Mirador de Vallehermoso

Alojera

TF713

Quemado 1136m

PARQUE NACIONAL DE GARAJONAY

Arure

Playa de Heredia

Mirador del Santo
Las Hayas

La Laguna Grande

❼

EL CERCADO ❻

Lomo del Balo

Chipude

△ *Garajonay 1487m*

△ *La Fortaleza 1050m*
Igualero

Playa de Ingles

La Calera

VALLE GRAN REY ❺

La Playa Calera

Imad

La Puntilla

Vueltas

Agalán

ALAJERÓ ❽

La Dama

Playa de la Rajita

Antoncoj

Punta Falcones

Punta del Becerro

The parador courtyard in San Sebastián de La Gomera

| 0 km | 3 |
| 0 miles | 3 |

GETTING THERE

The distance between La Gomera and Tenerife is 32 km (20 miles). The journey by ferry from Los Cristianos takes 1 hr 40 min, by hydrofoil it is 45 min. There are also ferry links with La Palma and El Hierro. The island has direct air links with Tenerife and Gran Canaria. All main routes on the island are served by buses, although these are not very frequent. It is therefore preferable to hire a car. A few unmade roads on the island are only suitable for a four-wheel-drive vehicle.

Black sand beach near the harbour in San Sebastián de La Gomera, one of the few beaches on the island

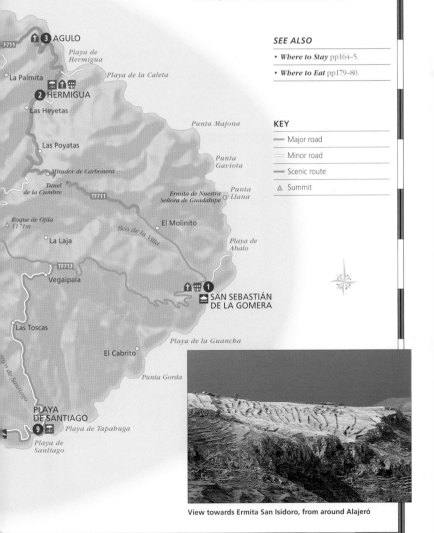

SEE ALSO

- **Where to Stay** pp164–5.
- **Where to Eat** pp179–80.

KEY

- ═══ Major road
- ─── Minor road
- ━━━ Scenic route
- △ Summit

View towards Ermita San Isidoro, from around Alajeró

Façade of Iglesia de la Virgen de la Asunción in San Sebastián

San Sebastián de La Gomera ❶

🏠 7,000. 🚌 ⛴ ℹ C/Real, 1, 922 141 512. 🎉 Fiesta de San Sebastián (20 Jan), Bajada de la Virgen de Guadalupe (5 Oct, every 5 years).

With the daily arrival of tourists on the Tenerife ferry, the island's sleepy capital and main harbour comes alive. The road from the harbour into town passes through the laurel-shaded **Plaza de las Américas**, which is lined with street cafés.

To the west of the square stands the **Torre del Conde**. This Gothic tower was built in 1447 by the first Spanish governor of La Gomera, Hernán Peraza the Elder. Restored in 1997, it is the only remaining fragment of the town's fortifications. Torre del Conde is a reminder of a tragic uprising in the town. In 1448, Beatriz de Bobadilla, wife of Hernán Peraza the Younger, barricaded herself within its walls after her husband was killed by a Guanche in revenge for his illicit affair with a native princess. When help arrived from Gran Canaria, Beatriz avenged herself by putting almost every male Guanche on Gomera to death.

The island's main church is the **Iglesia de la Virgen de la Asunción** in Calle Real. The foundations were laid in the mid-15th century and Christopher Columbus is said to have knelt down to pray in the church's dim interior

before continuing on his first voyage. **Casa de Colón**, at 56 Calle Real, is where Columbus is said to have stayed before setting off for the New World, while the **Pozo de Colón**, a well standing in the courtyard of a former customs building, has the inscription "With this

The Gothic defensive tower of Torre del Conde

water America was baptized". Another sight to look out for is the small **Ermita de San Sebastián**. Built around 1450, this is the oldest church on the island, and is dedicated to La Gomera's patron saint.

Heading towards **Mirador de la Hila**, which offers views over the whole of San Sebastián, the road leads to the **Parador de San Sebastián**. This comfortable hotel was built in 1976 and is a modern replica of a Canary colonial mansion.

Environs
Some 4 km (2 miles) north, the gravel road divides: one route descends towards the quiet beach at **Playa de Abalo**; the other leads to **Ermita de Nuestra Señora de Guadalupe** – every five years a statue of the Virgin Mary is carried to San Sebastián from here (the next "Bajada" is in 2013).

Hermigua ❷

🏠 500. 🚌 ℹ near Iglesia de la Encarnación, 922 880 990.

A winding road leads from San Sebastián to Hermigua. Along the route, the scenery is attractive and varied with weathered rocks, forests of willow and laurel, juniper groves, deep ravines and lush green valleys.

Hermigua, known as Mulagua during the times of Guanches, was once an important town but is today little more than a village. The fertile soil in the lower regions

---

CHRISTOPHER COLUMBUS (1451–1506)

The name "Isla Colombina" evokes La Gomera's links with Christopher Columbus. Columbus stopped here three times, in 1492, 1493 and 1498. The island provided his fleet with food and fresh water and was a good launch pad for his historic expeditions. The many stories surrounding his visits include an alleged romance with Beatriz de Bobadilla. Columbus will always remain an unofficial patron of the island and the Fiesta Colombina, held on 6 September each year, commemorates his first voyage.

Statue of Columbus in Playa de las Américas

of Barranco de Monteforte still allows cultivation of grapes, bananas and dates.

Today the only evidence of past glories is a handful of old buildings along the small scenic streets and the **Convento de Santo Domingo de Guzmán** in the Valle Alto district. Dating from the 16th century, the church's interior features a fine 19th-century image of the Madonna by Fernando Estévez.

Hermigua is famous for its handmade rugs and other woven products. These can be seen and purchased in **Los Telares**, the local handicraft centre. Nearby is **Playa de Hermigua** – covered with shingle, it is not the most beautiful of beaches and is subject to rough weather.

Environs
An hour's hike along the footpath, to the northeast, brings you to **Playa de la Caleta**, one of the best black sand beaches on the island.

The pretty Iglesia de la Encarnación in Hermigua

Agulo ❸

🏃 800. 🚌

The 17th-century town of Agulo lies in the north-eastern part of the island, high above the sea at the foot of a natural rock amphitheatre and surrounded by banana plantations. Together with the nearby hamlet of Lepe, inhabited by hardly more than handful of crofters, this is a picturesque little place and a popular destination for sightseers around La Gomera.

Banana plantation on the coast near Agulo

One unique feature of Agulo's architecture is the church of **San Marcos** (1939). Moorish in design, its four white domes are visible from far away. The town's best-known native son is the painter José Aguiar (1895–1976) who was born in Cuba of Gomeran parents, and spent his childhood in Agulo.

Environs
A steep, twisting road leads upwards from Agulo to **Mirador de Abrante**. This stone terrace offers a splendid view over the rocky coast and the ocean and is a fine spot to appreciate Mount Teide on Tenerife. A little further along the road, at the end of a ravine, is the village of La Palmita, renowned for its traditional lifestyle.

Vallehermoso ❹

🏃 900. 🚌 ℹ️ *Avda. de Guillermo Ascanio, 18, 922 800 000.*

Vallehermoso translates as "beautiful valley" and the surrounding agricultural landscape is evidence of the island's fertile soil. Some 17 km (11 miles) along a winding road from Agulo, this compact town, with its bustling centre (including shops, a post office, a bank and a petrol station) is a good starting point for sightseeing and walking tours around this green and pleasant region.

At the centre of the town is the Iglesia San Juan Bautista, which was designed by the Tenerife architect, Antonio Pintor. One of the town's other attractions is a small park enlivened by bizarre groups of roughly hewn sculptural figures.

Environs
A short way to the north is **Playa de Vallehermoso**, which is good for windsurfing. Those who prefer to swim in calmer waters can make use of the swimming pool built next to the pebble beach.

Some 4 km (2 miles) to the north is **Los Órganos** – an impressive section of steep cliff that can be seen only from the sea, on cruising trips from Valle Gran Rey, Playa de Santiago or San Sebastián. This basalt wall, 80 m (262 ft) high and 200 m (656 ft) wide, resembles the pipes of an organ and is one of the most unusual (and least accessible) attractions on La Gomera.

Just 2 km (1 mile) to the east, along the road to Agulo, is the **Roque Cano**. This 650-m (2,132-ft) high fang-shaped rock was created by erosion of a volcanic peak.

Las Rosas, situated just 11 km (7 miles) from Vallehermoso, is a popular stopping place for coach tours. It has a restaurant where tourists are treated to demonstrations of El Silbo – the island's famous whistle language *(see p128).*

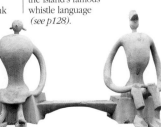

***Mother and Father** in Vallehermoso's park*

Black sand beach at Valle Gran Rey

Valle Gran Rey ❺

🏃 5,000. 🚌 🚢 🛈 *La Playa, Calle de la Noria, 922 805 458.*

The centre of tourism on the island, Valle Gran Rey ("valley of the great king") was known even before the Spanish conquest of Gomera, when it was named Orone after a Guanche leader. Today's Valle Gran Rey is really a complex of several seaside villages – **La Calera**, **La Playa**, **La Puntilla** and **Vueltas** – which are the measure of the tourism boom that has even reached La Gomera. The developing estates try hard to meet the demands of modern European guests, particularly Germans, who look for comfort but are also keen to sample a different lifestyle. The place attracts many visitors who come not only for the idyllic scenery, but also for the excellent new pensions and restaurants. The magnificent Atlantic waves will satisfy even the most demanding surfing fanatics.

La Calera, with its picturesque setting in the midst of banana plantations, has been nicknamed the Montmartre of La Gomera, thanks to its small boutiques and cosy restaurants. It is regarded as one of the archipelago's prettiest towns and the house prices here are some of the highest on the island. Like La Playa, it also has a small beach.

The harbour at **Vueltas** offers hydrofoil links to Los Cristianos on Tenerife, as well as short cruises along the coast of La Gomera and to

Los Órganos. It is also used by fishing boats and numerous yachts. Several restaurants tempt visitors with tasty dishes of freshly caught fish. The most scenic road on the island is surrounded by massive basalt rocks and runs through the valley, renowned for its fertility. Local crops include dates, bananas, papayas, avocados, mangoes and tomatoes. Small fields,

New houses at the mouth of the Valle Gran Rey

cutting into the valley slopes in the form of terraces, are similar to Balinese rice fields.

For hikers there are several walking trails, representing various degrees of difficulty. Above the town, at the entrance to the valley, is a **viewpoint** made according to a design by César Manrique, and featuring one of the island's best restaurants.

Environs
Perched above the valley, 11 km (7 miles) to the north, is the village of **Arure**, which prior to the island's conquest used to be its main centre. Today the place has a desolate look about it and is known mainly for its excellent *miel de palma* – "palm honey". The palms from which the honey is made have flanges fitted around their trunks to protect them against hungry ants.

The nearby **Mirador del Santo** offers a splendid view over the ravines and on to La Palma and El Hierro.

El Cercado ❻

🚌 *Chipude.*

This small village is best-known for its handicrafts, especially the primitively shaped earthenware products that are made of dark Gomera clay, without the use of a potter's wheel.

Local traditions are also being upheld by a small number of bars offering traditional cuisine.

EL SILBO GOMERA

Long before the invention of the telephone, Gomera's inhabitants needed a way of communicating across the island's inhospitable terrain. A unique whistle language, known as El Silbo, was the solution. Modulating the whistle by changing finger positions produced many different sounds to produce a limited vocabulary, which could be transmitted up to 4 km (2 miles). Nowadays the whistle is just used to impress tourists but the local Guanches once relied on it when threatened or during hunting expeditions.

Cupping the hands to carry the sound further

Terraced fields of El Cercado

living by growing bananas. The 16th-century **Iglesia del Salvador** is one of the few remains of the village's historic past.

From Alajeró a path leads westward, along a very deep ravine, to **La Manteca**. Though many of the people who were born in the area have left in search of a better life, this ghost village, set in a very picturesque spot, is one of the few villages to be totally abandoned.

Environs

Some 3 km (2 miles) to the south, at the foot of **La Fortaleza** – a large basalt rock that is almost as flat as a table top – lies **Chipude**. At 1,050 m (3,444 ft) above sea level, this is the highest village on La Gomera. It is known for its 16th-century church, the Iglesia de la Virgen de la Candelaria. Like El Cercado, Chipude is renowned as a pottery village. A steep country road that later becomes a walking trail leads from El Cercado to **La Laguna Grande** – an information point at the entrance to the Parque Nacional de Garajonay.

Some 15 km (9 miles) to the south is **La Dama**. Surrounded by banana plantations, this small village is poised high above the ocean.

Parque Nacional de Garajonay ❼

See pp130–31.

Alajeró ❽

🏠 *600.* 🚌 🎭 *Fiesta del Paso (Sep).*

A typical Gomera village, Alajeró sprawls along a mountain road in the southern part of the island. Most of the village's inhabitants make a

Environs

In Agalán, 2 km (1 mile) north of Alajeró down a cobbled road, is the island's only surviving dragon tree. The **Drago de Agalán** is about 150 years old.

Playa de Santiago ❾

🏠 *1,600.* 🚌 ℹ️ *Casa de Cultura, Avenida Marítima, 922 895 650.*

Playa de Santiago plays a vital role in La Gomera's transport system. It lies at the junction of two ravines – **Barranco de los Cocos** and **Barranco de Santiago** – and has a fishing harbour and a newly constructed airport, situated on a bare stretch of land to the west. In addition, the town lies along the road that runs in a loop around the southern part of the island.

Traditional pottery made in El Cercado

As recently as 50 years ago Playa de Santiago was probably the busiest centre on the island with a thriving food industry, a small shipyard and a harbour with facilities for the export of the local cash crops, including bananas and tomatoes. Then, in the 1970s, an economic crisis hit and the town went into a steep decline.

Affordable holidays provided the town's route back to prosperity and these days Playa de Santiago is orientated mainly towards tourism. It is the second largest resort on the island, besides Valle Gran Rey, and is slowly but surely returning to its past glory.

Visitors are attracted mainly by the weather, since the place is believed to be the sunniest spot on La Gomera. Further temptations include the local beaches and the modern hotel and beach club facilities.

If proof were needed of Playa de Santiago's tourist-friendly credentials then look no further than the **Jardín Tecina**. The complex has numerous bars, restaurants, tennis courts and a new golf course. Perched on top of cliffs, the complex consists of unobtrusive white bungalows, built in the local style. A lift, running in a shaft carved into the rock face, whisks guests to the beach and the Club Laurel beach club, which has a huge salt-water pool and a good restaurant. To the east of the hotel are other beaches, including **Tapahuga**, **Chinguarime** and **Playa del Medio**.

Shingle beach in Playa de Santiago

Parque Nacional de Garajonay

Covering an area of 40 sq km (15 sq miles), Gomera's
national park is the largest intact area of ancient
woodland in the archipelago. The unique weather
conditions, caused by the constant flow of mist produced
when the cool Atlantic trade winds encounter warm
breezes, ensure constant dew and humidity conducive to
the growth of some 450 species of plants and trees. The
vegetation often reaches unprecedented sizes, providing
an illustration of what a Mediterranean forest looked like
before the last Ice Age. So precious is this region that
it is the only national park in Spain to
be declared a World Heritage Site
by UNESCO.

Walking Trails
*The high viewpoints
situated along the park
trails provide fantastic
views over to Tenerife.*

Epina

TF-713

Banda de
las Rosas

VALLE GRAN RAY

▲ QUEMADO
1136

Las Hayas

El Cercado

El Cercado
The village,
enjoying a scenic
position and
easily reached by
bus, provides
a starting point
for walks around
the park.

Chipude

Iguala

La Laguna Grande
*Often shrouded in mist, La Laguna
Grande is a good stopping-off
point for walks around the park.
It also features an excellent
restaurant, a children's
playground and a picnic area.*

Chipude
This village, on the
outskirts of the park,
has a small hotel and
restaurant.

PLA
DE SANTIA

0 km   1

0 miles   1

KEY

═══ Major road

── Other road

··· Footpath

━━ Park boundary

⌐·⌐ Seasonal river

☀ Viewpoint

VEGETATION

The term *laurisilva*, meaning
"laurel grove", is used to
describe the ancient laurel
forest at the heart of the park.
The evergreen laurel trees
grow to 20 m (65 ft). These
trees provide large areas of
the park with a thick ceiling
of green, which keeps in
much of the mist and
provides enough shade to
keep walkers cool on the
many hiking trails that wind
through the forest. As well as
laurel trees, the park has
dense tree heather and
juniper groves.

**Lichen hanging from the
branches of tree heather**

Mirador de Vallehermoso
From this fine viewpoint, just inside the park boundary and surrounded by dense heather, you can get a magnificent overview of the park and the north side of the island.

Ravines
The park is criss-crossed by many densely wooded ravines, which provide shelter for numerous species of rare birds, including the long-toed Canary pigeon.

Visitors' Centre
The excellent visitor centre, near Las Rosas, has craft workshops, an exhibition on Gomera handicrafts, a well-labelled garden, and a pleasant Canary restaurant.

Garajonay
At 1,487 m (4,877 ft), El Alto de Garajonay is La Gomera's highest mountain. A marked trail leads to the summit.

Los Roques
The volcanic formations, including Zarcita (1,236 m/4,054 ft), Carmen (1,140 m/3,739 ft) and Agando (1,250 m/4,100 ft), are situated just outside the park's boundaries, and are best seen from Mirador El Bailadero.

EL HIERRO

l Hierro is the smallest and westernmost island of the archipelago. Known locally as "La Isla Chiquita" – the Small Island – it occupies a mere 278 sq km (107 sq miles). Rural and, for the most part, untouched by tourism thanks to its lack of sandy beaches, the entire island has only 6,000 or so inhabitants, a quarter of whom live in the island's capital – Valverde.

The shape of El Hierro is the result of a strong earthquake that struck the island some 50,000 years ago. At that time one third of the island broke away from its northern side and sank beneath the ocean waves, creating the El Golfo bay. The most recent volcanic eruption on this mountainous island, numbering 500 volcanic peaks, occurred more than 200 years ago.

Prior to the Spanish invasion of 1403, the island's population consisted of Bimbache tribes. Following the island's conquest most of these tribes fell victim to slave traders and their land was appropriated by Norman and Castilian settlers. A feudal system, introduced at that time, survived until the mid-19th century.

Aeonium, growing on the rocks

Today, the population lives mainly off agriculture, growing grapes and bananas, as well as almonds, peaches, potatoes and tomatoes. As elsewhere, fishing is another key element of the local economy, particularly on the southern coast.

Tourism plays little part in the economy of the island. The accommodation on offer extends to some 800 beds (taken mainly by Canary islanders in July and August). The pine forest camping site of Hoya del Morcillo is also very popular.

There is no industry on El Hierro, but handicrafts thrive, particularly pottery, weaving and woodcarving. Many tourists shop for local products, particularly at village markets where buyers and sellers are entertained by folk musicians and dancers.

Natural pools in Charco Manso lava near Valverde

◁ Red and yellow carpets of flowering plants covering the rocks

Exploring El Hierro

El Hierro's chief draw is its romantic wildness.
Before Columbus's voyages, this was the
westernmost point of the known world. Even
today the island is largely untouched by
tourism and retains its "end of the world"
feel. The magnificent mountain scenery
compensates for the lack of sandy beaches.
Wild terrain, shrouded in mist and often
overgrown with dense pine forest, attracts
nature lovers. Some less accessible places can
only be reached on foot. Equally attractive is
the maritime nature reserve, to the south, a
paradise for divers. The local cuisine revolves
around fresh fish and the island is known
for its delicious wines.

LOCATOR MAP

Giant junipers, twisted into fanciful
shapes by the wind, in El Sabinar

SEE ALSO
- **Where to Stay** pp165–6.
- **Where to Eat** p180.

0 km   2

0 miles   2

SIGHTS AT A GLANCE

El Sabinar ❺
Frontera ❷
Isora ❽
La Restinga ❼
Las Puntas ❸
Puerto de la Estaca ❿
Sabinosa ❹
San Andrés ❾
Santuario de Nuestra Señora
   de los Reyes ❻
Valverde ❶

Tiny Puerto de la Estaca, on the east coast – the island's
only ferry harbour

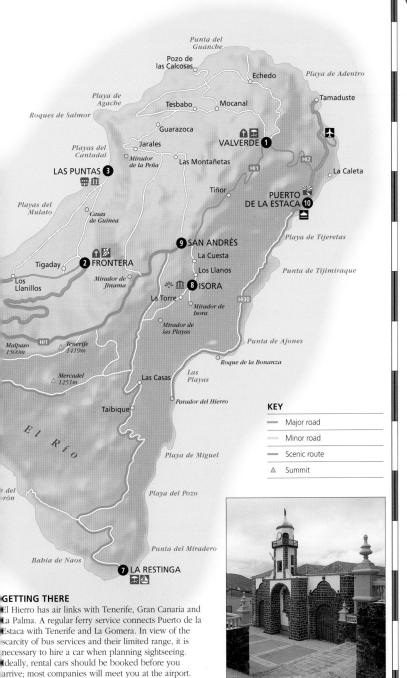

Punta del Guanche
Playa de Adentro
Pozo de las Calcosas
Echedo
Tamaduste
Playa de Agache
Tesbabo
Mocanal
Roques de Salmor
Guarazoca
Jarales
Mirador de la Peña
Las Montañetas
VALVERDE ❶
LAS PUNTAS ❸
Playas del Cantadal
Playas del Mulato
Casas de Guinea
Tiñor
La Caleta
PUERTO DE LA ESTACA ❿
Playa de Tijeretas
Tigaday ❷ FRONTERA
Los Llanillos
Mirador de Jinama
SAN ANDRÉS ❾
La Cuesta
Los Llanos
❽ ISORA
La Torre
Mirador de Isora
Punta de Tijimiraque
Mirador de las Playas
Malpaso 1500m
Tenerife 1419m
Punta de Ajones
Roque de la Bonanza
Mercadel 1251m
Las Casas
Las Playas
Playas del Pozo
Taibique
Parador del Hierro
El Río
Playa de Miguel
Punta del Miradero
Bahía de Naos
❼ LA RESTINGA

KEY

—	Major road
=	Minor road
—	Scenic route
△	Summit

GETTING THERE

El Hierro has air links with Tenerife, Gran Canaria and La Palma. A regular ferry service connects Puerto de la Estaca with Tenerife and La Gomera. In view of the scarcity of bus services and their limited range, it is necessary to hire a car when planning sightseeing. Ideally, rental cars should be booked before you arrive; most companies will meet you at the airport. The roads have recently been improved, but some more remote places require an all-terrain vehicle.

Iglesia de la Concepción in Valverde

Pools in Pozo de las Calcosas near Valverde

Valverde ❶

🏛 *2,000.* 🚌 ℹ️ *C/Dr. Quineiro, 11, 922 550 302.* 🎪 *Fiesta de San Isidro (15 May), Bajada de la Virgen de los Reyes (every 4 years in Jul).*

The full name of the island's capital is La Villa de Santa María de Valverde. Unlike the other island capitals, Valverde has no harbour. The small town is poised on the slope of an evergreen valley (hence the name), and is extremely quiet and often rather foggy.

The only noteworthy local historic sight is **Iglesia Santa María de la Concepción**. Built in 1767 on the site of a former 16th-century chapel, this vast church was erected in thanksgiving for the repulse of a pirate attack. The belfry includes a large clock brought from Paris in 1886. The main feature of the interior is the Baroque altar. The town hall, standing opposite the church, took 30 years to build (1910–40), and is in the local style.

Environs
Tamaduste, 10 km (6 miles) to the northeast, is the islanders' favourite resort, and has a quiet cove with a pleasant beach.

Charco Manso, 8 km (5 miles) to the north, is a complex of natural pools set in volcanic rock. These are reached by a narrow road

with hairpin bends. The sea here can be dangerous and swimming is not advisable.

Pozo de las Calcosas, 8 km (5 miles) to the northwest, is a good place to swim and features pools similar to those of Charco Manso, and a number of black stone huts on the ocean shore, all reached by steep steps.

An unforgettable view over **El Golfo** bay is to be had from **Mirador de La Peña**, 8 km (5 miles) to the west. The restaurant here was built in 1988 following a design by César Manrique.

Frontera ❷

🚌 🎪 *Fiesta de la Virgen de la Candelaria (Aug).*

Many of the inhabitants of the island's second largest town make their living by growing grapes. These are the source of Viña Frontera – wines famous throughout the archipelago.

The **Iglesia de la Candelaria**, standing on the outskirts of the town, was built in 1818 and occupies the entire square. The interior, covered with a wooden ceiling, features a striking, gilded altar. Standing above the church, on

a hill of red volcanic ash, is a belfry that is visible from afar.

Environs
Tigaday, 1 km (half a mile) to the west, is a relatively large village and a great wine-producing centre. It is the starting point for the road to Las Puntas.

Las Puntas ❸

ℹ️ *922 559 081* 🎪 *Fiesta de San Juan (24 Jun).*

Standing on the old wharf, where until 1930 ships arrived bringing supplies, is the Hotel Puntagrande, which had an entry in the *Guinness Book of Records* as the world's smallest hotel. It began life in 1884 as a harbour building until it was transformed into a hotel. It has four rooms, a bar and a restaurant. Although it is difficult to get a room here it is still worth coming in order to admire the beautiful sunset and enjoy a swim in one of the rocky coves.

Another noteworthy local feature is the **Roques de Salmor**. These scenic rock formations rise from the sea, and are one of the island's most important bird colonies.

Environs
A short way to the south, **Casas de Guinea** is an old Norman settlement dating from the early 15th century. Along with Las Montañetas, it claims to be the oldest village on El Hierro. Today it houses the Ecomuseo de Guinea – a complex of former shepherds' huts that have been restored and kitted out with furniture

The world's smallest hotel in Las Puntas

For hotels and restaurants in this region see pp165–6 and p180

from different periods. A small site known as **Lagartario**, above the museum, is used to provide natural breeding conditions for a rare species of lizard from Salmor, found only in El Hierro. A project to restore this species of giant, 1.5-m (5-ft) lizard, extinct since the 1930s, commenced in 1975. Public viewing of the giant lizards is limited; apply to the town hall in Tigaday. Skeletons of the extinct giant lizards can today be seen in London and Vienna's main natural history museums.

🏛 **Ecomuseo de Guinea**
Tel *922 555 056.* ⏰ *10am–2pm and 4–6pm Tue–Sun* ⏺ *Mon.* 📷

Pozo de la Salud, poised on the shore of El Golfo bay

Sabinosa ❹

🚌 📷 *San Simón (end Oct).*

Swamped with flowers, Sabinosa is pleasantly remote, with picturesque narrow streets and paths. Poised high up on a steep slope, overlooking almost all of El Golfo bay, it is known for its "well of health" – **Pozo de la Salud** – which can be found by the sea below Sabinosa. The water, which must be drawn up by bucket from a well, is highly radioactive and is believed to be something of a cure-all for any number of ailments. A modern hotel, built here in 1996 to cater to the needs of health-seeking visitors, is the only one of its type in the Canary Islands.

BAJADA DE LA VIRGEN DE LOS REYES

In the early 18th century, during a period of drought, the Madonna was carried down from the Nuestra Señora de los Reyes by villagers to Valverde and, hey presto, it rained. Since then a feast has been held every four years (2009, 2013) on the first or second Saturday in June. The statue of the Holy Mother follows the same route along unmade country lanes – the Camino de la Virgen – and is carried on a litter to Valverde. The ceremony, which begins at 5am and goes on till late, is accompanied by a week of merriment, with many villagers dressed in red and white costumes.

The "Descent of the Virgin"

Environs

Playa de Arenas, 6 km (4 miles) to the west, is a sandy beach, popular with tourists and locals alike.

Some 10 km (6 miles) to the west is **Playa de Verodal**. This small, scenic, windswept beach, with its rust-coloured volcanic sands, lies at the foot of a high cliff. Accessible via a bumpy, coarse-gravel road, it is generally considered to be the most beautiful stretch of beach on the island.

East of Sabinosa, the road runs to **Los Llanillos**, a tiny village with a small chapel built of blocks of volcanic rock. Standing by the roadside is a workshop producing all shapes and sizes of birdcages. A little further along, the road reaches **Charco Azul**, where rocky coves with turquoise water tempt visitors to swim.

El Sabinar ❺

The name of this upland, swept by Atlantic winds and crossed by a gorge, derives from the local word *sabina* (juniper). It features almost 300 white-trunked juniper trees that have bent and twisted into bizarre shapes.

El Sabinar is reached by a road that starts out as asphalt and later becomes a dirt track running among pastures and crossing cattle gates. It is a little under 4 km (2 miles) from the sanctuary of Nuestra Señora de los Reyes.

Environs

Mirador de Basco, 3 km (2 miles) to the north, offers a view (on sunny days) not only of El Golfo, but also of La Palma, La Gomera and Tenerife.

The island's symbol – a wind-twisted juniper tree in El Sabinar

Santuario de Nuestra Señora de los Reyes, surrounded by a low wall

Santuario de Nuestra Señora de los Reyes ❻

Set among wooded hills in the western part of the island, surrounded by a low wall, is the pilgrim sanctuary of the Holy Mother of the Kings (Magi) – the patron saint of El Hierro. Inside is a statue of the Madonna, kept on a silver litter. Every four years, in the course of a ceremonial procession known as the Bajada de la Virgen de los Reyes, the statue is carried to Valverde (see p137).

Legend has it that a French ship was becalmed near the shores of the island, and the crew were only able to survive thanks to the help of El Hierro's inhabitants. Having no money to pay for food and water, the captain presented the islanders with a statue of the Virgin Mary. On the same day, 6 January 1577, the day of the Epiphany, a strong wind sent the ship on her way.

Environs
The **Faro de Orchilla** lighthouse is 7 km (4 miles) to the southwest. The road leading to it is initially asphalt but later becomes an unmade track. In AD 150, the Greek geographer Ptolemy declared this western end of the island to be the end of the world. In 1634, the zero meridian was drawn through this point and remained recognized as such until 1884, when it was moved to Greenwich. Even so, El Hierro still refers to itself as "Isla del Meridiano" and visitors can buy a decorated certificate confirming that they have crossed the zero meridian.

La Restinga ❼

🚌 🎭 Fiesta de San Juan (24 Jun), Fiesta de la Virgen del Carmen (16 Jul).

La Restinga is a small fishing harbour and yacht basin, situated on the sunniest, southern end of the island. It is also one of the most popular resorts on El Hierro. There's a large hotel and a small apartment complex and the coastal road – Avenida Marítima – features a wide variety of shops, bars and restaurants. This is a good place to sit out and watch the world drift by.

In the centre is a small, black sand beach that is sheltered by the large harbour. Though generally rather quiet, La Restinga has plenty of facilities for water sports including diving. The local waters around here have protected status and feature rich marine fauna and flora combined with underwater gullies and interesting rock formations to explore. Diving centres are open all year round and offer trips and night-time expeditions.

Environs
A short way to the northwest is **Bahía de Naos** – which is

known principally as the place where Jean de Béthencourt landed in 1403.

Some 10 km (6 miles) to the northwest is **Cala del Tacorón** – a number of small coves carved into the volcanic shore of Mar de las Calmas. Here, swimmers find the clear waters and steps down to the sea particularly inviting.

Cueva Don Justo, 2 km (1 mile) to the north, within the Montaña de Prim massif, is a great attraction to potholers, with its 6-km (4-mile) labyrinth of underground volcanic tunnels.

Spectacular view from Mirador de las Playas

Isora ❽

🎭 Fiesta de San José (19 Mar).

Situated in the eastern part of the island, Isora is a picturesque assembly of several hamlets, and is famous for cheese production. It is well worth trying to arrive here at dawn to admire the magnificent sunrise.

Volcanic peaks around La Restinga

For hotels and restaurants in this region see pp165–6 and p180

Another attraction is the famous *lucha canaria* games, when feats of Canary-style wrestling take place at the local stadium.

Environs

About 1 km (half a mile) to the south, at the edge of the mountain range of El Risco de los Herrenos, is the **Mirador de Isora**, offering enchanting panoramic views over the ocean. A narrow footpath, some 4 km (2 miles) long, leads down to the coast.

About 3 km (2 miles) to the south is **Mirador de las Playas** – a high viewpoint, set among Canary pines. The broad terrace provides magnificent panoramic views over Las Playas bay, from Roque de la Bonanza up to the parador.

El Pinar, 6 km (4 miles) to the south, is the collective name often used to describe two villages – **Las Casas** and **Taibique** – which has a main street featuring bars, restaurants, shops, a hotel and bank. The local Artesanía Cerámica sells ceramics and handmade jewellery. There is also a small church – **Iglesia de San Antonio**.

San Andrés ❾

🚍 📷 *Fiesta de la Apañada (1st Sun in Jun).*

A heady 1,100 m (3,600 ft) above sea level, the prickly pear and fig trees of San Andrés are often shrouded in cold, damp mist for hours on end, and especially at night. This small agricultural town tends to be very hot in the summer, but winters are cold, and often battered with strong winds.

Its inhabitants live mainly off the land, cultivating crops and grazing sheep and goats. Despite the fertile soil, the unfavourable weather conditions cause many of them to leave this

Mist-shrouded fields around San Andrés

extremely rough and inhospitable terrain.

Environs

To the north, an asphalt road a little under 4 km (2 miles) long, which later becomes a footpath, leads to **Árbol Santo** – the holy Bimbache tree, known to locals as the *Garoé*. According to legend, water once flowed from the tree to give the island its entire supply (in fact the pine tree's needles had the ability to accumulate large quantities of water). The ancient tree was destroyed in 1949 by a hurricane; in its place grows a lime tree, planted here in 1957.

Goat's cheese produced in San Andrés

Some 2 km (1 mile) to the southwest is **Mirador de Jinama**. It is reached by road through fields divided by dry stone walls. In clear weather, the viewpoint provides a fine panorama over El Golfo bay.

Puerto de la Estaca ❿

📷 *San Telmo (14 Sep).*

Until 1972, when the airport opened, this small harbour, cut off from the land by high volcanic cliffs, was the island's only link with the world. The name of the harbour, built in 1906, is derived from the word *estaca*, which is a type of wooden pile, to which fishermen tied their boats.

Environs

The **Roque de la Bonanza**, a bare basalt rock rising vertically from the sea a few steps from the shore, is 9 km (6 miles) to the south. It can be reached via a beautiful coastline road that is in the shadow of a steep volcanic slope.

Take care: at one point, the road passes through a single-lane tunnel with intermittently functioning traffic lights.

Some 2 km (1 mile) further south, set amid picturesque scenery, stands the **Parador del Hierro** – the most comfortable hotel on the island. The hotel has an isolated waterfront location, with views of the cliff walls round the bay, and was built in the Castilian style between 1973 and 1976. Its opening was delayed by five years, due to the slow building of the road that terminates here.

Roque de la Bonanza or "Rock of the Silent Ocean" in Las Playas bay

LA PALMA

The Palmeros refer to La Palma as La Isla Bonita – "the Beautiful Island", or La Isla Verde – "the Green Island". Both nicknames are justified since the island is both extremely pretty and strikingly lush. The rich vegetation of ferns and laurel forests, together with the fine domestic gardens, regarded as the best-kept in the archipelago, make this one of the greenest spots in the region.

The island's greenery is in large part thanks to the highest rainfall in the Canary Islands. In spring and autumn the sun stays behind the clouds for an average of 63 days and the plants enjoy excellent growing conditions.

Statue of a "dancing dwarf"

The fifth largest island of the archipelago, La Palma is shaped like the head of a stone axe. It is claimed to be among the world's most mountainous islands, in terms of its height to area ratio (the island is 706 sq km/273 sq miles). The highest peak – Roque de los Muchachos – measures 2,426 m (7,957 ft). Like the rest of the archipelago, La Palma is a volcanic island and its volcanoes cannot be regarded as truly extinct. The last eruption occurred in 1971 in the south of the island, where the black lava fields and reddish brown volcanic rocks contrast with the lush greenery of the remaining part of the island. Opinion is divided as to when the next eruption is likely to take place.

The island's population engages mainly in agriculture. An abundance of water ensures good crops of grapes, avocados, bananas and tobacco. The latter is used to make cigars that are considered by experts to be as good as the cigars produced in Cuba. La Palma is also known for its production of honey while, like many of the islands, fishing plays an important part in the local economy. Mass tourism remains less of a feature here, due in part to the shortage of pleasant beaches along the island's craggy coastline, though there are good tourist centres on the west and east coasts.

Glittering volcanic rocks, providing a fairytale-like spectacle of colour around Pico de la Cruz

◁ Green areas of Caldera de Taburiente National Park

Exploring La Palma

La Palma is excellent for walking trips and can cater for all tastes from a gentle stroll to a strenuous hike. Its varied landscapes, from the volcanic ash region of Fuencaliente to the lush, almost tropical forests of Los Tilos, fully compensate for the lack of great historic sights. Free of the bustle of the larger resort islands, there's ample opportunity for rest and relaxation, while the coastal waters of La Palma, rich in aquatic life, will attract divers. An excursion along the volcano trail, in the south of the island, is one of the highlights of a visit here, as is sampling the local wines and cuisine.

Punta de Rabisca

Garafía

Barranco de Briestas

LA ZARZA

Puntagorda

Roque de los Muchach 242

Playa de Camarino   Cascajo

LP1

Tajarafe

Playa de Jurado

Bco de los Any

LOS LLANOS DE ARIDANE
8
Mirador del Time

EL P
TAZACORTE 7   Tajoy
La Laguna
Tria
Las Manc
PUERTO NAOS 10
Charco Verde

Colourful wooden balconies on the sea promenade at Santa Cruz de La Palma

0 km   3

0 miles   3

SIGHTS AT A GLANCE

Barlovento 5
Fuencaliente de La Palma 11
La Zarza 6
Las Nieves 2
Los Llanos de Aridane 8
Los Tilos 3
Mazo 13
Parque Nacional de la Caldera de Taburiente pp150–51 9
Puerto Naos 10
San Andrés 4
Santa Cruz de La Palma pp144–5 1
Tazacorte 7

Excursions

Ruta de los Volcanes 12

SEE ALSO

GETTING THERE

La Palma has air links with Tenerife, Gran Canaria and El Hierro, as well as with some cities of mainland Spain. There are charter flights to and from several Western European airports. Planes touch down at the airport on the east coast, which connects to Santa Cruz de La Palma via an 8-km (5-mile) motorway. Ferries from Tenerife and La Gomera sail to Santa Cruz de La Palma harbour. Most of the island's towns and villages have bus transport. However, in order to explore the more remote parts of La Palma, you will have to hire a car.

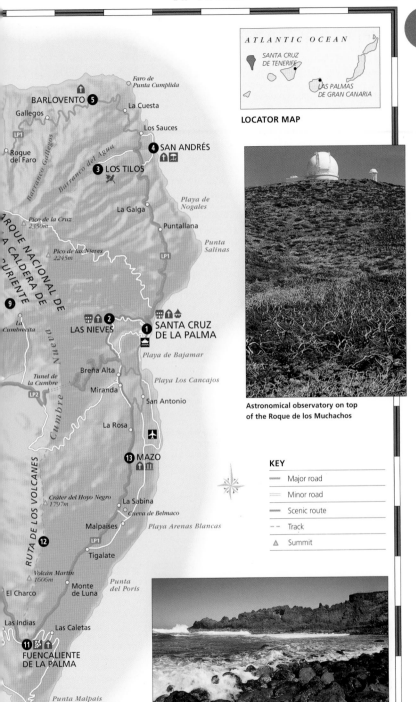

ATLANTIC OCEAN

SANTA CRUZ
DE TENERIFE

LAS PALMAS
DE GRAN CANARIA

LOCATOR MAP

Faro de
Punta Cumplida

BARLOVENTO 5

Gallegos

La Cuesta

LP1

Los Sauces

Roque
del Faro

4 **SAN ANDRÉS**

Barranco Gallegos

Barranco del Agua

3 **LOS TILOS**

PARQUE NACIONAL DE
LA CALDERA DE
TABURIENTE

Pico de la Cruz
2350m

La Galga

Playa de
Nogales

Pico de las Nieves
2245m

Puntallana

Punta
Salinas

LP1

9

La
Cumbrecita

2
LAS NIEVES

1
**SANTA CRUZ
DE LA PALMA**

Nueva

Playa de Bajamar

Breña Alta

Playa Los Cancajos

Tunel de
la Cumbre

LP2

Miranda

San Antonio

Cumbre

La Rosa

13 **MAZO**

RUTA DE LOS VOLCANES

Cráter del Hoyo Negro
1797m

La Sabina

Cueva de Belmaco

Malpaises

Playa Arenas Blancas

12

LP1

Tigalate

Volcán Martín
1606m

Punta
del Poris

El Charco

Monte
de Luna

Las Indias

Las Caletas

11
**FUENCALIENTE
DE LA PALMA**

Punta Malpais

Punta de
Fuencaliente

**Astronomical observatory on top
of the Roque de los Muchachos**

KEY

— Major road

— Minor road

— Scenic route

-- Track

△ Summit

Bathing area in Charco Azul, near San Andrés

Santa Cruz de La Palma ❶

Santa Cruz de La Palma, situated on a bay known to the Guanches as Timibucar, has from its early days played a vital role in the economic and political life of Spain. During the 16th century it was the third most important port in the entire Spanish empire, after Seville and Antwerp. It was also considered the best shipbuilding centre in the Canary Islands. The town's wealth attracted pirates, who plundered it on several occasions, including a particularly brutal raid in 1553 by Jean-Paul de Billancourt, otherwise known as "Pegleg". However, Santa Cruz de La Palma always managed to recover and today it is the capital of the island and an important communications centre.

Calle O'Daly, the main street of Santa Cruz's old town

Exploring Santa Cruz de La Palma

Poised on the slopes of a volcanic crater, this is one of the Canary Islands' loveliest towns. Its compact layout features many modern houses and a picturesque old town. The centre developed within a short space of time and consequently has a harmonious appearance.

But Santa Cruz de La Palma is more than a collection of colonial architectural relics. Numerous bars and restaurants along Avenida Marítima are popular with locals and tourists alike, and add to the town's atmosphere.

🏛 Calle O'Daly

The main street, now turned into a pedestrian precinct, bears testimony to the town's former wealth and prestige. It was named after an Irish banana merchant who settled here. The street is lined on both sides with historic houses and residences. The most outstanding of these are the **Palacio de Salazar** (No. 22), which dates from the early 17th century and features distinctive wooden balconies, and the 19th-century **Casa Pinto** (No. 2).

Statues of musicians in Calle O'Daly

🔒 Ermita de San Sebastían

Plaza de San Sebastian.

This small chapel, which is usually closed, is one of several in Santa Cruz; the others include the 16th-century **Ermita de Nuestra Señora de la Luz**, which stands in the picturesque San Sebastián Square. Inside is a statue of Saint Catherine, which was brought here from Antwerp.

🏛 Plaza de España

At the very heart of Santa Cruz lies the Plaza de España. This triangular space, with its 16th-century fountain, is surrounded by historic buildings. The statue in the middle is of Manuel Diáz Hernández (1774–1863), a priest of San Salvador church who preached political liberalism in his sermons.

🔒 Iglesia de El Salvador

Plaza de España. **Tel** 922 413 250.
◻ 8:30am–1pm & 4–8:30pm daily.
Built at the end of the 15th century, the church acquired its present shape in the second half of the 16th century. This is the most monumental example of the Canary Islands' Renaissance architecture. Its façade has a portal in the form of a triumphal arch (1503) – an allegory of Christ and his Church. The interior features a *mudéjar* (Spanish-Moorish) coffered ceiling and sculptures by Fernando Estévez.

🏛 Casas Consistoriales

Plaza de España.
Casas Consistoriales, formerly the bishop's palace and now the town hall, was built in 1559–63. Its Renaissance façade, resting on columned arcades, is decorated with the bust of Philip II, carved in low relief, and the crests of La Palma and the Habsburgs. The inside walls are decorated with paintings by Mariano de Cassio, depicting island life.

🏛 Avenida Marítima

Avenida Marítima is regarded as one of the Canary Islands'

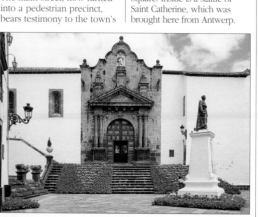

Iglesia de El Salvador in Plaza de España

For hotels and restaurants in this region see pp166–7 and p181

most beautiful and best-preserved shorelines. At its southern end stands a dragon tree *(see p16)*, with curiously twisted branches. At the northern end of the shore stands the **Casas de los Balcones** – a row of picturesque old houses, which have been wonderfully restored, with colourful elevations, featuring beautiful wooden balconies.

Main altar in Iglesia de San Francisco

🛡 Iglesia de San Francisco
Plaza de San Francisco. **Tel** 922 421 578. ◯ 9am–2pm & 4–6:30pm Mon–Fri. 📷

In 1508, Franciscan monks accompanying Alonso Fernándo de Lugo in his conquest of the island began to build their abbey in Santa Cruz. The church, built in the 16th–17th centuries, is one of the earliest examples of Renaissance architecture on La Palma. Outstanding features of the interior include the main altar and the coffered ceiling, as well as the richly painted décor. Today, the abbey houses the **Museo Insular** exhibiting local relics, along with Guanche skulls, stuffed animals and Spanish-school paintings.

🏛 Museo Naval
◯ 9am–2pm Mon–Fri. 📷

Near Plaza de la Alameda stands a 1940 replica of the *Santa María* – the tiny ship in which Christopher Columbus set off in 1492 to discover the New World. The inhabitants of Santa Cruz have named the ship *El Barco de la Virgen* – the Ship of the Holy Virgin. Inside is a modest maritime museum. The core of its collection consists of fascinating old charts, navigational instruments and a variety of ships' flags.

VISITORS' CHECKLIST

🏘 20,000. 🚌 🚢 ✈ 11 km (7 miles) south. 🛈 Plaza de la Constitucion, 922 412 106. 📅 Sat, Sun. 🎭 Carnival (Jan/Feb), Fiesta de la Cruz (3 May), Bajada de la Virgen (Jun/Jul, every 5 years).

♣ Castillo de Santa Catalina
Avenida Marítima.

This 16th-century castle is also known as Castillo Real. It was built as a defence against pirates who plundered ships as they left the port for the Americas with exports of goods such as sugar cane. In 1585, gunfire from the castle prevented Sir Francis Drake from taking over the island.

El Barco de la Virgen, a replica of Christopher Columbus's ship

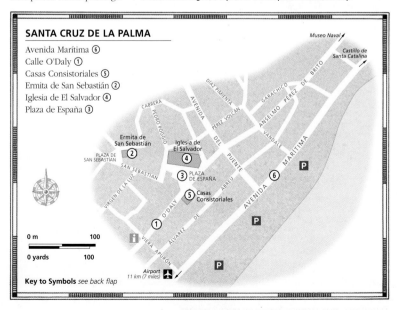

SANTA CRUZ DE LA PALMA
Avenida Marítima ⑥
Calle O'Daly ①
Casas Consistoriales ⑤
Ermita de San Sebastián ②
Iglesia de El Salvador ④
Plaza de España ③

0 m   100
0 yards   100

Key to Symbols see back flap

Airport 🛈
11 km (7 miles) ✈

Rich interior of Santuario de Las Nieves

Las Nieves ❷

🏛 🎏 *Bajada de la Virgen de las Nieves (Jun/Jul, every 5 years).*

This village, lying among green hills above Santa Cruz de La Palma, is the main pilgrimage centre and the most important religious shrine on the island.

Standing in a picturesque spot is the **Santuario de la Virgen de las Nieves**. Its small church was built in 1657 on the site of the original chapel. It forms a historic complex together with the neighbouring buildings: the 17th-century **Pilgrim's House**, the early 18th-century **Parish House**, and several houses that once belonged to members of the local aristocracy.

The church is a typical example of colonial Canary architecture, with wooden balcony façades, whitewashed walls and a lovely *mudéjar* (Spanish-Moorish) ceiling made of Canary pine. The lights of flickering candles, lit by the faithful, and the rich interior décor give the place its unique atmosphere. The central position on the gilded Baroque main altar is occupied by a 14th-century 82-cm (32-inch) high terracotta statue of the Madonna of the Snow, the island's patron saint, which was made in Flanders and stands on a base of Mexican silver. Her image refers not so much to the snowy peaks of the archipelago as to

her miraculous appearance during a freak August snowstorm in Rome. The side walls of the church are decorated with a row of *ex voto* canvases. These votive pictures are in thanks for numerous miracles performed by the island's patron saint, including saving a ship caught in a storm, calming the stormy seas and answering the prayers of couples hoping to have children.

Los Tilos ❸

3 km (2 miles) west of San Andrés.
🛈 *Centro de Investigaciones e Interpretación de la Reserva de Biosfera "Los Tilos".* 🕘 *9am–4pm Mon–Fri.*

The rocky, almost vertical sides of the deep Barranco del Agua ravine are overgrown with a misty, evergreen rainforest, which includes moss-covered laurel trees – the island's largest concentration of the ancient *laurisilva* – as well as lime, myrtle and ferns.

In 1983, Los Tilos was declared a biosphere reserve by UNESCO. A 3-km (2-mile) winding asphalt road, running along the bottom of the ravine, leads to the tourist centre, with its information point and restaurant.

The reserve area, measuring some 5 sq km (2 sq miles), has several marked walking trails. One of them leads to the **Mirador de las Barrandas**

viewpoint. A longer and much more difficult (6-km/4-mile) trail with steep ascents leads in a southwesterly direction to **Caldera de Marcos y Cordero**, where a determined tourist can admire the picturesque waterfalls.

San Andrés ❹

🚶 *1,100.* 🚌 🎏 *Fiesta de San Andrés (30 Nov).*

This pretty seaside village, with cobbled streets and squares planted with flowers and palms, is filled with typical local houses. At its centre stands the **Iglesia de San Andrés Apostól**. Built as a fortified church in the 16th century and extended in the 17th century, this is one of the oldest churches in the Canary Islands. The interior features a Baroque main altar and retable and a *mudéjar-style* coffered ceiling. Look out, too, for the paintings of assorted human limbs on the wall, hung here in thanks for the supposed healing powers of the church's patron saint.

San Andrés remains under joint administration with the larger town of **Los Sauces**, hence the combined name of San Andrés y Los Sauces. The environs of both towns are famous for the cultivation of bananas and sugar cane.

The only noteworthy building in Los Sauces is the **Iglesia Nuestra Señora de Montserrat**, the largest church on the island, which dates back to 1515. Its present Neo-Romanesque appearance

The modest Iglesia de San Andrés Apostól

is the result of refurbishment in 1960. Inside is a picture of the Madonna, attributed to the Dutch artist, Pieter Poubrus.

Environs
A short way to the south is **Charco Azul** – a tiny village set among banana tree plantations. High cliffs provide effective shelter for a natural tidal pool of a startling blue shade.

About 7 km (4 miles) to the south is **Puntallana**. One of its historic sights is the Iglesia San Juan Bautista. However, Puntallana owes most of its popularity to Playa de Nogales – a long, black sand beach backed by steep cliffs.

Mysterious rock carvings in La Zarza

Picturesque gullies criss-crossing the area around Barlovento

Barlovento ❺

🏚 750. 🚌 🎭 *Fiesta de la Virgen del Rosario (2 Aug, every 2 years).*

Besides the **Iglesia de Nuestra Señora**, with its altar of 1767 and some 16th–18th-century Spanish sculptures, Barlovento's main claim to fame is its fiesta held every two years in August, when the villagers recreate bloody scenes from the Battle of Lepanto (1571).

Environs
For a dip, try the **Piscinas de Fajana**, 6 km (4 miles) to the northeast where the Atlantic keeps a rock pool topped up with cool water. The nearby lighthouse at **Punta Cumplida** has been operating non-stop since 1860.

La Zarza ❻

10 km (6 miles) west of Barlovento.

The archaeological site of La Zarza provides visible evidence of the Benahoares – the former inhabitants of La Palma – who left strange signs carved into the rock in several sites throughout the north of the island, including Roque Faro, Don Pedro and Juan Adalid. These carvings consist mostly of spirals, circles and linear figures, and have survived in their natural environment, though their meaning remains unknown.

The information centre has a small museum illustrating the everyday life of the Benahoares. The exhibition includes a 20-minute video and shows how the ancient inhabitants of the island lived, and reveals their diet, medical practices and burial rites. The illuminated screens display images of erupting volcanoes, island scenery, its flora, fauna, and a map pointing out where the rock carvings were found.

When the carvings were discovered here in 1941 they became an archaeological sensation. Apart from the puzzling pictures, the ancient inhabitants of the island also left two Aztec-style carved images: one of a man, and an abstract figure of a woman with the head of an insect.

🏛 **Parque Cultural La Zarza**
La Mata, s/n. **Tel** 922 695 005.
🕐 winter: 11am–5pm; summer: 11am–7pm. 🅿️

Tazacorte ❼

🏚 3,000. 🚌 🎭 *Fiesta de San Miguel (29 Sep).*

In 1492, Alonso Fernandez de Lugo commenced the conquest of the island from Tazacorte. Today, the skyline of this small town, surrounded by banana plantations, is dominated by the **Iglesia de San Miguel Arcángel**. The church, built in the 16th century, was extended in 1992 and given a magnificent, abstract stained-glass window. Next to the church is a pergola lined with ceramic tiles and overgrown with bougainvillea – the traditional meeting place of the locals.

Environs
Just 12 km (7 miles) north is **Mirador del Time**, which offers a fine view over Los Llanos, Tazacorte, the surrounding mountains and the ocean.

Banana plantations growing almost in the centre of Tazacorte

Wide boulevard leading to Plaza España in Los Llanos de Aridane

Los Llanos de Aridane ❽

🚶 20,000. 🚌 🎭 Fiesta de los Remedios (2 Jul, every 2 years).

The second largest town of La Palma is a modern affair, with the exception of the **Plaza de España**. This charming square, with laurel trees casting a pleasant shade over café tables, is a venue for concerts.

One side of the square is occupied by the **town hall**. Opposite it stands the **Iglesia de Nuestra Señora de los Remedios**. This white 16th-century church is built in the Canary colonial style. Its Baroque main altar features a 16th-century Dutch statue of its patron saint.

Environs
About 3 km (2 miles) to the east is **El Paso**, a small town famous for its handmade cigars. Its main feature is the old quarter, with traditional Canary-style buildings surrounding the **Ermita de la Virgen de la Concepción de la Bonanza**. Next to the chapel stands a modern church with Neo-Gothic furnishings, dedicated to the same saint.

A short way south of El Paso is the **Parque Paraíso de las Aves** – a combination of botanical garden and miniature zoo, housing exotic birds from many corners of the world.

Parque Nacional de la Caldera de Taburiente ❾

See pp150–51.

Puerto Naos ❿

🚶 500. 🚌

A small, quiet resort, Puerto Naos was once a fishing village, but now features an ever-increasing number of low-built apartment complexes. Its main tourist attraction is the guaranteed good weather, with some 3,300 annual hours of sunshine.

Running along the black sand palm-lined beach, the longest on La Palma, is a small promenade with cafés, restaurants and small shops. It also features the four-star Hotel Sol Palma, opened in 1990. This modern, tiered hotel was once the biggest on the island and can accommodate nearly 1,000 guests.

Environs
Charco Verde, about 2 km (1 mile) to the south, is a scenic sandy beach. The beach is sheltered from the Atlantic waves, and ideal for families.

Fuencaliente de La Palma ⓫

🚶 1,800. 🚌 🎭 La Vendimia (14–30 Aug), San Martín (11 Dec).

The name of this place derives from the words *fuente caliente*, meaning "hot spring". However, the spring has long since been swallowed by a series of volcanic eruptions.

Set amid vineyards, the small town is best-known for its sweet, heavy wine and is

the home of the oldest and largest winery on the island, established in 1948. Evidence of the town's historic past can be seen in the parish church of **San Antonio Abad** (1730).

Environs
A little over 10 km (6 miles) to the south is **Punta Fuencaliente**, the southernmost point of La Palma. It features a lighthouse and salt pans.

Mazo ⓭

🚶 5,300. 🚌 🚢 Sat, Sun. 🎭 Corpus Christi (May–Jun).

Mazo is famous for its handmade cigars *(puros)*. Tourists also shop here for handicrafts including woven baskets and lacework. The **Escuela Insular de Artesanía** has these for sale and also holds demonstrations of how they are made.

Other sights include the **Cerámica el Molino**, known for its production of replica black Guanche vessels, and the **Museo de Corpus**, in a villa called Casa Roja, which exhibits street decorations for the feast of Corpus Christi.

The **Iglesia de San Blás** (1512), which looks out towards Tenerife, was extended in the 19th century and features a beautiful Baroque altar and richly carved decorations.

A Madonna from Mazo's San Blás

Environs
Just 4 km (2 miles) to the south is the **Cueva de Belmaco**, a cave with original Guanche inscriptions.

San Antonio volcano near Fuencaliente de La Palma

Ruta de los Volcanes ⑫

A somewhat arduous trail leads along the Cumbre Vieja mountain ridge, from Refugio el Pilar (alt. 1,450 m/4,756 ft) towards Fuencaliente. The hike, which should take a fit walker some 6-7 hours, is an unforgettable experience. Winding round steep volcanic rims, the path leads past striking geological formations and provides magnificent views of the eastern and western coasts of the island.

Refugio del Pilar ①
This ridge, with a walkers' shelter, is a popular picnic spot. It can be reached by car and is a good starting point for hikes.

Fuencaliente ⑥
From here the trail continues further south, towards the nearby volcanoes of San Antonio (last eruption in 1677) and Teneguía (last eruption in 1971).

Montaña de los Charcos ②
A powerful eruption of this volcano took place in 1712 when a vast flow of lava swamped much of the southwestern part of the island.

Volcán Martín ⑤
The eruption of the volcano in 1646 destroyed the former springs (believed to be a cure for leprosy) that gave the nearby town its name.

LOS LLANOS DE ARIDANE

SANTA CRUZ DE LA PALMA

• El Charco

LP 1

LP 1

Cráter del Hoyo Negro ③
The trail runs along the edge of the San Juan volcano, which most recently erupted in 1949. The crater, with its rubble of solidified lava, is a reminder of how relatively recent the eruption was.

Cráter del Duraznero ④
This crater, rising 1,902 m (6,238 ft) above sea level, was left after the eruption of San Antonio in 1949. To the left of it stands the peak of Nambroque.

Las Indias

| 0 km | 1 |
| 0 miles | 1 |

TIPS FOR WALKERS

Length: 19 km (12 miles).
Stopping-off points:
Fuencaliente is a good place to halt for a meal.
Note: Don't stray from the marked trail, and make sure you carry a supply of drinking water.

KEY

▬ Main trail
▬ Scenic route
═ Other road
••• Footpath
☼ Viewpoint

Parque Nacional de la Caldera de Taburiente ❾

La Caldera de Taburiente, a massive crater formed in the course of several powerful volcanic eruptions, is a natural fortress and served as a refuge for the last Benahoares when the Spanish invaded in the 15th century. Some of its walls reach up to 2,000 m (6,560 ft). Awarded national park status in 1954, the crater has many walking trails (some walks require a very good head for heights!). No roads run right through the park, and walkers should make sure they take with them enough water and a snack.

Roque de los Muchachos
Six telescopes have been placed along the steep, mountain road around Roque de los Muchachos, which passes through scrubland.

Caldera de Taburiente
The lush vegetation, much of it unique to the region, and the bare, rugged summits of the park, often shrouded in mist, appeal to lovers of nature.

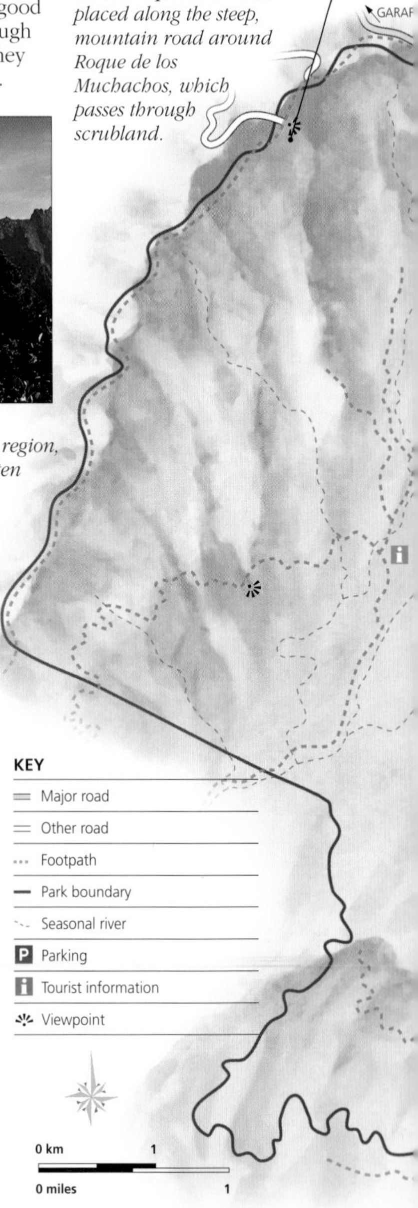
GARAF
KEY
Major road
Other road
Footpath
Park boundary
Seasonal river
Parking
Tourist information
Viewpoint
0 km
1
0 miles
1

ASTRONOMICAL OBSERVATORY

Thanks to their clear skies, the Canary Islands are regarded as one of the best places for conducting observations of the cosmos. The International Astrophysical Observatory near Roque de los Muchachos was opened in 1985, in the presence of King Juan Carlos and many European heads of state. Several telescopes, including the largest Anglo-Dutch one, named after William Herschel and measuring 420 cm (165 inches) in diameter, are used for night observations. There is therefore a ban between 8pm and 9am on the use of lights while driving in the park (once a year the entire island switches off its lights to make certain experiments possible).

The Herschel telescope inside the observatory

Mirador de los Andenes
These bare rocks, eroded by wind and moisture over thousands of years, have been shaped into curious natural works of art.

Pico de la Cruz
This is one of park's highest peaks. A challenging 4–5 hour walking trail, connecting Pico de las Nieves with Roque de los Muchachos, leads over the peak through some breathtaking scenery.

SANTA CRUZ
DE LA PALMA

Trail to Roque de los Muchachos
The trail, running along the highest peaks of Caldera de Taburiente, provides a view over the stunningly steep walls of the crater, shrouded with dense fog.

La Cumbrecita
A good asphalt road leads to La Cumbrecita, which has an information point. This is a good viewpoint from which to see the park.

Lomo de las Chozas
A short and easy trail leads through Canary pines from La Cumbrecita westwards, to Lomo de las Chozas, where the views are at their best at sunset and sunrise.

P

EL PASO

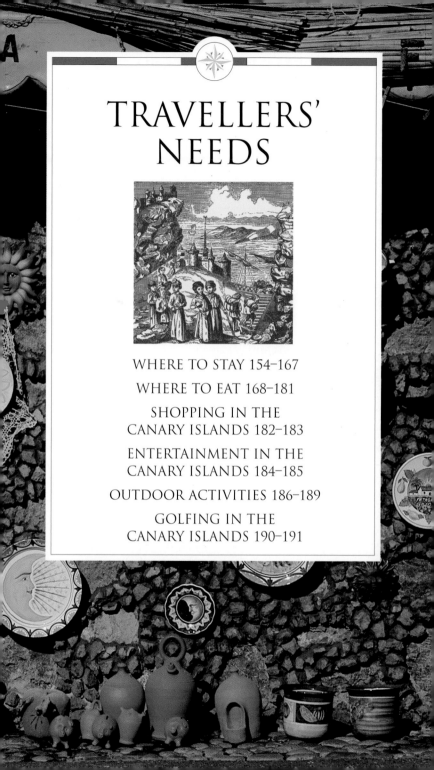

TRAVELLERS'
NEEDS

WHERE TO STAY

The Canary Islands are seventh on the list of the world's most frequently visited places, with a sophisticated and highly organized tourist industry. Popularity has its downside, however, and the accommodation prices can be high. This applies in particular to the larger islands, such as Tenerife and Gran Canaria, where it can be difficult

Tenerife's parador

to find cheap places to stay in high season. The smaller, less-frequented islands, such as El Hierro and La Gomera, offer lower prices, but do not have many hotels. In recent years, *casas rurales* have become more widespread. Usually in country properties of charm and character, they provide much more varied and individual alternatives to conventional hotels.

Guest lounge in Las Cañadas del Teide parador on Tenerife *(see p163)*

HOTELS

Hotels are the most expensive form of accommodation on the Canary Islands. Many of them belong to international hotel chains, such as NH Hotels, Riu, TRYP or the Spanish chains (Sol Meliá, H10 Hoteles and Paradores Nacionales) and are block-booked by foreign package tour operators for most of the year.

The hotels in large town centres cater mainly for business visitors. Popular coastal resorts have huge hotel complexes, aimed squarely at the tourist market. These have been built relatively near the beaches and are generally surrounded by lush tropical gardens. Hotels are designed so that most rooms have sea views.

Complexes vie with each other to offer their guests maximum fun, day and night. Many have tennis courts, large swimming pools, mini-golf, gymnasia or exercise rooms.

It is certainly advisable to check in advance to find out whether these facilities are included in the price or are charged for separately.

PARADORS

The six state-run parador hotels (one on each island except Lanzarote) are attractively located in coastal or national park settings.

They provide a first-class service and usually have excellent restaurants. Despite their high prices, they offer good value and are well worth considering.

APARTMENTS

Apartments are the most popular form of accommodation on the islands and there are many more of these than there are hotels. They can either be situated within hotel buildings or as separate blocks or complexes.

Quality varies, but most include a lounge, fully equipped kitchen, bathroom and one or two bedrooms. Most sleep between two and six people, but it is sometimes possible to combine two apartments into one. Apartments are especially suitable for families with young children.

Apartments are generally better value for couples or families than staying in a hotel, though many require you to stay at least three to five nights and sometimes a week is the minimum.

Some apartments form part of a complex and provide similar facilities to those offered by hotels. Most of these have a swimming pool and a small playing field or tennis courts. Some have much more.

Hacienda del Buen Suceso, Gran Canaria *(see p156)*

◁ **Pottery shop in Fataga, Gran Canaria**

CASAS RURALES

Rural hotels *(casas rurales)* are generally converted farms or village houses and are aimed at those seeking quiet, out-of-the-way places. Most of them are located far from the traditional resorts and can be found in small towns and villages. Some have no public transport so it is wise to check whether you will need to hire a car.

However, they are not necessarily a cheap option. Neither can they offer the same variety of facilities as the large hotel complexes, but this is the very reason that many visitors seek them out. *Casas rurales* offer a degree of authenticity and individuality not found elsewhere and the rooms and communal spaces are often characterful and furnished with local handicraft items. This is definitely the best choice for those who appreciate a personal touch.

All tourist information offices have full lists of organizations offering this type of service. Information can also be found on the Internet or in the *Guía de Alojamiento en Casas Rurales de España* publication.

CAMPING SITES

Camping sites are rather primitive and most islands have only one or two sites at most. Before travelling it is wise to find out about the situation on a particular island. Just turning up and pitching your tent on the beach is generally forbidden.

BOOKING

Most of the islands' hotel rooms and apartments are booked by travel agents and tour operators in advance. They then sell on the holidays, including flights and half-board. Such holidays do not suit everyone but are the cheapest way to visit the Canary Islands.

One of the few camp sites to be found on Lanzarote

It is obviously possible to make a booking without using a travel agent. It is best to do so well in advance, although it is sometimes possible to find something at short notice.

Hotels and pensions can be booked over the telephone, or via the Internet. Some places, particularly the smaller hotels and *casas rurales*, may require a deposit. When booking, bear in mind peak tourist times, and festivals and carnivals, especially when going to Gran Canaria or Tenerife.

Entrance to Jardín Tropical hotel in Costa Adeje

PRICES

Hotel prices depend on the season and the island. The dates when prices change are determined by individual hoteliers, so it is worth finding out in advance what prices apply at particular times. Tariffs will obviously be higher during popular holidays and carnivals. It

The stunning Hotel San Roque *(see p162)*, Tenerife's first boutique hotel

should be understood that hotels quote their prices in various ways. Some are per night in a twin room; others are per person per night. Check this when you book.

The price is subject to 5 per cent IGIC tax, which is generally included in the quote. Prices quoted by apartments, pensions and *casas rurales* do not usually include breakfast. Until recently, hotels always included breakfast in the price of the room, but this habit seems to be gradually disappearing.

Most hotels accept credit cards. Pensions and *casas rurales* usually prefer to be paid in cash.

DIRECTORY

OVERNIGHT ACCOMMODATION

www.hotelsearch.com

www.tourspain.es

PARADORS

www.parador.es

@ info@parador.es

CASAS RURALES

www.canary-islands.com

www.toprural.com

CAMPING SITES

Federación Española de Empresarios de Camping

C/San Bernardo, 97–98, 28015 Madrid.

Tel 914 481 234.

Fax 914 481 267.

Choosing a Hotel

Hotels have been selected across a wide price range for facilities, good value and location. They are listed separately for each island, in the order in which they appear in the guide. For each island, they are listed in alphabetical order, according to location and then price. For more information on hotels see page 154.

PRICE CATEGORIES
For a standard double room per night including breakfast, service and tax.

€ Under €50
€€ €50–€100
€€€ €100–€150
€€€€ €150–€200
€€€€€ Over €200

GRAN CANARIA

AGAETE Finca Las Longueras Hotel Rural
€€

Finca Las Longueras, 35480 **Tel** *928 898 145* **Fax** *928 898 752* **Rooms** *10*

An intimate hotel in the grounds of a tropical plantation of bananas, oranges and papaya. This renovated 19th-century mansion, with bedrooms straight out of a Jane Austen novel, retains much character from its days as an autumn residence. A detached house sleeping four offers even more tranquillity. **www.laslongueras.com**

AGAETE Hotel Puerto De Las Nieves
€€€

Avda Alcalde José de Armas, 35489 **Tel** *928 886 256* **Fax** *928 886 267* **Rooms** *30*

This four star hotel, located near the beach in the village of Agaete, has a spa, Jacuzzi, gym and sauna. The restaurant serves local dishes in bright, nautically-themed surroundings. The reception area and rooms are tastefully decorated in dark woods and primary colours. Staff are very friendly. **www.hotelpuertodelasnievas.com**

AGÜIMES Casa de los Camellos
€€

C/Progreso 12, 35260 **Tel** *928 785 003* **Fax** *928 785 053* **Rooms** *12*

This small rural hotel in the centre of a peaceful, historic town has 12 traditionally furnished rooms surrounding two inner patios brimming with flowers and ferns. The hotel was formerly a granary where travelling merchants lodged. Its restaurant, El Oroval, has a reputation for serving excellent, typically Canarian cuisine. **rcamellos@hecansa.com**

ARUCAS Hacienda del Buen Suceso
€€€

Finca del Buen Suceso, Ctra. de Arucas a Bañaderos, 1 km, 35400 **Tel** *928 622 945* **Fax** *928 622 942* **Rooms** *18*

Located 15 minutes from Las Palmas, this stunning hacienda dating from 1572 was lovingly converted to a hotel in 1997. Canopied four-poster beds, exposed sloping wooden ceilings and a Jacuzzi set in local blue brick and overlooking lush greenery are some of the imaginative touches here. **www.haciendabuensuceso.com**

CRUZ DE TEJEDA El Refugio
€€

Cruz de Tejeda, 35328 **Tel** *928 666 513* **Fax** *928 666 520* **Rooms** *17*

This 19th-century traditional Canarian-style hotel is located in the remote Cruz de Tejeda area in the centre of the island. Surrounded by pine forests, mountains and valleys, and set away from the coast and tourist resorts, it is an ideal base for exploring the old rural trails that criss-cross the area. **www.hotelruralelrefugio.com**

FATAGA Molino de Agua de Fataga
€

Ctra. Fataga–San Bartolomé 1 km, 35814 **Tel** *928 172 089* **Fax** *928 172 244* **Rooms** *20*

A unique, rural hotel with traditional Canarian architecture, some of which dates back to the 16th century. Set in the stunning Valley of a Thousand Palms, 20 minutes north of Playa del Inglés, its treasures include an 18th-century water mill and a small farm with ponies, donkeys and ostriches. **www.molinodeagua.com**

LAS PALMAS DE GRAN CANARIA Fataga & Centro de Negocios
€€

C/Néstor de la Torre 21, 35006 **Tel** *928 290 614* **Fax** *928 292 786* **Rooms** *94*

Located in a city centre commercial zone and 10 minutes from Las Canteras beach is this luxurious contemporary hotel, which is geared towards leisure and business travellers alike. The hotel's five floors have different bold colour schemes and each room displays delightful individual touches. **www.hotelfataga.com**

LAS PALMAS DE GRAN CANARIA Parque
€€

C/Muelle de las Palmas 2, 35003 **Tel** *928 368 000* **Fax** *928 368 856* **Rooms** *102*

Centrally located near the bus station and overlooking Parque San Telmo, this typical city centre hotel is used by business people as well as holidaymakers. Rooms are comfortably furnished. The 6th-floor restaurant terrace offers fantastic views over the park and the ocean. **www.hparque.com**

LAS PALMAS DE GRAN CANARIA Reina Isabel
€€€

C/Alfredo L. Jones 40, 35008 **Tel** *928 260 100* **Fax** *928 274 558* **Rooms** *224*

This grand hotel offers old-fashioned charm and high standards. Its location, with the picturesque Las Canteras beach on one side and a shopping area on the other, makes it ideal for enjoying two very different aspects of the city. Amenities include Turkish baths and a lovely terrace bar on the beach. **www.bullhotels.com**

Key to Symbols *see back cover flap*

LAS PALMAS DE GRAN CANARIA Santa Catalina   €€€€

*C/ León y Castillo 227, 35005 **Tel** 928 243 040 **Fax** 928 242 764 **Rooms** 202*

An historic, English Colonial-style hotel with its own casino, sits in extensive sub-tropical gardens. Dating from 1890, previous guests include Winston Churchill, Agatha Christie and Prince Charles. Rooms are tastefully decorated in pastel colours, with ensuites finished in marble. Free bus to Las Canteras beach. **www.hotelsantacatalina.com**

LAS PALMAS DE GRAN CANARIA Aldiana Mirador   €€€€€

*Oficial Mayor José Rubio, San Bartolomé de Tirajana, 35290 **Tel** 928 123 000 **Fax** 928 123 023 **Rooms** 60*

Scenery and tranquillity are major attractions of this Alpine-styled hotel located in the island's interior. A breathtaking mountain backdrop and surrounding pine trees make it ideal for countryside activities, many of which are organized by the hotel. Excellent wines from the hotel's own vineyard are a bonus. **www.aldiana.com**

MASPALOMAS IFA Hotel Faro   €€€

*Plaza de Colon, 35100 **Tel** 902 450 010 **Fax** 928 141 940 **Rooms** 188*

Located on the beach on the island's southernmost tip, under the gaze of the 19th-century Maspalomas lighthouse. This hotel's unprepossessing façade fronts a friendly hotel with a commitment to personal attention. The well-equipped rooms have balconies with sun loungers. **www.ifahotels.com**

MASPALOMAS Gran Hotel Costa Meloneras   €€€€

*C/Mar Mediterraneo 1, 35120 **Tel** 928 128 100 **Fax** 928 128 122 **Rooms** 1136*

Set in 8 hectares of tropical gardens, close to the lighthouse at Maspalomas, this hotel offers outstanding facilities in idyllic surroundings close to golf courses. Spacious, elegant rooms are beautifully decorated and have views over the mountains or pools and gardens. Facilities include pools, restaurants, a spa and sports facilities. **www.lopesanhr.com**

MASPALOMAS Palm Beach   €€€€

*Avenida del Oasis s/n, 35100 **Tel** 928 721 032 **Fax** 928 141 808 **Rooms** 328*

Although rather bland looking from the outside, this stylish, luxury hotel proves to be a real eye-opener inside. Retro 1970s design has been employed throughout, with glorious zig-zag carpets and chintzy fabrics; the result is playful and fun rather than tacky. It's just yards from Maspalomas beach. **www.hotel-palm-beach.com**

MASPALOMAS Riu Grand Palace Maspalomas Oasis   €€€€

*Plaza de las Palmeras, 35106 **Tel** 928 141 448 **Fax** 928 141 192 **Rooms** 332*

Set amid subtropical gardens with artificial lagoons and roaming peacocks is this palatial hotel with friendly staff. On the golden sands of Maspalomas beach, the hotel has a wide selection of restaurants including a Japanese one. The spacious bedrooms have balconies overlooking the sea or gardens. **www.riu.com**

PLAYA DE INGLÉS Hotel Intercontinental   €€

*Avda. De Italia 2, 35100 **Tel** 928 760 249 **Fax** 928 771 484 **Rooms** 410*

Rooms at the Intercontinental are bright and comfortable, and most have superb views of the ocean. The attractive grounds include pools and whirlpools, and an extensive entertainment programme attracts clients with a young outlook. It has a reputation for good food and recently won an award for the quality of its cuisine. **www.ifahotels.com**

PLAYA DEL INGLÉS Hotel Sahara Playa   €€

*Avda. Alfereces Provisionales 1, San Bartolomé de Tirajana, 35100 **Tel** 928 762 900 **Fax** 928 762 914 **Rooms** 56*

This modest, good-value hotel, is located 50 metres from the beach and marina, and a few minutes' walk from the town centre. It consists of two buildings – one has 56 comfortable rooms with sea views, the other was recently refurbished to a high standard and has 35 one-bedroom apartments. Both have pools. **www.saharaplaya.com**

PLAYA DEL INGLÉS Barcelo Las Margaritas   €€€

*Avda. Gran Canaria 40, 35100 **Tel** 928 761 112 **Fax** 928 765 380 **Rooms** 490*

A good choice for people wanting to be near the lively bars and restaurants of the resort's most popular tourist area. An all-inclusive option and a wide range of facilities make this hotel attractive for families. It also boasts a swimming pool with a waterfall and a rooftop terrace for nude sunbathing. **www.barcelo.com**

PLAYA DEL INGLÉS Catarina   €€€

*Avda. De Tirajana 1, 35100 **Tel** 928 762 812 **Fax** 928 760 615 **Rooms** 402*

Close to the sand dunes of Maspalomas, with a free bus to Playa del Inglés, is this family-oriented hotel with entertainment and organized sports. Facilities for children include a baby-sitting service, children's club, library and pool. There are extensive, landscaped gardens with swimming pools, whirlpools and a waterfall. **www.ifahotels.com**

PLAYA DEL INGLÉS IFA Dunamar   €€€

*C/Helsinki 8, 35100 **Tel** 928 772 800 **Fax** 928 773 465 **Rooms** 273*

This high-rise hotel sits in terraced, landscaped gardens with extensive water features. Facilities include swimming pools, whirlpools, a massage area and health and relaxation centres. Use of the sauna, Turkish bath and Jacuzzi are all included in the room price. Lively nightlife with a piano bar, fashion shows and entertainment. **www.ifahotels.com**

PLAYA DEL INGLÉS Riu Palace Maspalomas   €€€

*Avda. Tirajana s/n, 35100 **Tel** 928 769 500 **Fax** 928 769 800 **Rooms** 368*

Located 2 km (1 mile) from the main town is this attractive modern hotel in the shape of an amphitheatre, with architecture inspired by the island's colonial past. Rooms have spectacular views across the famous Sahara-like Maspalomas dunes to the ocean. Amenities include lagoon-sized swimming pools in tropical gardens. **www.riu.com**

PLAYA DEL INGLÉS Riu Waikiki
€€€
Avda. Gran Canaria 20, 35100 **Tel** *928 773 880* **Fax** *928 761 769* **Rooms** *505*

Five, seven-storey circular buildings offer all-inclusive value for families on a budget. Activities on offer include tennis, volleyball and water polo, and two 18-hole golf courses are located nearby. Excellent facilities for children include an entertainment programme. The hotel is close to the city and shops, and provides a free bus to the beach. **www.riu.es**

PUERTO RICO Marina Suites Aparthotel
€€€
Puerto Base s/n, Puerto Rico, Mogán, 35128 **Tel** *902 996 093* **Fax** *928 083 333* **Rooms** *216*

Modernist aparthotel with glass and chrome design, located in an exclusive position on the harbour at Puerto Base. The well-equipped, spacious rooms are decorated to a high standard in contemporary design. Large freshwater swimming pool, hot tubs, a whirlpool and a bar are set right on the ocean front. **www.marinesuitesgrancanaria.com**

SAN AGUSTÍN Costa Canaria
€€
Las Retamas 1, 35100 **Tel** *928 760 220* **Fax** *928 720 413* **Rooms** *246*

The Costa Canaria sits in extensive gardens leading to the beach and promenade of San Agustín. Rooms in the main building have balconies and sea views, while rooms in the gardens have terraces and superior décor. Facilities include two freshwater pools, a Jacuzzi, a children's pool and entertainment. **www.costa-canaria.com**

SAN AGUSTÍN Hotel Don Gregory
€€
Avda. Las Dalias 11, 35100 **Tel** *928 773 877* **Fax** *928 799 996* **Rooms** *244*

This hotel is located directly on Las Burras beach, 4 km (2 miles) from the centre of Playa del Inglés. The San Agustín commercial centre opposite the hotel should satisfy shopping needs. All rooms have views over subtropical gardens or the sea. Facilities include a freshwater pool, piano bar and entertainment most evenings. **www.hotelesdunas.com**

SAN AGUSTÍN IFA Interclub Atlantic
€€€
C/Los Jazmines 2, 35100 **Tel** *902 450 010* **Fax** *928 760 974* **Rooms** *419*

All-inclusive hotel set in a vast water park with sub-tropical flora in San Agustín, offering excellent views over the ocean and Maspalomas sand dunes. A good choice for families, offering entertainment for both adults and children. Suites and bungalows are a good family option. **www.ifahotels.com**

TAFIRA ALTA Escuela Santa Brígida
€€€
C/Real de Coello 2, 35017 **Tel** *928 355 511* **Fax** *828 010 401* **Rooms** *41*

Situated ten minutes from the Alfredo Kraus auditorium, this hotel offers large, superior rooms that are pleasantly furnished. It is a training school for the catering industry so great care is taken in the service and preparation of meals. The swimming pool is next to a busy road so it can be a bit noisy. **www.necansa.com**

TAURITO Taurito Princess
€€€
C/Alhambra 8, Urb. Costa Taurito, 35138 **Tel** *928 565 250* **Fax** *928 565 566* **Rooms** *402*

This large hotel has a tranquil beachside location near the mountains in the beautiful Valle de Taurito. Families come to enjoy the wide range of facilities, including two large swimming pools and a mini club with entertainment for children aged 5–12 years. There's also lively nightlife. Jet ski hire is available. **www.princess-hotels.com**

VEGA DE SAN MATEO Las Calas
€€
El Arenal 36, La Lechuza, 35320 **Tel** *928 661 436* **Fax** *928 660 753* **Rooms** *9*

This charming 19th-century traditional Canarian rural hotel is set in delightful orchards and gardens. Each of its nine bedrooms is individually styled with antique furniture and assorted curios. Gardens and common areas offer eclectic corners of stone and wood, dotted with African art and sculptures. **www.hotelrurallascalas.com**

FUERTEVENTURA

ANTIGUA Era de la Corte
€€
La Corte 1, 35630 **Tel** *928 878 705* **Fax** *928 878 710* **Rooms** *11*

A quiet village is the setting for this 19th-century building with a vivid red sandstone façade. Each room is individually furnished, some with four-poster beds. The hotel's restaurant serves dishes made with traditional ingredients like *gofio* and local cheeses. There's a small swimming pool and an atmospheric attic reading room. **www.eradelacorte.com**

ANTIGUA Hotel Elba Palace Golf
€€€€€
Urb. Fuerteventura Golf Club, 35610 **Tel** *928 163 922* **Fax** *928 163 923* **Rooms** *61*

This hotel offers unadulterated luxury at the heart of Fuerteventura Golf Course and doubles as the Club House. Rooms have acres of wooden floor space and opulent furnishings. The hotel has one of the best restaurants on the island, offering gourmet cuisine and fine wines. Heath, spa and fitness facilities available. **www.hoteleselba.com**

CALETA DE FUSTE Bungalows Fuertesol
€
Avda. Virgen de La Peña 2, 35630 **Tel** *928 163 017* **Fax** *928 163 071* **Rooms** *110*

Located just 800 metres from the beach, this good-value aparthotel with two- and three-bedroom bungalows set around a large pool is very popular with families. A mini train provides the transport and the complex is close to a shopping centre with bars and restaurants. **www.canarias-hotel.com**

Key to Price Guide *see p156* **Key to Symbols** *see back cover flap*

CALETA DE FUSTE Barceló Club El Castillo

Caleta de Fuste s/n, 35610 Tel 928 163 101 Fax 928 163 042 Rooms 420

Situated on Caleta de Fuste beach, this hotel offers accommodation in individual bungalows and has good facilities for families. Sited around a swimming pool complex, the bungalows are light, with roomy terraces. The friendly and helpful staff organize family entertainment. Two restaurants, buffet and pizzeria. **www.barceloclubelcastillo.com**

CORRALEJO Club Las Olas

Avda. Las Palmeras s/n, 35660 Tel 928 536 299 Fax 928 536 297 Rooms 250

This self-catering complex in a quiet part of Corralejo offers bars and restaurant, two large pools, two children's pools and evening entertainment for both adults and children so it's a good choice for couples and families. Situated just 300 metres from the beach, it also attracts a surfing clientele.

CORRALEJO Corralejo Beach

Avda. Nuestra Señor del Carmen 3, 35600 Tel 928 068 000 Fax 928 866 317 Rooms 118

In a great location, two minutes' walk from Corralejo beach with views over the harbour, Lobos Island and the beach, this aparthotel prides itself on good service and is known for its friendly staff. The standard rooms are compact while the suites offer a more spacious option. **www.corralejobeach.com**

CORRALEJO Hesperia Bristol Playa

Urb. Lago de Bristol, 35660 Tel 928 867 020 Fax 928 866 349 Rooms 186

Situated on the seafront, five minutes from the harbour, is this modern aparthotel with attractive architecture and functional one-bedroom self-catering apartments. Amenities include a swimming pool, snack bars and a disco. The restaurant closes in the evening, but there's a good selection of restaurants nearby. **www.hesperia-bristolplaya.com**

CORRALEJO Atlantis Duna Park

C/General Franco s/n, 35660 Tel 928 535 251 Fax 928 535 491 Rooms 79

This hotel with spacious rooms and landscaped gardens occupies a great location in the centre of Corralejo, one minute from the beach and 100 metres from bars and restaurants. Although close to these attractions, it remains quiet and tranquil, and is suitable for all ages. Facilities include a pool, gym and sauna. Efficient service.

CORRALEJO Club Hotel Riu Olivia Beach Resort

Avda. Grandes Playas, 35660 Tel 928 535 334 Fax 928 866 154 Rooms 814

An all-inclusive hotel situated on Grandes Playas sand dune beach, surrounded by extensive gardens. It offers two large swimming pools and two children's pools, which are heated in winter. The elegantly furnished rooms have satellite TV and a balcony or terrace. There are Canarian-and Asian-themed restaurants. **www.riu.com**

CORRALEJO Riu Palace Tres Islas

Avda. Grandes Playas, 35660 Tel 928 535 700 Fax 928 535 858 Rooms 375

This stylish, five-storey hotel on the seafront is surrounded by palm trees. Rooms are tastefully decorated and have satellite TV and balconies with a sea view. Facilities include two large swimming pools and a children's pool (all heated in winter), floodlit tennis courts, massage and sauna, a piano bar and nightly entertainment. **www.riu.com**

COSTA CALMA Risco del Gato

C/Sicasimbre 2, 35627 Tel 928 547 175 Fax 928 547 030 Rooms 51

This hotel offers impeccable style in peaceful, private and luxurious surroundings. The accommodation is in private, individual bungalows built around an interior courtyard. Spacious both inside and out, they are furnished to the highest standards. Facilities include three restaurants and a spa centre. **www.hotelriscodelgato.com**

COSTA CALMA H10 Playa Esmerelda

C/Punta del Roquito 2, 35627 Tel 928 875 353 Fax 928 875 350 Rooms 314

An award-winning hotel on the seafront with excellent customer care. The buildings are designed to blend in with their surroundings and offer high standards of decoration. The landscaped gardens are the setting for three pools. Other facilities include a sports centre, diving club, sauna, and mini-club and park for children. **www.h10hotels.com**

COSTA CALMA Club Barlovento

C/Barranco de Damas, 35627 Tel 928 547 002 Fax 928 547 038 Rooms 255

This appealing low-level modern hotel sits beside a beautiful white-sand beach near the yachting marina. The hotel's imaginative pool area is particularly attractive, featuring a semicircular waterfall. Rooms have balconies overlooking the pool or the beach. Facilities include a gym and a sauna. **barlovento@intercom.es**

COSTA CALMA Hotel Tindaya

C/Punta del Roquito s/n, 35627 Tel 928 547 020 Fax 928 547 461 Rooms 215

Hotel Tindaya bears all the hallmarks of the H10 chain with high standards throughout. There are luxurious touches, elegant colour schemes, ambitious North African influenced architecture and tastefully furnished rooms. The range of facilities includes a nightclub and a thalasso health and beauty centre. **www.h10.com**

JANDIA Iberostar Fuerteventura Park

Las Gaviotas s/n, 35626 Tel 902 995 555 Fax 928 541 280

In this bright hotel adjacent to Jandia beach the studios and two-bedroom apartments are colourfully decorated. There's a large swimming pool complex and a Wellbeing Centre offering Thai Zen therapies. The children's swimming pool and a mini-club for 4–12 year olds make this a good choice for families. **www.iberostar.com**

MORRO JABLE Altamarena

Avda. del Saladar 28, 35625 **Tel** *928 540 430* **Fax** *928 540 218* **Rooms** *238*

Only the lush tropical plants and trees of the hotel's gardens separate the Altamarena from one of the best beaches on the island. It offers guests picturesque and relaxing surroundings, friendly staff, a choice of Canarian or international cuisine and the opportunity to try their hand at archery. **www.lopesanhr.com**

MORRO JABLE Robinsón Club Jandía Playa

Avda. del Saladar, 35625 **Tel** *928 541 375* **Fax** *928 541 025* **Rooms** *362*

This light, sunny all-inclusive hotel will suit sports enthusiasts with its wide range of facilities, including beach volleyball, tennis, surfing and sailing. For health and relaxation, there's a gym, massage, Jacuzzi and beauty centre. Rooms are spacious and tastefully decorated. Evenings offer a nightclub and theatre. **www.robinson-espana.es**

PÁJARA Casa Isaitas

Pájara, 35626 **Tel** *928 161 402* **Fax** *928 161 482* **Rooms** *4*

Sited in a small village in the centre of the island is this 200-year-old restored rural house with wooden balconies and two courtyards. One courtyard is the setting for the guest rooms, which are simply and rustically furnished; the other houses the dining area, with a traditional oven, BBQ and *paella* pan. **www.casaisaitas.com**

PÁJARA Faro Jandia

Avda. del Saladar s/n, 35626 **Tel** *928 545 035* **Fax** *928 545 240* **Rooms** *214*

Voted by an internet travel site as one of the 100 best hotels in the world, this stylish, semi-circular building overlooks a tear-shaped swimming pool and offers spacious rooms and suites with panoramic windows. Facilities include fine grill and à la carte restaurants, a spa centre, international shows and a children's playground. **www.grupomur.com**

VILLAVERDE Mahoh

Sitio de Juan Bello, 35660 **Tel** *928 868 050* **Fax** *928 868 612* **Rooms** *9*

These 19th-century buildings, built with volcanic stone and timber, offer a contrast to the hotels on the coast. Bedrooms with exposed stone walls, some with four-poster bed, possess a rustic charm. There's also a restaurant, a pool, a riding stable and it's a ten-minute drive to the nearest beach. **www.mahoh.com**

LANZAROTE

ARRECIFE Lancelot

Avda. Mancomunidad 9, 35500 **Tel** *928 805 099* **Fax** *928 805 039* **Rooms** *112*

Situated in the centre of Arrecife, close to good restaurants is this modern hotel. Facilities include a restaurant with sea views, a compact swimming pool with views over the town and a small fitness centre. Its most attractive feature is its location beside the pale golden sands and turquoise waters of El Reducto beach. **www.hotellancelot.com**

ARRECIFE Miramar

C/Coll 2, 35500 **Tel** *928 812 600* **Fax** *928 801 533* **Rooms** *85*

This contemporary town-centre hotel, with chic interior design, is situated beside the sea and the picturesque drawbridge of Puente de las Bolas in the old town. All rooms have sea views, satellite TV, internet access and bold, rich colour schemes. The hotel is ideally located for exploring Arrecife's historic quarter. **www.hmiramar.com**

COSTA TEGUISE Occidental Allegro Oasis

Avda. Del Mar, 35509 **Tel** *928 590 410* **Fax** *928 590 791* **Rooms** *372*

All the rooms have sea views at this large, family-oriented hotel next to a pretty cove, which can be accessed via the hotel's palm-fringed gardens. The excellent facilities include two restaurants, five swimming pools, a pub-style bar, a pétanque court, shops, a children's park and snorkelling and diving from the beach. **www.occidental-hoteles.com**

COSTA TEGUISE Gran Meliá Salinas

Avda. Islas Canarias, Urb. Costa Teguise, 35509 **Tel** *928 590 040* **Fax** *928 590 390* **Rooms** *325*

This modern, opulent hotel with a large atrium offers large rooms with chic décor and spacious balconies. There's a wide variety of restaurants offering cuisine from around the world and occasional cooking shows. It also offers mini-golf, pitch and putt, bowling, beauty and wellbeing facilities, and evening entertainment. **www.solmelia.com**

PLAYA BLANCA H10 Lanzarote Princess

C/Maciot Urb. Playa Blanca, 35570 **Tel** *928 517 108* **Fax** *928 517 011* **Rooms** *407*

Its location – 300 metres from the beach and 500 metres from the resort and fishing village of Playa Blanca – makes this ocean-front hotel a good option for relaxing by the sea. It has lovely gardens and a large swimming pool with a thatched, desert island-style bar at its centre. **www.h10hotels.com**

PLAYA BLANCA Hesperia Playa Dorada

Urb. Costa Papagayo, 35570 **Tel** *928 517 120* **Fax** *928 517 432* **Rooms** *466*

Located on the seafront at Costa del Papagayo is this hotel with extensive gardens and sun terraces surrounding three pools. The spacious bedrooms are nicely furnished and have either a balcony or a terrace. Fitness facilities include a Jacuzzi, gym, two squash courts, an indoor swimming pool, and pitch and putt. **www.hesperia-playadorada.com**

Key to Price Guide *see p156* **Key to Symbols** *see back cover flap*

PLAYA BLANCA Iberostar Lanzarote Park

Avda. Canarias 5, 35570 **Tel** *928 517 048* **Fax** *928 517 348* **Rooms** *332*

This large hotel is right on the beachfront and offers views over Fuerteventura. It's a good choice for families who will appreciate the children's pool, playground and mini-club with entertainment for 4–12 year olds. Varied sports facilities include four swimming pools, volleyball, archery, squash courts and a tennis school. **www.iberostar.com**

PLAYA BLANCA H10 Bahia Blanca Rock

C/Janubio s/n, 35570 **Tel** *928 517 037* **Fax** *928 517 055* **Rooms** *200*

An attractive apartment complex with traditional Canarian-styled architecture offers 200 well-equipped apartments set around tropical gardens. The packed day and night activities programme and the restaurant's buffet with plenty of child-friendly options make this hotel a popular location for families. **www.h10hotels.com**

PLAYA BLANCA H10 Rubicon Palace

Urb. Montaña Roja, 35570 **Tel** *928 518 500* **Fax** *928 518 498* **Rooms** *584*

A chic, low-rise, all-inclusive hotel on the seafront with a courtesy bus to the beach. Rooms are fashionable and elegantly furnished with large private terraces. The extensive grounds include eight pools, a poolside BBQ restaurant, Beefeaters English Pub and Piano Bar, and a health and beauty centre. **www.h10hotels.com**

PLAYA BLANCA H10 Timanfaya Palace

Urb. Montaña Roja, 35570 **Tel** *928 517 676* **Fax** *928 517 035* **Rooms** *305*

This prestigious hotel has beautiful Arabic architecture which blends with its surroundings, and is an ideal location for guests who want luxury with environmental awareness. Inside, a fern-filled atrium and mosaic fountains display touches of class. Rooms are large and facilities include a live music bar, disco, gym and sauna. **www.h10hotels.com**

PUERTO DEL CARMEN Hotel Magec

Calle Hierro 11, 35510 **Tel** *928 515 120* **Rooms** *11*

The rooms at this basic pension are simply furnished and clean. This location suits budget travellers and those wishing to eschew the larger, purpose-built hotels by the coast in favour of the atmosphere of Puerto del Carmen's fishing quarter. When booking state whether an ensuite bathroom is required.

PUERTO DEL CARMEN Lanzarote Village

Avda. de Suiza 1, 35510 **Tel** *928 511 344* **Fax** *928 512 030* **Rooms** *211*

In a good location on Pocillos beach in Puerto del Carmen, Lanzarote Village is an all-inclusive aparthotel. White, low-rise apartments are clustered around a pleasant swimming pool and sun terrace area. Facilities include tennis courts, table tennis, darts and billiards. A cocktail bar and disco liven up the evenings.

PUERTO DEL CARMEN Los Fariones

C/Roque del Este 1, 35510 **Tel** *928 510 175* **Fax** *928 510 202* **Rooms** *248*

Located on the beach, a few metres from the leisure and restaurant area of La Tiñosa, is this hotel with beautiful tropical gardens and freshwater pools. Rooms are large, modern and bright, with balconies and sea views. Facilities include a diving centre, tennis court, mini-golf, sauna and massage, and nightly entertainment. **www.farioneshotels.com**

PUERTO DEL CARMEN San Antonio

Avda. Las Playas, 84 **Tel** *928 514 200* **Fax** *928 513 080* **Rooms** *331*

All rooms here are a good size, with balconies overlooking the beach. Pools include a high pool with views to Fuerteventura, a large main pool and a children's pool. The hotel also boasts a gym and sauna with Turkish baths, two floodlit tennis courts, a BBQ restaurant and a cocktail bar with live music. **www.hotelsanantonio.com**

PUERTO DEL CARMEN La Geria

Júpiter 5, 35510 **Tel** *928 510 441* **Fax** *928 511 919* **Rooms** *240*

This modern hotel is a stone's throw from the long, sandy los Pocillos beach. Although close to shops, bars and restaurants, the hotel's spacious grounds and pool are tranquil and relaxing. There's a second pool indoors. Water sports, including diving, can be arranged on the beach. **www.hipotels.com**

PUERTO DEL CARMEN Riu Olivina

C/Grecia 11, 35519 **Tel** *928 514 393* **Fax** *928 510 851* **Rooms** *102*

Just 300 metres from Playa de los Pocillos is this hotel set in elegant landscaped gardens surrounded by lush tropical vegetation. Rooms are large and bright with a private balcony or terrace. Facilities include table tennis, volleyball and two tennis courts. The children's mini-club and playground are in Riu Olivina Apartments next door. **www.riu.com**

YAIZA Finca de las Salinas

C/La Cuesta 17, 35570 **Tel** *928 830 325* **Fax** *928 830 329* **Rooms** *19*

Peace and quiet reigns in this beautiful, 18th-century mansion with wooden floors and ceilings and a glass-covered courtyard. Bedrooms are converted stables and styled in impeccable taste with antique and modern furnishings. A wine bar serves local wines. Tennis court, Jacuzzi and fitness centre. **www.fincasalinas.com**

YAIZA Iberostar Papagayo

C/Princesa Ico 2, San Marcial del Rubicon, 35570 **Tel** *928 519 251* **Fax** *928 518 658* **Rooms** *208*

A three-storey hotel in quiet location overlooking the bay of Playa de las Coloradas. Papagayos beach is a 10-minute walk and the marina is just 500 metres away. Rooms are large with cheery décor. The hotel has plenty of sporting activities and the wellness and spa centre offers a good selection of treatments. **www.iberostar.com**

TENERIFE

COSTA ADEJE Fañabe Costa Sur
⬚⬚⬚⬚⬚⬚   €€

Avda. Bruselas 13, 38660 **Tel** *922 712 900* **Fax** *922 712 769* **Rooms** *425*

A good-value hotel in a quiet part of Costa Adeje's upmarket area. The facilities, entertainment and activities programmes are well suited to a family holiday. Fañabe and the fashionable Playa del Duque beach are a few minutes' walk down quite a steep hill. **www.gfhoteles.com**

COSTA ADEJE Hotel Gran Tinerfe
⬚⬚⬚⬚⬚⬚   €€€

Avda. Rafael Puig, 13, 38660 **Tel** *922 791 200* **Fax** *922 791 265* **Rooms** *348*

This high-rise seafront hotel is situated within easy reach of the bars and restaurants of Playa de las Américas and close to a beach. Facilities include three large swimming pools, four bars and a relaxing outdoor restaurant overlooking the sea. Guests have free entrance to the casino located within the hotel. **www.h10hotels.com**

COSTA ADEJE Iberostar Bouganville Playa
⬚⬚⬚⬚⬚⬚   €€€

Urb. San Eugenio, C/Eugenio Dominguez, 23 **Tel** *922 790 200* **Fax** *922 794 173* **Rooms** *489*

At this lively hotel on the coast rooms are modern, spacious and bright. There's a large swimming pool and sun terrace area, while facilities for families include a mini-club, a children's pool and a playground. There's also a karaoke bar, tennis, bowls and squash courts, and as a fitness centre with sauna and massage. **www.iberostar.com**

COSTA ADEJE Guayaymina Princess
⬚⬚⬚⬚⬚⬚   €€€€

Playa de Fañabe – C/Londres, 1, 38670 **Tel** *922 712 584* **Fax** *922 712 000* **Rooms** *513*

A stylish frontage of white and glass and a vast atrium welcome you to this hotel's reception area. A beautiful, free-form swimming pool criss-crossed by bridges fronts the hotel, which is in an excellent location, two minutes' walk from the beach, shops, restaurants and bars. The stylish piano bar is a popular spot for cocktails. **www.princess-hotels.com**

COSTA ADEJE Jardín Tropical
⬚⬚⬚⬚⬚⬚   €€€€

C/Gran Bretaña, 38660 **Tel** *922 746 000* **Fax** *922 746 060* **Rooms** *390*

This hotel offers Arabian-inspired architecture set in tropical gardens with pools and sunset views over La Gomera. It is popular with families for the children's club, entertainment and baby-sitting services, and with golf enthusiasts for the organized green fee bookings, transport and preferential access to the best courses. **www.jardin-tropical.com**

COSTA ADEJE Torviscas Playa
⬚⬚⬚⬚⬚   €€€€

Urb. Torviscas, Avda. Ernesto Sarti, 5, **Tel** *922 712 300* **Fax** *922 713 155* **Rooms** *470*

A popular hotel located on the promenade, 50 metres from beach and a few minutes' walk from Puerto Colon Marina. The rooms are a good size and have large balconies. The hotel has shops, including a newsagent, bars and restaurants, and its expansive swimming pool is surrounded by palms. **www.iberostar.com**

COSTA ADEJE Gran Hotel Bahía del Duque Resort
⬚⬚⬚⬚⬚⬚   €€€€€

Playa de Fañabe, 38660 **Tel** *922 746 900* **Fax** *922 746 916* **Rooms** *482*

This hotel offers opulence, service and style on a grand scale. Pools, waterfalls, botanical gardens, terraces and lawns front the Playa del Duque beach. The eclectic collection of buildings and grounds covers an area the size of a small village and includes 12 restaurants and an inexhaustible list of recreation facilities. **www.bahia-duque.com**

GARACHICO Hotel San Roque
⬚⬚⬚⬚   €€€€€

C/Esteban de Ponte 32, 38450 **Tel** *922 133 435* **Fax** *922 133 406* **Rooms** *20*

In a historic north coast town away from the island's tourist resorts is this charming boutique hotel. It occupies an 18th-century house built around two pretty patios and decorated with avant-garde art. All rooms have Jacuzzis, flat-screen TVs and video and DVD players. Dinner and breakfast are served at poolside tables. **www.hotelsanroque.com**

GUIA DE ISORA Abama Resort
⬚⬚⬚⬚⬚⬚   €€€€€

Guia de Isora, 38687 **Tel** *902 105 600* **Fax** *922 866 402* **Rooms** *330*

This vast deluxe hotel with Moorish village architecture sits on a headland just a few minutes' drive from Playa San Juan. It has eight restaurants, a tennis academy, spa, blues club and a world-class golf course. Rooms have spacious terraces with spectacular views. There are also luxury villas to rent. **www.abamahotelresort.com**

LA CALETA Hotel Costa Adeje Palace
⬚⬚⬚⬚⬚⬚   €€€€

Playa La Enramada, 38670 **Tel** *922 714 171* **Fax** *922 719 206* **Rooms** *467*

A chic and fashionable hotel in upmarket Costa Adeje. Hushed pastel tones, lush tropical planting and stylized furnishings make the most of the sunlight hours, while clever lighting adds romance after dark. Beautiful rooms and good dining complement the wide range of recreation facilities. **www.h10hotels.com**

LA CALETA Hotel Riu Palace Tenerife
⬚⬚⬚⬚⬚⬚   €€€€

Urb. La Herradura, 38670 **Tel** *922 714 191* **Fax** *922 719 045* **Rooms** *296*

One of a breed of prestigious hotels with imaginative architecture which characterize the quiet western edge of Costa Adeje. The extensive gardens offer pools and views to La Gomera. With themed restaurants, a "body love" centre, children's areas and entertainment, it's suitable for families and couples alike. **www.riu.com**

Key to Price Guide *see p156* **Key to Symbols** *see back cover flap*

LA CALETA Hotel Sheraton La Caleta

La Enramada, Poligono 9, 38670 **Tel** *922 162 000* **Fax** *922 162 010* **Rooms** *284*

This hotel and spa, set in extensive gardens on the ocean front, offers contemporary style with warm colours and lots of glass. All bedrooms have a private balcony or terrace and plenty of floor space. Four restaurants, including a *Teppanyaki* (Japanese cuisine cooked on a griddle), offer variety and excellence in dining. **www.starwoodhotels.com**

LA LAGUNA Costa Salada

Camino La Costa, Finca Oasis, Valle de Guerra, 38270 **Tel** *922 690 000* **Fax** *922 541 055* **Rooms** *13*

An idyllic get-away-from-it-all rural hotel, located within a subtropical nursery, standing on a series of terraces overlooking the rocky northern coast of Tenerife. Rooms combine modern décor with traditional features and have terraces and sea views. There's also a wine cellar in a natural cave. **www.costasalada.com**

LA LAGUNA Nivaria

Plaza del Adelantado, 38002 **Tel** *922 264 298* **Fax** *922 259 634* **Rooms** *79*

This 18th-century mansion in the heart of La Laguna's old quarter features comfortable rooms, a bar and a squash court. It faces the bustling Plaza del Adelantado alongside convents, the market and the historic town hall, making it the perfect location for delving into the culture and history of the former capital. **www.hotelnivaria.com**

LA OROTAVA Hotel Rural La Orotava

C/ Carrera 17, 38300 **Tel** *922 322 793* **Fax** *922 322 725* **Rooms** *8*

Located in heart of the old quarter of historic La Orotava, this hotel occupies one of the island's oldest buildings, dating from 1585. Within its charming courtyard, surrounded by typical Canarian wooden balconies, is the Sabor Canario restaurant where breakfast is served. Each stylish bedroom is uniquely furnished. **www.saborcanario.net**

LA OROTAVA Parador de Cañadas del Teide

Las Cañadas del Teide, 38300 **Tel** *922 374 841* **Fax** *922 382 352* **Rooms** *37*

This modern Alpine chalet-styled *parador* is the only place to stay inside the national park. It occupies an unparalleled location in a stunning crater below Mount Teide. During daytime, the cafeteria and surrounding area is very busy with day-trippers, but at night it's just you, the stars and the volcano. **www.parador.es**

LOS CRISTIANOS Princesa Dacil

Avda. Juan Carlos I, 25 **Tel** *922 753 030* **Fax** *922 790 658* **Rooms** *364*

Centrally located close to beach and all amenities, this busy, friendly hotel has extremely large rooms with balconies overlooking mountains or gardens. A full programme of daytime entertainment includes competitions and organized sports, and there's a mini-club for 5–12 year olds. Evening entertainment and shows too. **www.solmelia.com**

LOS CRISTIANOS Paradise Park

Urb. Oasis del Sur, 38650 **Tel** *922 75 72 27* **Fax** *922 75 01 93* **Rooms** *394*

This hotel lies in the upper reaches of Los Cristianos. Rooms with lounges have views of the mountains and the sea. Although there are facilities in the hotel, those on offer at its adjoining Paradise leisure park are exceptional with a traditionally styled Canarian restaurant and stylish pools and spa area. **www.hotelparadisepark.com**

LOS CRISTIANOS Arona Gran Hotel

Avda. Los Cristianos **Tel** *922 750 678* **Fax** *922 750 243* **Rooms** *401*

A popular hotel at the eastern end of Los Cristianos with views over the old port and the town. An impressive atrium forms the reception and lobby area while outside, terraces have pretty gardens surrounding two pools and sunbathing decks. Rooms are generously sized with large balconies, most with sea views. Good service. **www.springhoteles.com**

PLAYA DE LA ARENA Hotel Barcelo Varadero

Avda. La Gaviota, 1, 38680 **Tel** *922 869 814* **Fax** *922 867 726* **Rooms** *317*

This low-rise hotel in a quiet residential area, in the family resort of Playa de la Arena, is a 10-minute stroll away from a blue flag beach. Large apartments overlook a long pool. Evening entertainment is varied and a very good buffet attracts a lot of Spanish guests at the weekend. **www.barcelo.com**

PLAYA DE LAS AMERICAS Bitácora

Calle California, 1, 38660 **Tel** *922 791 540* **Fax** *922 796 677* **Rooms** *314*

Located in the centre of Playa de las Américas, a short walk from the beach and close to a selection of stylish bars and restaurants, is this large, modern hotel set in subtropical gardens. There's a very good buffet and a great range of facilities and activities for adults and children. **www.springhoteles.com**

PLAYA DE LAS AMERICAS Hotel Gala

Avda. A. Gomez Cuesta, 3, 38660 **Tel** *922 794 513* **Fax** *922 796 465* **Rooms** *308*

Centrally located near to bars, clubs and discos, the bedrooms at this hotel have double-glazed windows to ensure nights finish when you want them to. Rooms are pleasant and amply sized, with flower-laden balconies; some have sea views. Facilities include two large heated swimming pools and a health and fitness centre. **www.hotelgala.com**

PLAYA DE LAS AMERICAS Hotel Mediterranean Palace

Avda. de las Américas, 38660 **Tel** *922 757 545* **Fax** *922 753 479* **Rooms** *535*

A vast swimming pool with fountains forms the centrepiece of this hotel with a distinctive blue exterior. The sun terraces have hammocks, as well as sun loungers and parasols. Rooms have yellow and blue décor with ensuites finished in marble. Guests can use the spa facilities at the Mare Nostrum resort next door. **www.expogrupo.com**

PLAYA DE LAS AMERICAS Vulcano

Avda. Domínguez Alfonso, 38660 **Tel** *922 787 740* **Fax** *922 792 853* **Rooms** *371*

Just 300 metres from the beach and 1 km (half a mile) from a golf course, this large modern hotel occupies a great location for exploring shops, bars and restaurants in both Playa de las Américas and its neighbour Los Cristianos. The hotel's grounds include two large swimming pools. Popular with mature visitors. **www.springhoteles.com**

PUERTO DE LA CRUZ Tigaiga

C/Parque de Taoro 28, 38400 **Tel** *922 383 500* **Fax** *922 384 055* **Rooms** *83*

This small hotel has been around since the early days of tourism here and is renowned for its personal touch. The peaceful, prime location above the town centre can be reached via the Taoro's beautiful exotic gardens. Rooms are generously sized, with views of Mount Teide or the gardens. **www.tigaiga.com**

PUERTO DE LA CRUZ Botánico

C/Richard, J. Yeoward 1, 38400 **Tel** *922 381 400* **Fax** *922 381 504* **Rooms** *252*

Located 2km (1 mile) from the centre of town, this hotel offers opulent marble interiors with sweeping staircases and sumptuous red-and-gold themed bedrooms. The vast sub-tropical gardens include a Japanese lake with Koi carp and black swans, while the Oriental spa offers a bewildering array of treatments. **www.hotelbotanico.com**

SANTA CRUZ DE TENERIFE Pelinor

C/Bethencourt Alfonso 8, 38002 **Tel** *922 246 875* **Fax** *922 240 833* **Rooms** *73*

This city-centre hotel is geared more towards business than leisure stays, but provides a perfect location for the city, with easy access to parks, restaurants, museums, galleries and theatres, and easy walking distance to the port and Auditorium. Rooms are comfortably furnished. The snack bar-cafeteria serves breakfast. **www.hotelpelinor.com**

SANTA CRUZ DE TENERIFE Taburiente

C/ Dr José Navieras 24A, 38001 **Tel** *922 276 000* **Fax** *922 270 562* **Rooms** *171*

Modern elegance combines with old-fashioned class at this chic city-centre hotel, which faces the beautiful Parque García Sanabria. Guests are well-provided for with a swimming pool, Jacuzzi, sauna and solarium, as well as a boutique, shop and restaurant. There are also stylish bars and restaurants nearby. **www.hoteltaburiente.com**

SANTA CRUZ Iberostar Mencey

Avda. José Naveiras 38, 38004 **Tel** *922 609 900* **Fax** *922 280 017* **Rooms** *286*

This classically grand, luxury hotel opposite Parque García Sanabria makes a great location for exploring the city. Its plush rooms, opulent décor and attentive staff have welcomed movie stars and royalty over the years. Add beautiful gardens, pools and a casino and you can enjoy a slice of old fashioned grandeur. **www.hotelmencey.com**

SANTA CRUZ DE TENERIFE Hotel Contemporaneo

Rambla Santa Cruz 116, 38001 **Tel** *922 120 329* **Fax** *922 271 223* **Rooms** *150*

This modern, high-rise hotel is in the heart of the city. All the rooms are stylishly decorated in shades of brown and cream and have mod-cons such as flat screen TVs, Wi-Fi, and satellite televisions (although the Wi-Fi is not free). The restaurant is popular with business people. **www.hotelcontemporaneo.com**

LA GOMERA

HERMIGUA Ibo Alfaro

C/General 121, 38820 **Tel** *922 880 168* **Fax** *922 881 019* **Rooms** *17*

Located in the centre of the village, in a former manor house dating from more than 150 years ago, this hotel affords views right across the valley. There are palm and cactus gardens and a sun terrace, while the rooms are impeccably decorated, retaining all their original features, and all rooms have balconies. **www.hotel-gomera.com**

PLAYA DE SANTIAGO Apartamentos Bellavista

C/Santa Ana, 38811 **Tel** *922 895 570* **Fax** *922 895 208* **Rooms** *10*

Ten spacious one- and two-bedroom apartments, with balconies offering views of the sea and the town, are situated in a peaceful area, a five-minute walk through a banana plantation. The hotel reception can arrange hiking, boat and diving trips. **www.casascanarias.com**

PLAYA DE SANTIAGO Jardín Tecina

Lomada de Tecina, 38811 **Tel** *922 145 850* **Fax** *922 145 851* **Rooms** *434*

A fabulously dramatic clifftop location above Playa de Santiago is the setting for two-storey blocks scattered around extensive landscaped, tropical gardens. A lift built into the cliffside leads to the leisure complex and an à la carte restaurant (*see p179*). Facilities include a golf course, five pools, sauna, massage and diving lessons. **www.jardin-tecina.com**

SAN SEBASTIÁN DE LA GOMERA Hesperides

C/Ruiz De Padrón, 38800 **Tel** *922 871 305* **Rooms** *9*

A small, friendly, budget hotel-pension in the centre of the capital, giving easy access to shops, restaurants and the beach. Rooms are clean and comfortable with shared bathrooms. This hotel is a good, value-for-money option for exploring the city and as a base for hiking.

Key to Price Guide *see p156* **Key to Symbols** *see back cover flap*

SAN SEBASTIÁN DE LA GOMERA Villa Gomera €

C/Ruiz De Padrón 68, 38800 **Tel** *922 870 020* **Fax** *922 870 235* **Rooms** *16*

This small, bright and friendly hotel is modern and welcoming. Pleasantly decorated throughout, it is situated in the centre of the capital. Rooms are comfortable, clean and bright, some with their own balconies, and offer very good value for money. The hotel also has apartments with separate living rooms and terraces. **www.hotelvillagomera.com**

SAN SEBASTIÁN DE LA GOMERA Hotel Garajonay €€

C/Ruiz De Padrón 15, 38800 **Tel** *922 870 550* **Fax** *922 870 554* **Rooms** *29*

Good value, three-storey, town-centre hotel within easy reach of shops, bars and the harbour. The town's beach is 300 metres away. Rooms are a decent size, clean and bright with balconies overlooking the town. The hotel has a dining area serving breakfast only and a sun terrace on the roof.

SAN SEBASTIÁN DE LA GOMERA Hotel Torre del Conde €€

C/Ruiz De Padrón 15, 38800 **Tel** *922 870 000* **Fax** *922 871 314* **Rooms** *38*

This town-centre hotel is situated within close proximity to the park and historic tower which share its name. Rooms are comfortable and have satellite TV, while the sun terrace on the roof has good views of the town, especially the Torre del Conde opposite. The hotel's restaurant serves local cuisine. **www.hoteltorredelconde.com**

SAN SEBASTIÁN DE LA GOMERA Parador de la Gomera €€€€

Lomo de la Horca, 38800 **Tel** *922 871 100* **Fax** *922 871 116* **Rooms** *60*

In a stunning clifftop position above La Gomera's main town and port is this *parador*, built in traditional Canarian style and decorated with maritime paraphernalia. The bedrooms are simply furnished with dark wood fittings and tiled bathrooms. Guests can enjoy the subtropical gardens and fabulous views across the sea to Tenerife. **www.parador.es**

VALLE GRAN REY Casa Bella Cabellos €

La Calera, 38870 **Tel** *922 805 182* **Rooms** *5*

This restored rural house is located in palm groves above the small resort of Valle Gran Rey. Typically Canarian in style, the five bedrooms are pleasantly decorated and retain many of their original features. This is a friendly, comfortable option and a good base for hiking.

VALLE GRAN REY Gran Rey €€€

La Puntilla, 38870 **Tel** *922 805 859* **Fax** *922 805 651* **Rooms** *99*

In an excellent seafront location, near some sandy coves, midway between the main tourist area of La Playa and the harbour at Vueltas is this eco-friendly hotel with attractive marble, stone and wood décor. All rooms and the rooftop swimming pool have views of the sea and the valley. **www.hotel-granrey.com**

VALLEHERMOSO Hotel Rural Tamahuche €€

La Hoya 20, 38840 **Tel** *922 801 176* **Fax** *922 801 176* **Rooms** *10*

This lovingly restored 19th-century traditional house with wooden floors, carved window seats and wooden, canopy ceilings offers stunning views over the valley and Roque Cano. Rooms exude romance, with fine, white linen, private balconies and beautiful bathrooms. The cosy dining room offers good home cooking. **www.hoteltamahuche.com**

EL HIERRO

FRONTERA Apartamentos Frontera €€

Principal de Tigaday, Valle del Golfo, 38913 **Tel** *922 559 291* **Fax** *922 559 291* **Rooms** *18*

Located in the centre of El Golfo valley, in the wine-producing town of Tigaday, this friendly, family-run hotel consists of 12 apartments and six studios with fully-equipped kitchens, satellite TV and balconies affording good views of the sea and the valley. A good base for hikers. **www.apartamentosfrontera.com**

FRONTERA Ida Inés €€

Camino del Hoyo Belgara Alta 2, 38911 **Tel** *922 559 445* **Fax** *922 556 088* **Rooms** *12*

This small hotel overlooks the Atlantic Ocean from its El Golfo valley setting. Its 12 cosy bedrooms have superb views of either the sea or the valley. The small swimming pool has a solarium and guests have Internet access. A good base for walking or mountain biking. **www.hotelitoidaines.com**

LA RESTINGA Kai Marino €

La Restinga, 38915 **Tel** *922 557 034* **Fax** *922 557 034* **Rooms** *7*

A low-rise aparthotel overlooking the small beach and harbour. German owned, this was the first bar to open in the area and remains popular with divers due to the clear waters and variety of marine life in the area. Rooms are clean and bright, service is friendly and welcoming.

LAS PUNTAS Apartamentos Roques Salmor €€

Ctra. Punta Grande s/n, 38911 **Tel** *922 559 016* **Fax** *922 559 401* **Rooms** *2*

These modest, fully-equipped bungalows are set around a small pool with sweeping views towards the natural rock pools of Cascadas de Mar, home of the famous giant lizard. The nearest town is Tigaday, 5 km (3 miles) away, while Valverde is a 20-minute journey by car.

LAS PUNTAS Hotel Punta Grande

Embarcadero de Punta Grande 2, 38911 **Tel** *922 559 081* **Fax** *922 559 081* **Rooms** *4*

Consisting of just four bedrooms and a restaurant, this hotel once appeared in the *Guinness Book of Records* as the smallest hotel in the world. As it is so close to the water that you can actually fish from out of the window, it may not come as a surprise that the restaurant's speciality is seafood.

PINAR Hotel Pinar

Travesia del Pino 64, 38910 **Tel** *922 558 008* **Fax** *922 558 090* **Rooms** *10*

Situated in the centre of the peaceful hillside village of El Pinar, this small hotel has 10 basic rooms with TVs and bathrooms. The hotel has a popular restaurant and bar which serves freshly caught fish of the day, typical Herreño home cooking and a selection of tapas. **www.hierrosur.com**

SABINOSA Balneario Pozo La Salud

Pozo La Salud, 38911 **Tel** *922 559 561* **Fax** *922 559 801* **Rooms** *18*

Distinguished as being Spain's westernmost hotel, the Pozo La Salud sits next to the natural spa of the same name and offers a range of health treatments courtesy of the warm, healing waters. Guests can enjoy treatments such as an anti-stress package. **www.el-meridiano.com**

VALVERDE Boomerang

C/Dr. Gost 1, 38900 **Tel** *922 550 200* **Fax** *922 550 253* **Rooms** *17*

This small, reasonably priced, basic hotel in the centre of town offers clean, simply furnished bedrooms equipped with TV and bathroom. The hotel's limited facilities include a restaurant, pleasant gardens and a terrace. Its location makes it a suitable base for hiking. **www.hotel-boomerang.com**

VALVERDE Hotel Residencia Casañas

Calle San Francisco 9, 38900 **Tel** *922 550 254* **Fax** *922 550 254* **Rooms** *15*

Situated close to the church of Nuesta Señora de la Concepción and the town's restaurants, this hotel is an ideal base for exploring. The rooms are clean, simple and equipped with a TV. The hotel offers panoramic views across the coast and sea, and good, friendly service.

VALVERDE Casa Rural El Tesón I

Calle Esquina Campo 14, San Andrés, 38916 **Tel** *922 551 824* **Fax** *922 550 575* **Rooms** *2*

A charming rustic Canarian cottage in a serene location, surrounded by fields and tropical fruit orchards in the hills near San Andrés. The cottage sleeps four and is equipped with a washing machine, TV and wood-burning stove. There's a shop close by and two restaurants 1 km (half a mile) away. **www.ecotourismcanarias.com**

VALVERDE Parador de El Hierro

Las Playas 15, 38910 **Tel** *922 558 036* **Fax** *922 558 086* **Rooms** *45*

Black cliffs are the backdrop for this modern hotel, which stands on an isolated beach facing the Roque de Bonanza. It has an elegant colonial décor with white walls, and wooden balconies with sea views. This is an ideal option for walking or relaxing. El Hierro specialities are served in the restaurant. **www.parador.es**

LA PALMA

BARLOVENTO La Palma Romántica

Las Llanadas s/n, 38726 **Tel** *922 186 221* **Fax** *922 186 400* **Rooms** *41*

Personal, friendly service and attention to detail are the watchwords of the management and staff at this hotel set at 600m above sea level and often "floating" on a sea of mist. Style, elegance and luxury combine in generously sized rooms. Facilities include bars, fine dining in the restaurant and fitness facilities. **www.hotellapalmaromantica.com**

BRENA BAJA Hacienda San Jorge

Playa de los Cancajos 22, 38712 **Tel** *922 181 066* **Fax** *922 434 528* **Rooms** *155*

At this lovely finca with traditional Palmero architecture and lush tropical gardens, the apartments are bright and spacious with balconies overlooking the sea, gardens or mountains. Facilities include a panoramic restaurant, large gym and sauna, a pool and a delightful bar. Paths lead through the gardens to the beach. **www.hsanjorge.com**

BRENA BAJA Hotel Las Olas

Playa de los Cancajos, 38712 **Tel** *922 434 052* **Fax** *922 434 085* **Rooms** *182*

On the beach at Los Cancajos are these modern, elegant apartments with bedroom, bathroom and kitchen-diner with balcony or terrace affording views over sea, mountains or pool. The hotel has swimming pools and sunbathing terraces, including a private one for nude sunbathing. Offers diving lessons for beginners. **www.a-caledonia.com**

BRENA BAJA Aparthotel Breñas Garden

Finca Amado II 68, 38712 **Tel** *922 433 175* **Fax** *922 433 181* **Rooms** *40*

These apartments are clustered in a quiet area at the foot of Montaña Breja. They have basic furnishings but are fully equipped and feature wooden ceilings, fireplaces and sea views. Each room has a terrace, and there's a restaurant serving breakfast and dinner. The beach at Cancajos is 4 miles (6km) away. **www.brenasgarden.com**

Key to Price Guide *see p156* **Key to Symbols** *see back cover flap*

BRENA BAJA Taburiente Playa

Urb. Las Salinas, Playa de los Cancajos, 38712 **Tel** *922 181 277* **Fax** *922 181 285* **Rooms** *293*

At this modern hotel situated 300 metres from the black sands of Los Cancajos beach, rooms are large with stunning views along La Palma's coastline. The hotel has three swimming pools, gym, sauna, buffet restaurant and children's play park. Santa Cruz and the airport are only a short drive away. **www.h10hotels.com**

FUENCALIENTE Hotel Teneguia Princess

Ctra. La Costa Cera Vija 10, 38740 **Tel** *922 425 500* **Fax** *922 425 509* **Rooms** *378*

A vast, timbered lobby and lounge area greets you as you enter this extensive new coastal hotel complex. There are 12 swimming pools, including one with simulated waves and a small beach. Five restaurants, seven bars, a disco and professional shows offer evening diversion. Sports and relaxation facilities fill the days. **www.princess-hotels.com**

LOS LLANOS DE ARIDANE Hotel Eden

Plaza de España s/n, 38760 **Tel** *922 460 104* **Fax** *922 460 183* **Rooms** *19*

This is a good-value hotel in a perfect city centre location, on the corner of the historic Plaza de España. It offers a lounge overlooking the plaza and comfortable decent-sized rooms. It also provides a pavement bar-cafeteria. The staff are friendly. **www.hoteledenlapalma.com**

LOS LLANOS DE ARIDANE Valle Aridane

Glorieta Castillo Olivares 3, 38760 **Tel** *922 462 600* **Fax** *922 401 019* **Rooms** *42*

Located near the city centre is this hotel with an interesting retro-style façade, large rooms and friendly service. There's a breakfast room and a sun terrace with a bar on the roof, affording views to La Caldera de Taburiente, which can be reached by car in 10 minutes. **www.hotelvallearidane.com**

LOS LLANOS DE ARIDANE Amberes

Avda. General Franco, 38760 **Tel** *922 401 040* **Fax** *922 402 441* **Rooms** *7*

In this lovingly restored 17th-century mansion, set in romantic cloistered courtyards and gardens, rooms are all deluxe-sized and individually styled with original features, natural materials and impeccable taste by their Dutch, interior designer owner. The restaurant offers vegetarian specialities and fine wine. **www.hotel-amberes.com**

LOS LLANOS DE ARIDANE Hotel Trocadero Plaza

C/Las Adelfas 12, 38760 **Tel** *922 403 013* **Fax** *922 402 903* **Rooms** *18*

This small, contemporary hotel is a good choice for a central stay as it is close to restaurants and shops in the town. There's a sun terrace and café, and reception staff are happy to assist with information on excursions around the island. They will also help with car hire, and private parking is available. **www.hoteltrocaderoplaza.com**

PUERTO NAOS Sol Elite La Palma

Punta del Pozo, 38769 **Tel** *922 408 000* **Fax** *922 408 014* **Rooms** *307*

A large hotel and three apartment buildings overlooking the small beach resort of Puerto Naos. The spacious rooms have satellite TV and sea or mountain views. Apartments are built in traditional Canarian style and have one or two bedrooms and a large terrace. Facilities include an on-site supermarket, laundry and observatory. **www.solmelia.com**

SANTA CRUZ DE LA PALMA Castillete

Avda. Maritima 75, 38700 **Tel** *922 420 840* **Fax** *922 420 067* **Rooms** *42*

An aparthotel in an excellent location on the promenade and only a few minutes stroll from the city centre. Comfortable apartments have fully equipped kitchen, TV and a small balcony, most with views of the sea. The hotel has a restaurant and rooftop sun terrace with swimming pool. **www.aparthotelcastillete.com**

SANTA CRUZ DE LA PALMA Maritimo

Avenida Maritima 75, 38700 **Tel** *922 414 302* **Fax** *922 414 302* **Rooms** *96*

This is a simple yet comfortable three-star, well-positioned for bracing walks along the promenade and a stroll through the Old Quarter. Don't expect luxury, but you will find friendliness and comfort and there is free Internet in the restaurant café. **www.hotelmaritimo.com**

SANTA CRUZ DE LA PALMA Parador de la Palma

Ctra. de el Zumacal, Breña Baja, 38720 **Tel** *922 435 828* **Fax** *922 435 999* **Rooms** *78*

This purpose-built *parador*, in the traditional Canarian style, features towers and wooden balconies and cool, relaxing inner courtyards. From the large rooms and expansive gardens with swimming pool, there are breathtaking views along the coast to Santa Cruz. **www.parador.es**

TAZACORTE Apartamentos Atlantis

Mariano Benlliure 14, 38770 **Tel** *922 406 146* **Fax** *922 406 146* **Rooms** *23*

Situated at the edge of the village of Tazacorte, these clean, bright apartments have a kitchen-dining room, bathroom and one or two bedrooms with sliding doors to a balcony. Attractions include a garden, swimming pool, rooftop laundry room and views over banana plantations, Caldera de Taburiente and El Time. **www.atlantis-lapalma.com**

VILLA DE MAZO Arminda

Lodero 182, 38730 **Tel** *922 428 432* **Rooms** *5*

This charming intimate rural hotel is located in a 300-year-old traditional house in a banana plantation, on Villa de Mazo's slopes. Five lovely rooms with bathrooms are fronted by a flower-filled patio, where breakfast is served overlooking the gardens and swimming pool, and with views to the sea and La Gomera.

WHERE TO EAT

The Canary Islands can offer a good selection of restaurants, able to satisfy the most discerning palates. Traditional Canary cuisine is in plentiful supply, as are dishes from other regions of Spain. In addition, speciality food, which includes German, French, Italian, Chinese, Arab and Indian cuisine, can easily be found to cater for the varied tastes of tourists.

Decorative tiles in a Canarian restaurant

Numerous restaurants offer hybrid menus and many chefs create sophisticated dishes by experimenting with a range of local ingredients and various culinary traditions. Some of these restaurants are highly regarded and very popular. The majority of Canary Island restaurants, however, are actually small bars near beaches and tourist centres, which cater for the fast-food market.

A modest restaurant in one of El Golfo's quiet streets

WHERE TO EAT

The islands offer countless bars and restaurants, with diverse menus. The majority of restaurants open for lunch and dinner. Tourists and locals alike enjoy going to restaurants, which accounts for the variety on offer, including *marisquería* (seafood) and *cervecería* (pubs).

There is no dress code in restaurants, apart from a very few exclusive places that require evening dress. Apart from the fast-food bars close to the beaches, swimming costumes are not acceptable in bars and restaurants.

There are also fast-food chains, local and foreign, including McDonald's, Tele Pizza, Slow Boat (Chinese), Little Italy (pizza and pasta) and Bocatta as well as cafés serving English-style breakfasts, fish and chips and pizzas. For the genuine article, visitors will need to head inland, away from the popular resorts, where the majority of authentic Canary restaurants (*típico*) can be found.

WHAT TO EAT

The islands' cuisine is the basic Mediterranean diet. Ingredients include fish, meat, rice, sweetcorn, potatoes, vegetables and tropical fruit.

The most popular meats are goat and lamb, although beef is also becoming popular. Typical species of fish include *dorada* (sea bass) and *pez espada* (swordfish).

Canary dishes are quite easy and quick to prepare. Most types of fish and meat are fried or roasted. They are usually served with the local *mojo* sauces, made of olive oil, seasoning and herbs.

Local bars serve basic *raciones* (portions), including *tortilla de patata* (omelette with potatoes), *jamón Serrano* (Spanish ham), *queso* (cheese) and many others.

Another option are the so-called *platos combinados* – inexpensive combinations of basic dishes, including chips, fried egg and cutlet. These are large helpings, and usually competitively priced.

Also available are "single pot" courses. These consist mainly of potatoes and pulses, along with any combination of meat, fish and vegetables.

One should also not forget *gofio*. This roasted sweetcorn flour can be added to everything: soups, stews, desserts and even ice cream!

WHEN TO EAT

As with the rest of Spain, mealtimes on the Canary Islands have fairly irregular hours. Lunchtime (*la comida*) is usually between 1pm and 3pm, but restaurants that cater principally for locals tend to have unusually late meal times. Regardless of the hour, however, having ordered a meal you are generally allowed to finish it in peace.

Lagomar restaurant, Lanzarote (see p175)

Restaurants by the harbour in Puerto de Mogán

Outside traditional mealtimes it is always possible to eat in bars, which offer a wide variety of food. Beachside restaurants are good for snacks any time of day.

Dinner *(cena)* starts late, at about 9pm. It is served in all restaurants until 11pm or midnight. After this, it is generally only possible to buy sandwiches, kebabs or hot dogs in small bars.

Dinner in Spain is usually a hot meal. Like lunch, it may include two courses. During dinnertime, the restaurants offer only meals *à la carte*. Spaniards like to meet from time to time for dinner, in bars that serve *tapas* or *raciones*. When in a group it is fun to order a selection of *tapas* and sample a little bit of each dish.

The Spanish breakfast *(desayuno)* tends to be a light affair and usually consists only of coffee with milk and a sweet bun. An alternative is toast with ham and cheese. Many bars offer a set breakfast, generally including coffee, natural orange juice and a snack. If you want a bowl of breakfast cereal or a fry-up you had better head for a hotel restaurant.

BOOKING

The large number of restaurants on the islands means that there are no problems with finding a table. Nevertheless, sometimes it is worth booking in advance in order to avoid disappointment, particularly when you fancy a specific restaurant.

VEGETARIANS

All restaurants offer some vegetarian dishes, but the concept of a strictly meatless or fishless diet is not always understood. It is wise to check before ordering whether vegetarian dishes contain meat stocks or ham.

Orangerie restaurant in Hotel Palm Beach, Gran Canaria *(see p173)*

PRICES

Prices in the islands' restaurants can vary enormously. In smart, exclusive establishments a full meal, including wine, may cost up to €50 per head. In other, provincial restaurants, the same meal could cost around €15.

During lunch hours many restaurants offer, besides *à la carte* dishes, an inexpensive and tasty *menu del día* (menu of the day). Such menus always include a selection of starters, main courses desserts, as well as bread and often beverages (wine, beer or soft drinks). The average price of such a meal is from €4 to €10.

Some more upmarket restaurants also offer "taster" menus. The dishes from these menus are much more expensive, since they include all of the specialities recommended by the chef.

PAYING

Almost all restaurants accept credit cards to pay *la cuenta* (the bill). Even bars are willing to accept this form of payment, if it is more than a certain amount. You must, however, be prepared to pay in cash in smaller restaurants, not oriented towards tourists. Also, bills of under €30 are usually settled in cash. It is best to ask before ordering, if in doubt. Traveller's cheques are sometimes accepted.

TIPPING

Tips are not obligatory and may be left depending on the quality of service. If the service was bad, then don't tip! Generally, tips are below ten per cent. As a rule, you leave loose change or round up the bill. The IGIC tax is included in the price.

Restaurants lining the ocean boulevard in Playa de las Américas

The Flavours of the Canary Islands

The exotic fruits and vegetables which grow in the sub-tropical Canaries climate, and the unusual fish which are caught in local waters, have led to a cuisine very different from that of the Iberian peninsula. From the original inhabitants, the Guanche, culinary traditions survive in local staples like *gofio* (maize meal). Over the centuries, Spanish, Portuguese and North African influences have been incorporated into the local cuisine, but the underlying theme is always one of simplicity and a reliance on ultra-fresh local produce. All kinds of unusual delicacies are available, from sweet-fleshed parrot-fish to succulent tropical fruits.

Maize (corn)

Fish straight from the ocean, being dried in the sun to preserve them

SEAFOOD AND MEAT

The Canaries offer an incredible array of seafood, with varieties unknown on the Spanish mainland. Delicacies like *lapas* (limpets) are around only for a few months during the summer, and are usually served simply grilled (*a la plancha*). Other unusual varieties include wreckfish, damselfish, dentex and parrot-fish. These, along with more common varieties, are usually fried, baked in a salt crust, or dried in the sun.

Meats include standard Iberian favourites like pork, kid and beef, but they are often prepared according to ancient Guanche tradiions.

FRUIT AND VEGETABLES

The mild, stable Canarian climate is perfect for growing luscious tropical fruits (the most famous crop of the islands being bananas). Exotic vegetables thrive, too, as well as potatoes and tomatoes, which were introduced here 500 years ago from the newly discovered Americas. The islands boast varieties of potato unknown elsewhere, and these feature in the local favourite *papas arrugadas* ("wrinkly potatoes"), which are made by boiling potatoes in their skins in very salty water – sometimes seawater.

Dates   Bananas   Pineapple   Papayas (paw paw)

Mangoes

Guavas

Mouthwatering fresh fruits from the Canary Islands

CANARIAN DISHES AND SPECIALITIES

Almonds

The Greeks named the Canaries "the fortunate islands", and they are certainly blessed in terms of the freshness and abundance of the local produce. Whatever you choose to eat, you can be sure of encountering a bowl of the ubiquitous *mojo* sauce. This aromatic Canarian creation accompanies almost every dish, and appears in countless versions: the main ones are red *picón*, which is spiced up with pepper and paprika, and green verde, with parsley and coriander. The Canarian staple, *gofio* (roasted maize meal), is served for breakfast and used in local dishes such as *gofio de almendras*, a rich almond dessert. The islands are also known for delicious pastries like the honey-drizzled *bienmesabes* (meaning "tastes good to me") and traditional cheeses.

Sopa de pescados tinerfeña
This Tenerife fish soup of sea bass and potatoes is scented with saffron and cumin.

Choosing a Restaurant

The following restaurants have been chosen for their fine food, with particular emphasis on regional cuisine, as well as for the quality of their location and décor. They are listed in the order in which the islands appear in the guide, and then in alphabetical order by location. For more details on food and restaurants, see pages 168–170.

PRICE CATEGORIES
For a three-course meal, including wine and tax (without a tip).

€ Under €15
€€ €15–€20
€€€ €20–€25
€€€€ €25–€30
€€€€€ Over €30

GRAN CANARIA

AGAETE Casa Pepe €
Alcalde Armas Galván, s/n, 35480 **Tel** *928 898 227*

Situated in the beautiful Valle de Agaete, you'll find one of the oldest restaurants in the area. This is an informal dining venue, with maritime décor, that specializes in fish and seafood. Daily specials include favourites such as grilled fish platter and *papas arrugadas* (potatoes boiled in sea salt). Closed Wed.

AGAETE La Palmita €€
Ctra. de las Nieves, s/n, 35480 **Tel** *928 898 704*

Typical Canarian dishes using fresh fish and local herbs are the specialities of this restaurant. Particularly recommended are the *sama à la espalda* (butterfly grilled fish), and the vegetable stew of the day. A large terrace and garden area make it family-friendly. Closed Tue.

AGAETE Puerto de Laguete *Tapas* €€
Nuestra Señora de las Nieves 9, Puerto de las Nieves, 35489 **Tel** *928 554 001*

This traditional Canarian restaurant is situated in Puerto de las Nieves, a sleepy port, with uniform white and blue houses. Always crowded at weekends, it offers an international menu with traditional Canarian specialities and is very popular with visitors arriving on the ferries from Tenerife. Children's menu available.

AGÜIMES La Farola €€€€€
C/Alcalá Galiano 3, 35260 **Tel** *928 180 410*

Situated on Arinaga beach, a short distance from the airport, La Farola specializes in fish and seafood. The oven-baked salted fish or the *paella* made with fish or shellfish are particularly recommended. Home-made desserts include delicious *tarta de turrón*. Open 1–6pm Tue–Sun.

ARGUINEGUIN Qué Tal €€€€
Puerto de Mogán, 35138 **Tel** *928 565 534*

This contemporary and stylish restaurant in the pretty harbour of Puerto de Mogán serves a limited range of freshly cooked international dishes in a laid-back ambience. Make a reservation for the gourmet dinner if you are especially hungry – it offers ten courses of creative cuisine. Closed Sun, Mon and May.

ARUCAS El Mesón de la Montaña *Tapas* €€
C/Montaña de Arucas, 35400 **Tel** *928 600 844*

A spiralling road leads to this restaurant perched on the top of a mountain outside Arucas, offering great views of the northern part of the island. It serves a selection of international and Canarian dishes – some of the latter need to be ordered in advance. Good fish and seafood. The restaurant caters largely for groups and there's a children's playground.

ARUCAS Casa Brito €€€€
Pasaje Del Teror 17, 35400 **Tel** *928 622 323*

Argentinean meats are the main specialities of this rustic restaurant, but the fish dishes are just as good. Both are cooked in a wood-fired oven. Start with *potaje de berros* (watercress soup) and finish with a dessert of flaky pastry with almonds and honey. Good selection of wines. Closed Mon & Tue.

LAS PALMAS DE GRAN CANARIA Asturias €
C/Capitán Lucena 6, 35468 **Tel** *928 274 219*

You'll find Asturias in a maze of tiny streets, near Playa de las Canteras. As the name suggests, the cuisine is typically Asturian, both hearty and plentiful, originating from the northern Spanish region of the same name. Asturian cuisine specializes in meat and bean stews, as well as seafood, hams, chorizos and cheeses.

LAS PALMAS DE GRAN CANARIA La Cabana Criolla €€
Los Martínez de Escobar, 35017 **Tel** *928 270 216*

A simply furnished, rustic restaurant serving good quality food at very reasonable prices. The restaurant specializes in grilled meats prepared South American style, particularly Argentinean. A limited number of fish dishes are also available. The service is friendly and the ambience is relaxed. Limited wine menu. Closed Mon, Sun lunch.

Key to Symbols *see back cover flap*

LAS PALMAS DE GRAN CANARIA La Hacienda   *Tapas* 目   €€

Edificio Venegas, Profesor Augustín Millares Carló 9, 35003 **Tel** *928 373 197*

The serious approach to food here is accentuated by a minimalist décor. La Hacienda offers creative cuisine with Mediterranean origins, serving dishes such as duck with ginger and moschatel, and cod with fried green tomatoes. For dessert, the *soufflé cremoso* is highly recommended. Try the *menú de degustación* at lunchtime. Closed Sun.

LAS PALMAS DE GRAN CANARIA Kamakura   目 🍴   €€€

C/Galileo Galieli 4, 35010 **Tel** *928 222 670*

At this small Japanese restaurant near the Playa de las Canteras, diners can sit at the sushi bar or at one of the tables. The specialities here include *tempura* (lightly battered vegetables and prawns), fish tartar with aromatic herbs and *sashimi* (slices of raw fish), all served with attention to detail. Closed Mon lunch, Sun.

LAS PALMAS DE GRAN CANARIA La Chacalote   *Tapas* 目🔊🎵📷🍴   €€€

C/Proa 3, 35017 **Tel** *928 312 140*

A nautical theme pervades at this large, friendly seafood restaurant with fisherman-themed paraphernalia lining the walls. Established for over 30 years, the restaurant has a loyal clientele of regulars returning for the Spanish cuisine. Fish baked in salt and live shellfish are some of the specialites. Large groups are also catered for.

LAS PALMAS DE GRAN CANARIA La Dolce Vita   🍴   €€€

C/Augustín Millares 5, 35017 **Tel** *928 310 463*

There's no need to guess the theme when you walk into this authentic Italian pizzeria-restaurant. Italian movie posters line the walls and the menu is crammed with all manner of excellent fresh pasta dishes. Vegetarians will find a good choice of non-meat dishes too. There's a good selection of wines. Closed Sun & Wed evening.

LAS PALMAS DE GRAN CANARIA Cho-Zacarias   *Tapas* 目🔊📷🍴   €€€€

Audiencia 7, Vegueta, 35001 **Tel** *928 331 374*

Canarian antiques festoon the walls of this beautifully elegant restaurant set in an historical house within the old quarter of Vegueta. Serving traditional home-cooked Canarian dishes, it has deservedly earned an excellent reputation. The wine cellar is the envy of many island restaurateurs, with its stunning array of Spain's finest labels. Closed Mon, Sun.

LAS PALMAS DE GRAN CANARIA La Marinera   目🔊📷   €€€€

Alonso Quesada, S/A Plaza de la Puntilla, 35017 **Tel** *928 468 802*

One of the best restaurants in the resort, La Marinera offers excellent quality food and service, as well as stunning views over Las Canteras beach. The fish is sourced from local fishing boats and is of the best quality. A large terrace seats 250 diners and private dining rooms are also available.

LAS PALMAS DE GRAN CANARIA Mesón La Cuadra   *Tapas* 目🔊   €€€€

C/General Mas Gaminda, 32, 35018 **Tel** *928 243 380*

A beautiful restaurant with a menu to match. Many of the dishes include home-grown ingredients produced by the owner himself. The chef specializes in traditional Castillian and Canarian dishes such as watercress soup, roast lamb and grilled sea bass. There's a decent selection of wines on offer, mostly Spanish. Closed Mon.

LAS PALMAS DE GRAN CANARIA Rias Bajas   *Tapas* 目🍴   €€€€

C/Simon Bolivar 3, 35007 **Tel** *928 271 316*

Renowned as one of the capital's top dining venues, this Galician restaurant in the heart of the nightlife area provides an oasis of luxury and calm. High quality seafood dishes are the speciality at Rias Bajas, and the wine list is as impressive as the food menu.

LAS PALMAS DE GRAN CANARIA Amaiur   目📷🍴   €€€€€

C/Pérez Galdós 2, 35002 **Tel** *928 370 717*

Housed in a 19th-century colonial home in the Barrio de Triana, this restaurant is run by two brothers who offer traditional Basque cooking with innovations, depending upon the fresh market produce available. Among the tempting items on the menu are foie gras with grape sauce and Armagnac, and hake with seafood. Closed Sun.

LAS PALMAS DE GRAN CANARIA Casa de Galicia   目🍴   €€€€€

C/Salvador Cuyás 8, 35008 **Tel** *928 279 855*

With ingredients regularly flown in from Galicia, this restaurant goes to great lengths to recreate a taste of this historic region. The restaurant is very popular with locals who come to enjoy various meat pies and stews, as well as excellent seafood. There's an extensive wine list.

LAS PALMAS DE GRAN CANARIA El Novillo Precoz   目🔊🍴   €€€€€

C/Portugal, 35017 **Tel** *928 221 659*

Fillet steak cooked over a wood-burning grill is the number one dish in this popular family-run restaurant. Established over 30 years ago, El Novillo Precoz is something of an institution with locals. Booking is therefore advisable, especially for Sunday lunch. Closed Mon.

LAS PALMAS DE GRAN CANARIA La Sama   目🔊📷🍴   €€€€€

C/Marina 87, 35016 **Tel** *928 321 428*

Situated in the harbour area of San Cristobal, this seafood restaurant specializes, though not exclusively, in preparing various dishes with its namesake, a locally caught fish from the snapper family. Whether baked, fried or salted, the quality is always of a good standard. Car park and disabled access available.

Key to Price Guide *see p171* **Key to Symbols** *see back cover flap*

LAS PALMAS DE GRAN CANARIA 17°

🗐 🕭 🎵 🎠 🍴 €€€€€

Paseo de Tomás Morales 14, 35003 **Tel** *928 384 475*

Located in the heart of Las Palmas and close to the university, this highly regarded restaurant serves creative cuisine with Canarian, Colombian and Portuguese influences. Dishes include parrot fish steamed in banana leaves and oxtail with rosemary mash. The décor is white and pastel with bare stone walls. Closed Sun, Aug.

MASPALOMAS Chili

🗐 🕭 €€

Avda. de Tenerife 17, 35100 **Tel** *928 770 047*

If you like your food hot and spicy, try this Tex-Mex restaurant where the bright décor matches the colourful Mexican food. Expect to find the usual assortment of *nachos, tacos* and *fajitas*. The staff are friendly and provide special meals, games and other distractions for young children. Closed May.

MASPALOMAS El Portalon

🗐 🕭 🎵 🎠 🍴 €€€€€

Avda. Tirajana 27, 35100 **Tel** *928 772 030*

Specializing in Basque cuisine, this excellent restaurant within the Hotel Barbacan provides good quality food and service. A garden terrace provides outside seating for al fresco dining. The leg of lamb stuffed with foie gras and truffles, and the tropical fruit sorbets are highly recommended. Good wine list.

MASPALOMAS Orangerie

🗐 🕭 🎠 🍴 €€€€€

Hotel Palm Beach, Avenida Oasis, 35100 **Tel** *928 140 806*

Considered by many to be one of the best restaurants on the island (*see p169*), Orangerie is situated within the Hotel Palm Beach and offers both inside and outside dining. Contemporary and creative, the well-presented dishes show off an imaginative use of international and local ingredients. Closed Tue, Thu & Sun.

MOGÁN Acaymo

Tapas 🕭 🎠 €€

El Tostador 14, 35138 **Tel** *928 569 263*

In the pretty village of Mogán, this simple rustic restaurant offers creative Canarian cuisine and international meat and fish dishes. Those less hungry can order a selection of tapas. Reservations are recommended for Sunday lunch. Good parking. Limited wine list. Closed Mon, Sun dinner.

PLAYA DEL INGLÉS Las Cumbres

🗐 🕭 🍴 €€€

Avda. Tirajana 11, 35100 **Tel** *928 760 941*

Farming tools and other rustic accessories furnish the interior of this pretty beach-side restaurant serving traditional Canarian dishes. Although its local fame stems from its succulent lamb dishes, the menu also includes excellent seafood. If you have room afterwards, don't miss the *Crema Catalana*. Closed Tue & May.

PUERTO DE MOGÁN Tu Casa

Tapas 🗐 🕭 🍴 €€€

Avda. de las Artes 18, 35120 **Tel** *928 565 078*

At this friendly restaurant situated next to the golden sands of Mogán Beach, diners can either eat inside or on a large covered terrace. Tu Casa is famed for its *paella*, and for the home-grown tropical fruits served as a dessert or as a thick, creamy milkshake.

SAN AUGUSTÍN Anno Domini

🗐 🕭 🎠 🍴 €€€€€

Centro Comercial, Local 82–85, 35100 **Tel** *928 762 915*

Owner and chef Jacques Truyol manages to maintain an air of elegance at this impeccable French restaurant situated in a busy and somewhat chaotic shopping centre. Try the Burgundy-style snails or *tournedos rossini* with a glass of wine from the excellent wine list. Closed Sun & Sep.

SANTA BRIGIDA Las Grutas de Artiles

Tapas 🕭 🎵 🎠 🍴 €€

Las Meleguinas, Valle de la Angostura, 35300 **Tel** *928 640 575*

This restaurant is part of a leisure complex built around two natural caves and various outdoor spaces, including terraces and a pool. The food is Canarian, with specialities including *pescado al mojo verde* (fish with a spicy green sauce) and *buñuelos de plátano al vino tinto* (banana dumplings in red wine). There are pool-side tables.

SANTA BRIGIDA Bentayga

Tapas 🗐 🕭 🎠 🍴 €€€

Carretera del Centro 130, 35308 **Tel** *928 355 186*

This large, family-run restaurant is always packed at the weekend with local families, drawn by the friendly service and the huge range of dishes. Recipes are based on local cuisine but fused with more international flavours. The fillet steak is particularly good. Children can choose from their own menu. Large parties are welcomed.

SANTA BRIGIDA Satautey

🗐 🕭 €€€€€

Real de Coello 2, Monte Lentiscal, 35310 **Tel** *928 355 511*

Based in the Hotel Santa Brigida, the restaurant of this hotel training school has an excellent reputation for fine food prepared by the eager and inventive students. The Canarian starter selection provides a fine introduction to some of the more popular dishes found on the island. The desserts are also highly regarded. Open Fri, Sat & Sun.

VEGA DE SAN MATEO La Veguetilla

Tapas 🕭 🎠 €€€

Ctra. General del Centro 20 km, 35328 **Tel** *928 660 764*

A spacious chalet-type restaurant with wooden beams and an outside terrace with garden. The menu is a combination of international dishes and Canarian cuisine. Specialities include pumpkin stuffed with cod, fillet steak in green pepper sauce and *sole meunière*.

FUERTEVENTURA

BETANCURIA Valtarajal
♿ 🎵 🔳 €

Roberto Roldán s/n, 35510 **Tel** *928 878 007*

For a true Canarian dish try the *carne de cabra*, or goat meat, at this down-to-earth restaurant. Located in one of the prettiest areas of the island, what the interior lacks in sophistication, the staff make up for in friendliness. Popular with local families, this is the place to sample a taste of authentic island cooking. Open lunch only. Closed Wed.

BETANCURIA Casa Santa María
Tapas 🍽 ♿ 🔳 €€€€€

Plaza de la Concepción, 35510 **Tel** *928 878 036*

Situated on the same square as the 15th-century Iglesia de Santa María, this restaurant-museum in a 16th-century house is worth a visit. It has its own bodega and a garden. Try the traditional *puchero canario* (Canarian stew) and for dessert, the *crema Canaria*. Reservations only. Closed Mon.

CORRALEJO Gibson's Continental Restaurant
📑 🔳 €

Juan Sebastián, 35660 **Tel** *636 029 696*

This popular family restaurant offers a large menu with an eclectic theme, from traditional British food like fish and chips to Indian curries and Mexican *fajitas*. Vegetarians are well catered for and there's a children's menu. The staff are young, friendly and entertaining. Take-away service also available. Closed Wed.

CORRALEJO Cofradia de Pescadores
Tapas 🔳 €€

Muelle Chico 5, 35660 **Tel** *928 867 773*

The atmosphere is always lively at this fishermen's cooperative situated on the town beach, overlooking Corralejo Bay. It is ideal for families as children can play in the sand while parents eat in peace. Very reasonably priced fresh fish is the speciality. The choice of wines is limited.

CORRALEJO La Marquesina
Tapas 🍽 ♿ 🔳 €€

Muelle Chico, 35660 **Tel** *928 535 435*

This family-friendly restaurant offers stunning views over Corralejo's town beach and bay. The international menu features grilled meat and fresh fish with a Canarian twist. The lobster is very popular and, like everything else here, is reasonably priced. Limited selection of wines.

COSTA CALMA Don Quijote
Tapas 🍽 ♿ 🔳 🍴 €€€€

Apartamento Santa Ursula s/n, 35627 **Tel** *928 875 158*

Dine like a medieval lord at this elegant, award-winning restaurant furnished with suits of armour and coats of arms. Roast suckling pig and roast lamb are two of the recommended specialities. There's a terrace for outside dining. It's expensive, but worth it. Closed Sun.

JANDIA–PAJARA El Marinero Esquinzo
🔳 €€€€

Montaña de la Muda 2, 35628 **Tel** *928 544 075*

Located within the lush, tropical grounds of El Quinzo Aparthotel, this international restaurant is open to hotel guests and visitors. Diners can eat in the simply furnished restaurant or at the outside tables. Italian cuisine dominates the menu, and both the food and the service are generally of a good standard. Limited wine list. Open evenings only.

PLAYA BLANCA L'Artista
🍽 ♿ 🔳 🍴 €€

C/ La Tegal, 18–20, 35570 **Tel** *928 517 578*

This authentic pizza and pasta restaurant occupies two storeys on the sea front. Fresh pasta is the speciality of the house, but the *pizza artista* is just as good. Go for the views and the lively ambience. There is also a sister restaurant in Puerto del Carmen.

PUERTO DEL ROSARIO Benjamín
Tapas €€

C/León y Castillo 139, 35600 **Tel** *928 851 748*

A large selection of authentic island cuisine is served at this small and inexpensive Canarian restaurant. The service is efficient, the ambience relaxed and the quality of the food is consistent. Particularly recommended are the spicy *mojo* sauce, the goats' cheese and the prickly pear sorbet. Limited wine menu. Open for lunch only. Closed Sun, public hols.

PUERTO DEL ROSARIO La Barca del Pescador
🍽 ♿ 🔳 🍴 €€€€

Franchi Roca, El Castillo, Caleta de Fuste, 35510 **Tel** *928 163 500*

Built on two levels and decorated with maritime paraphernalia, this restaurant offers traditional cuisine based mainly on fish and seafood brought directly from Galicia. For a starter, try the *crema de berros* (watercress soup), followed by salt-crusted sea bass and for dessert, *tocino de cielo* (caramel custard). Pescador serves classic Spanish wines.

PUERTO DEL ROSARIO La Manduka
🍽 🍴 €€€€

C/Leon y Castillo 3, 35600 **Tel** *928 355 657*

This is a great, if somewhat expensive, choice in the island's capital. The decor is creative, with wall hangings and large abstract paintings adorning the walls and unsual tableware. The menu is inventive too; try the ostrich sirloin with chard, pine nuts and pistachio sauce. Closed Sun.

Key to Price Guide *see p171* **Key to Symbols** *see back cover flap*

LANZAROTE

ARRECIFE Altamar
Arrecife Gran Hotel, Parque Islas Canarias, 35550 **Tel** *928 800 000*

This restaurant is on the top floor of the Arrecife Gran Hotel, the city's only five-star hotel, and the views are excellent. The menu has both Mediterranean and international cuisine, and there's a great selection of local wines. Don't miss the cheesecake for dessert. The service is excellent.

ARRECIFE Castillo de San José
Castillo de San José, Ctra. de Puerto Nao, 35340 **Tel** *928 812 321*

Puerto Nao's converted fortress was built in 1779 and restored by the Lanzarote architect César Manrique in the 1970s. It now houses a contemporary art gallery and a restaurant. Enjoy international and regional specialities as you admire the art and views of the harbour. The reasonably priced menu of the day offers good value.

COSTA TEGUISE Chu-Lin
Centro Comercial Tandarena, local 8, 35509 **Tel** *928 592 011*

A taste of the orient in the heart of Costa Teguise, this popular, well-established Chinese restaurant offers the usual assortment of *chow mein* and *chop suey* dishes, as well as a number of set banquets. All meals are available to eat in or to take away. There's a good selection of wines.

COSTA TEGUISE Neptuno
Tapas
Avda. del Jabillo, Centro Comercial Neptuno, local 6, 35509 **Tel** *928 590 378*

This airy restaurant in a shopping centre serves traditional Canary Islands cooking, accompanied by local wines and cheeses. The menu is strong on all types of meat, but there are also some excellent fresh fish dishes such as *atun adobado al horno* (oven-cooked tuna fish) and *salmón ahumado de Uga* (smoked salmon). Closed Sun, 20 Jun–22 Jul.

COSTA TEGUISE Mesón La Jordana
Centro Comercial de Lanzarote Bay, Avda. de los Geranios, 35509 **Tel** *928 590 328*

King Hussein of Jordan was once a customer at this popular restaurant in one of Costa Teguise's shopping centres. Local fare is given a French touch so one of the starters is Burgundy snails; main courses include stewed partridge, braised duck, and sole with almonds; and desserts include papaya sorbet and *crêpes suzettes*. Closed Sun & Sep.

MACHER La Tegala
C/ de Tias a Yaiza 60, 35572 **Tel** *928 524 524*

An upmarket and fashionable restaurant aimed at the business sector and those who don't mind paying a little more for top-notch Canarian cuisine. La Tegala also has two 12-seater dining rooms available for private parties. Floor-to-ceiling windows afford panoramic views of the coastline and neighbouring Fuerteventura. Closed Mon lunch & Sun.

NAZARET Lagomar
Tapas
C/Los Loros 6, 35509 **Tel** *928 845 665*

A bright, airy restaurant set in a villa designed by César Manrique. The property was once owned by Omar Sharif who lost it in a game of bridge. Lagomar offers Mediterranean cuisine with specialities such as duck *magret* with caramelized apple, and salmon *papillotte*. There's live jazz on Sunday afternoons. Open for lunch only. Closed Mon.

PARQUE NACIONAL DE TIMANFAYA El Diablo
Parque Nacional de Timanfaya, 35509 **Tel** *928 840 057*

Situated right at the heart of the lunar-like Timanfaya National Park, this must be one of the very few restaurants in the world where the food is cooked using the heat from a volcano. Curved windows allow spectacular views of the surrounding moonscape. Children are well catered for. Open 9am–5pm daily.

PLAYA BLANCA Casa Brigida
Tapas
Puerto Marino Rubicon, Playa Blanca, 35570 **Tel** *928 519 190*

At this quaint and intimate restaurant, which specializes in fresh fish and seafood, diners pay reasonable prices for good quality fare and a friendly welcome from the owner. For such a small venue the wine list is surprisingly extensive and includes several of the best Lanzarote labels. Closed Jul.

PLAYA BLANCA Almacen de la Sal
Maritimo 12, 35570 **Tel** *928 517 885*

A former salt storehouse, this unique restaurant overlooking the beach is one of Lanzarote's star attractions. Stone walls, original decorations and live piano music add to an almost ghostly ambience, warmed by the superb service and Segovian cuisine. Shoulder of lamb Segovian style is highly recommended. Terrace seating available.

PLAYA BLANCA La Cocina de Colacho
C/La Destiladera, Castillo de Águila 35580 **Tel** *928 519 691*

Art meets cuisine at this trendy glass-fronted restaurant. Co-owner Anabel Machin is a painter, evident from the many wall hangings. Her husband and chef, Nicolas, also applies an artistic touch to beautifully presented Mediterranean/Canarian fusions such as fillet steak in calvados with caramelized apple, mushrooms and goats cheese. Closed lunch, Sun.

PUERTO DEL CARMEN El Tomate €€

Calle los Jameos, 35510 **Tel** *928 511 985*

Popular and well-established, El Tomate often welcomes visiting dignitaries to its bright, contemporary interior to enjoy international cuisine. The restaurant is famed locally for its delicious Joachim Rosenthal warm green salad with bacon and garlic, and also for its tempting home-made desserts. Booking is advisable. Open daily for dinner only.

PUERTO DEL CARMEN El Asador €€€€

Avda. Varadero s/n, 35510 **Tel** *928 512 821*

Boasting Lanzarote's only wood-burning stove, this typical Spanish carvery is deservedly popular, especially among families. This relaxed and unpretentious restaurant offers good views of the harbour. The undoubted star of the menu is the crispy roast suckling pig, though the spare ribs are also worthy of a special mention.

PUERTO DEL CARMEN La Canada *Tapas* €€€€

C/ César Manrique 3, 35510 **Tel** *928 512 108*

Michelin recommended, this fine dining venue serves a blend of international and traditional Canarian meals. Specialities include flambéed sole with green peppers, and roast lamb. The warm, intimate interior has wooden beamed ceilings, and private rooms are available.

PUERTO DEL CARMEN O Botafumeiro *Tapas* €€€€

C/Alemania 9, Centro Comercial Costa Luz, 35510 **Tel** *928 511 503*

A Galician restaurant with a lively atmosphere created by a regular local following and the very friendly staff. Seafood is the speciality, with flambéed langoustines in cava highly recommended. Meats are also available, including lamb, veal and huge T-bone steaks. A good selection of tapas is also served. Closed Mon.

YAIZA La Casona de Yaiza *Tapas* €€€€

C/ El Rincon 11, 35570 **Tel** *928 836 262*

Once named as the best restaurant in Lanzarote, this small bodega is part of the boutique hotel of the same name. The interior was put together by a group of artists and hotel professionals. The chef creates magical blends of Canarian/ Mediterranean cuisine using many fresh and local products. Closed Thu.

TENERIFE

ADEJE Restaurante Oasis €

C/El Grande s/n, 38670 **Tel** *922 780 827*

The town of Adeje is famed for its garlic chicken restaurants. While Oasis may not be the smartest, it's secret recipe chicken is one of the best. It offers simple furnishings, simple service and exceptionally tasty poultry (the only option on the menu) at bargain prices. There's a small pavement terrace but watch your elbows on the passing cars. Closed Wed.

ARONA Mesón Las Rejas €€€

Ctra. General del Sur, 1, La Camella, 38626 **Tel** *922 720 894*

This highly regarded restaurant is considered to be one of the most elegant eateries in the south. Canarian artefacts and furniture bedeck the vaulted dining room. The owner is rightly proud of his cellar, which contains a selection of over 200 fine Spanish wines. Specialities include fillet steak baked in salt, and roast wild boar. Closed Sun & Jul.

LA CAMELLA Verna's Restaurante €€€€€

Calle General 21, 38627 **Tel** *922 725 643*

This relaxed and friendly restaurant is located in the hills above the village of La Camella. The menu has the usual favourites, such as steak, fish and paella, but also features authentic Canarian dishes. The chef's specials are always worth a try. Fresh and local produce is used as much as possible and there's a good wine list. Closed Mon.

BUENAVISTA El Burgado *Tapas* €

Avda. Playa de las Arenas s/n **Tel** *922 127 831*

With stunning views of the Atlantic Ocean, this seafood restaurant serves up an impressive array of fresh fish caught daily, *paella* and other rice dishes. Try one of the many simple, freshly prepared fish dishes or an authentic Canarian dessert at this traditional coastal restaurant.

CANDELARIA El Archete *Tapas* €€€

Calle Arola 2, 38530 **Tel** *922 500 115*

This Canarian-themed restaurant manages to exude a rustic elegance, with tabletop candelabras and timber ceilings. Marinated rabbit and salted cod are two of the specialites. The owner takes great pride in his wine collection. Unusually for Tenerife, a large private car park is available for diners.

EL SAUZAL Casa Del Vino La Baranda *Tapas* €€€€

Autopista General del Norte 21 km (Enlace de El Sauzal, La Baranda), 38360 **Tel** *922 563 886*

Tenerife's wine industry is explained by this museum in an old house on the northwest coast near Tacoronte. There's also a restaurant that serves modern Canary Islands cuisine based on fresh local market produce though, of course, the wine is the centre of attention here. There are sometimes concerts in summer on the central patio. Closed Mon.

Key to Price Guide *see p171* **Key to Symbols** *see back cover flap*

GRANADILLA DE ABONA Bodega El Jable

Tapas 📋 ♿ 🍴   €€€€€

C/ Betejüi 9, San Isidro, 38611 **Tel** *922 390 698*

This Canary Islands' eatery serves both traditional and creative cooking, with the emphasis on fish dishes. The menu includes *potaje de berros*, warm fish salad with thyme, and bass with tomato vinaigrette and lentils. Try the *tarta de millo* for dessert. Only local wines are served here. Open every evening and Mon and Tues lunch. Evenings only. Closed Oct.

GUIA DE ISORA El Patio

📋 ♿ 🎵 🎰 🍴 🍴   €€€€€

Abama Hotel Resort, Guia de Isora, 38687 **Tel** *922 126 000*

The restaurant of the luxurious Abama Hotel Resort (*see p162*) provides an enchanting setting for a special, but overpriced, evening. Imaginative, modern dishes are created using local produce. Try the lobster on a pyramid of fresh pasta or the roasted young pigeon with walnut cream and wild mushroom sauce. Booking recommended. Closed lunch & Tue.

LA CALETA Restaurante La Vieja

Tapas 📋 ♿ 🍴   €€€€€

La Caleta 4, 38670 **Tel** *922 711 548*

This is the best of a cluster of seafood restaurants in the fishing village of La Caleta. The nautical-themed interior features a gaily painted fishing boat as a bar, crisp linens deck the tables, and there's a sea-facing terrace for al fresco dining. A fish of the same name, *vieja*, is just one of the local specialities. Closed Tue from May–Sep.

LA CALETA Rosso Sul Mare

♿ 🍴 🍴   €€€€€

Avenida Las Gaviotas 4, La Caleta, 38670 **Tel** *922 782 374*

This is a stylish Italian restaurant overlooking La Caleta Bay. It's great for lunch or dinner or just a drink with sea view. Dishes include warm octopus with new potatoes or lobster spaghetti. A kids' play park at the side of the restaurant makes this a good choice for families too.

LA MATANZA Casa Juan

Tapas ♿ 🍴   €€€

C/Acentejo 77, 38370 **Tel** *922 577 012*

This friendly, family-run restaurant focuses on home-smoked fish and various grilled meats, but vegetarians are also catered for. A large garden, log fire and elegant table settings exude a country-house atmosphere, but without the stuffiness. Children will enjoy the play area among the banana palms. Closed Mon, Sun & May.

LOS ABRIGOS Los Roques

📋 🍴 🍴   €€€€€

Calle Marina 16, Los Abrigos, 38618 **Tel** *922 749 401*

At Los Roques, Mediterranean cuisine is fused with Moroccan and Asian influences. With excellent food, great wine list and a fantastic sunset-viewing terrace, this is the perfect dusk dining venue. The king scallops stuffed with foie gras, and the tiger prawn and lobster *tangine* are highly recommended. Booking advisable. Closed Mon, Sun & Jun.

LOS CRISTIANOS La Tasca de mi Abuelo

Tapas 🍽 ♿ 🍴 🍴   €€€

Centro Comercial San Marino, local 13, 38660 **Tel** *922 794 466*

This tiny restaurant has no menu – the proprietor sits with diners and tells them the day's specials. Typical Castillian and Canarian dishes are cooked to order. Tapas are also available and surprisingly for such a tiny venue, there's also a very good selection of wines. On Friday evenings the owner entertains on his guitar. Closed Sun.

LOS CRISTIANOS The Surrey Arms

🍴   €€€

Paloma Beach, 38660 **Tel** *922 797 070*

A taste of Britain at the very edge of Los Cristianos. Expect all the old teatime favourites, but don't miss Paco's flambéed steak speciality. This pub-style restaurant has a lively atmosphere, friendly and efficient service, and is very reasonably priced. Closed Wed.

LOS REALEJOS La Finca

Tapas ♿ 🍴 🍴   €€€

El Monturio 12, 38410 **Tel** *922 362 143*

This award-winning restaurant in the north is famed not only for its tapas, but also for its creative main course dishes. The interior has a nautical theme with walls covered by parts of boats, fishing nets and other marine bric-a-brac. It's unsurprising then that seafood features highly on the menu. Closed Sun & Jun.

PALM MAR Rancho El Palm Mar

♿ 🍴   €

Ctra. Palm Mar–Guaza, 38627 **Tel** *922 732 424*

This off-the-beaten-track, rustic ranch-style eatery is hugely popular with large groups and parties who come for its friendly and lively ambience and good-value food. The menu is commendable for its variety and low prices, featuring fish, grilled meats and pasta. Closed Tue.

PLAYA DE LA ARENA Casa Pancho

♿ 🍴 🍴   €€€€€

C/Playa de la Arena, 38683 **Tel** *922 861 323*

Pancho's boasts possibly one of the most delightful settings in the south, with its magnificent terrace garden facing the ocean. It serves creative Canarian and Spanish cuisine, with the emphasis on seafood, and the home-made desserts are highly recommended. An air-conditioned cellar houses over 200 labels. Closed Mon & Jun.

PLAYA DE LAS AMERICAS Bianco

📋 ♿ 🍴 🍴   €€€

Centro Comercial Safari, Playa de Las Americas, 38670 **Tel** *922 788 697*

This contemporary restaurant is located in the heart of the Playa de las Americas. There are two menus; one is Italian and wide-ranging, with pasta, meat and fish and the other, served in an all-white room, serves Mediterranean dishes such as crayfish carpaccio with salmon eggs or a champagne risotto with cheese gratin and strawberry coulis.

PUERTO DE LA CRUZ La Gañania   *Tapas* 🖹 ♿ 🚻 🍴   €€€
Camino Del Durazno 11, 38400 **Tel** *922 371 000*

One of Puerto de la Cruz's top restaurants, La Gañania is a large restaurant surrounded by gardens and favoured by many a happy couple for their wedding banquet. The menu is a little limited, but typifies traditional Canarian cuisine with the odd creative surprise thrown in. There's a good selection of local wines. Closed Mon, Tue.

PUERTO DE LA CRUZ Régulo   *Tapas* 🖹 ♿ 🚻 🍴   €€€
C/ Pérez Zamora 14, 38400 **Tel** *922 384 506*

In an old house dating from the 18th century, with an agreeable inner patio, Régulo is close to the Plaza del Charco in the centre of town. The menu is noted for its locally caught grilled fish and Argentinian roast lamb. Try the fig mousse for dessert. Closed Sun.

PUERTO DE LA CRUZ Magnolia   🖹 🚻 🍴   €€€€
Avda. Marques de Villanueva del Prado, 38400 **Tel** *922 385 614*

Catalan and international dishes are served in this informal yet smart restaurant close to the Hotel Botánico (*see p164*). Specialities include *carpaccio* of salmon and hake, fillet steak stuffed with avocados and prawns, and roast shoulder of lamb. The service is friendly and the wine list adequate. Closed Tue.

SAN JUAN DE LA RAMBLA Las Aguas   *Tapas* 🚻 🍴   €€€
La Destila 20, 38420 **Tel** *922 360 428*

One of only two restaurants in the area, Las Aguas draws a regular clientele from the island's capital to savour its spectacular rice dishes. With a cosy interior and sea-front terrace, the restaurant provides a pretty setting for both lunch and dinner. Las Aguas boasts a good selection of Spanish and local wines. Closed Mon, Sun.

SAN MIGUEL DE ABONA Los Braseros Criollos   *Tapas* 🖹 🎵 🚻 🍴   €€€€€
Cruce Las Chafiras 62 km, 38620 **Tel** *922 735 137*

Typically Canarian in both décor and menu, this fine steak restaurant situated in the developing commercial area of Las Chafiras is a carnivore's paradise. Large slabs of meat are cooked in front of you at your table. The home-made desserts are highly recommended. Closed Wed & Apr.

SANTA CRUZ DE TENERIFE Cofradía de Pescadores   *Tapas* ♿ 🚻   €
Playa de Teresitas, 38001 **Tel** *922 549 024*

Cheap, cheerful and always buzzing with the sound of local chatter, this small restaurant near Las Teresitas beach is an ideal venue to end the day with a plate of superb fresh seafood and a chilled bottle of wine while watching the sun go down.

SANTA CRUZ DE TENERIFE El Líbano   🖹 ♿   €€
C/Santiago Cuadrado, 26, 38001 **Tel** *922 285 914*

Tucked away on a small side street, this locally popular restaurant has been serving Lebanese food for over 25 years. The interior may be simple but the food certainly isn't, with an extensive menu of exotic Middle Eastern cuisine, ranging from kebabs to stuffed vine leaves. Vegetarians are well catered for.

SANTA CRUZ DE TENERIFE La Hierbita   🖹 ♿ 🍴   €€
El Clavel 19, 38001 **Tel** *922 244 617*

This extremely popular restaurant is housed in a 100-year-old Canarian mansion complete with creaking floorboards and tiny cubby-holes. The high-class Canarian cuisine and extensive wine list draw both locals and visitors alike. For a lofty street view, reserve one of the secluded balcoy tables well in advance. Closed Sun.

SANTA CRUZ DE TENERIFE Viva Mexico   🖹 ♿   €€
C/Santa Clara 8, 38002 **Tel** *922 296 088*

If you like your food with a little zing, you'd be hard pressed to find a more fitting restaurant in the island's capital. The typically Tex-Mex menu matches the tasteful Mexican themed interior. Children are catered for with their own menu. Closed Mon.

SANTA CRUZ DE TENERIFE Da Gigi   🖹 ♿ 🚻 🍴   €€€
Avda. De Anaga 43, 38001 **Tel** *922 242 017*

A classic Italian restaurant in the heart of Santa Cruz de Tenerife dishing up the usual pasta and pizza plus a selection of Mexican offerings such as *burritos* and *enchiladas*. In addition to the large interior, there's an outside terrace, but it's only for those who don't mind dining next to a constant flow of traffic.

SANTA CRUZ DE TENERIFE El Solarijo   🖹 ♿   €€€
C/General Goded 11, 38006 **Tel** *922 293 249*

A union of Basque cuisine, with the emphasis on multiple ways of cooking cod, and Canarian ideas. Try the toast served with home-made foie gras and onion marmalade and, instead of fish, order the *cerdo iberico en salsa de vino tinto* (pork in red wine sauce). End with *tarta de queso fresco y mango* (cheesecake with mango). Closed Sun dinner.

SANTA CRUZ DE TENERIFE Marisquería de Ramón   *Tapas* 🖹 ♿ 🍴   €€€
C/Dique 23, 38002 **Tel** *922 549 308*

This simple and clean restaurant near Las Teresitas beach, just outside Santa Cruz de Tenerife, won't win any awards for interior design, but the live seafood, *paellas* and rice dishes are regarded as some of the best in the north. This fact is reflected in the relatively high prices.

Key to Price Guide *see p171* **Key to Symbols** *see back cover flap*

SANTA CRUZ DE TENERIFE La Cazuela
Tapas 📋 🖥 📶 €€€€

C/Robayna 34, 38004 **Tel** *922 272 300*

Situated in a pretty, historic house, this reputable restaurant in the old quarter of the island's capital has aquired a faithful following from lovers of fine food. It specializes in creative Basque cuisine using local Canarian produce. Try the grilled tuna steak with fried garlic and Tenerifian black potatoes. Excellent wine cellar. Closed Sun.

SANTA CRUZ DE TENERIFE Rasoi
📋 €€€€

Rambla de General Franco 25, 38006 **Tel** *922 244 505*

Meaning "The Kitchen" in Hindi, this ornate Indian restaurant has quickly gained a huge and loyal following in Santa Cruz. The signature dish is *murgh pastoom*, butter chicken with a creamy tomato sauce, but this is just one of the many dishes that have earned the restaurant its fine reputation.

SANTA CRUZ DE TENERIFE El Coto Antonio
📋 🎵 📶 €€€€€

C/ Perdon 13, 38006 **Tel** *922 272 105*

One of Tenerife's most celebrated restaurants where you can expect excellent food and good service but, of course, there is a price to match. This is a serious place which welcomes business people and VIPs. The black potato salad with salt cod, peppers and olive oil, and the bass in a coriander sauce are favourites. Closed Sun dinner, Sep.

SANTA CRUZ DE TENERIFE Los Menceyes
Tapas 📋 ♿ 🎵 📶 €€€€€

Avda. Dr. José Naveiras, 38, 38001 **Tel** *922 609 900*

Situated in the upmarket Sheraton Mencey Hotel (*see p164*), this restaurant is often the choice of visiting dignitaries and high-flying businessmen whether staying at the hotel or not. The food more than lives up to the classically elegant décor, with dishes such as sea bass on puff pastry from the award-winning chef. Open every evening from 8pm.

SANTA CRUZ DE TENERIFE Mesón Castellano
Tapas 📋 📶 €€€€€

C/Callao Lima, 4, 38002 **Tel** *922 271 074*

This basement restaurant specializes in Castillian meat and fish dishes, with a particular emphasis on sausage-based recipes. The prices aren't cheap but you are rewarded with the quality of cooking and lively atmosphere. The roast veal is highly recommended. Closed Sun evenings and Aug.

TACORONTE Los Limoneros
📋 ♿ 📶 €€€€€

Ctra. General del Norte 15.5 km Los Naranjeros, 38350 **Tel** *922 636 637*

At this starched linen and shiny silverware restaurant, set in an old Canarian house, the menu is international, the service impeccable and the furnishings regal. Los Limoneros is rightly held in high regard among the island's gastronomes. A private car park is available to diners. Closed Sun evening.

LA GOMERA

AGULO La Vieja Escuela
Tapas ♿ €

C/Poeta Trujillo Armas 2, 38830 **Tel** *922 146 004*

The old village school, a charming whitewashed cottage with beamed ceilings, is home to this simple restaurant-bar. Try typical local dishes, including home-made soups, fresh seafood, goat and *almogrote*, a piquant pâté made with cured Gomeran cheese, tomatoes and hot pepper. Closed Sun.

PLAYA DE SANTIAGO El Laurel
Tapas 🎵 🖥 📶 €€€€

Lomada de Tecina **Tel** *922 145 850*

At this award-winning à la carte restaurant within the sprawling Jardín Tecina hotel complex (*see p164*), polished cutlery and starched tablecloths are combined with rustic stone walls and beamed ceilings. Diners can enjoy the lovely views of the ocean and tropical gardens. Reservations recommended.

SAN SEBASTIÁN DE LA GOMERA Casa del Mar
Tapas 📋 ♿ €

Avda. Fred Olsen 2, 38800 **Tel** *922 870 320*

Harbourside family-owned restaurant serving simple and reasonably priced seafood dishes and traditional Canarian meals. Take your pick from stews, *paella* or grilled catch of the day. This is an ideal friendly spot to catch a bite while waiting for the ferry. There's a very limited wine selection but a good choice of spirits. Closed Tue.

SAN SEBASTIÁN DE LA GOMERA El Charcon
🖥 €€

Playa de Cuevilla, 38800 **Tel** *922 141 898*

Eat in a cave in this curious little seafood restaurant, which is built into a rock face close to the harbour. As well as a good selection of high quality fish dishes, the restaurant has great views of the ocean and the neighbouring island of Tenerife. Closed Mon, Sun.

SAN SEBASTIÁN DE LA GOMERA El Silbo
Tapas ♿ 🖥 €€

Ctra General 102, Hermigua, 38800 **Tel** *922 880 304*

This restaurant on the Hermigua beach offers no-frills dining. Instead, it serves simple food and a small selection of mainstream wines. For a typical lunchtime meal, you can start with the *croquetas de pescado* (fish croquettes), followed by *filetes de atun en adobo* (tuna fish in sauce) and finish with bananas covered with the local palm honey.

SAN SEBASTIÁN DE LA GOMERA Meson el Pejin €

Avda. Colon 26, 38800 **Tel** *922 870 033*

At this great little seafood restaurant in the heart of the island's pint-sized capital diners can expect a limited array of inexpensive but delicious fish dishes, including *paella*. The jolly owner and chef occasionally entertain with impromptu musical performances. Closed Wed & Jun.

SAN SEBASTIÁN DE LA GOMERA Cuatro Caminos €€€

Ruiz de Padrón 36, San Sebastian, 38800 **Tel** *922 141 260*

This is the place for no-frills Canarian cooking at a reasonable price, served in a tiny patio dining room. It's not fancy and it's not haute cuisine, but it offers value for money. Dishes include stews and soups, grilled meats and Castilian specialities like *cochinillo* (piglet).

SAN SEBASTIÁN DE LA GOMERA Hotel Parador de la Gomera *Tapas* 🗏 🕭 🖩 🖫 €€€€€

Llano de la Horca, 38800 **Tel** *922 871 100*

An elegant air-conditioned restaurant within the a *parador* overlooking San Sebastián (*see p165*). Waiting staff in traditional costume and traditional Canarian dishes add to the authentic experience. The somewhat limited menu is centred around seafood – try the sea bass baked in salt.

VALLE DEL GRAN REY El Palmarejo *Tapas* 🗏 🖩 €€

Ctra. General De Arure s/n **Tel** *922 805 868*

A restaurant and panoramic viewpoint with stunning views of the lush Valle Gran Rey. The restaurant is also a cooking school for young chefs who manage to consistently produce creative spins on traditional Canarian recipes. Reservations are recommended for a "table with a view". Closed Sun, Jun.

EL HIERRO

FRONTERA Restaurant La Maceta *Tapas* 🖩 €€

C/Las Lajas, 38911 **Tel** *922 556 020*

Although it has an enclosed dining room, eating al fresco within view of the area's natural saltwater swimming pools is the best way to appreciate this ocean-front restaurant. La Maceta specializes in locally caught fresh fish and traditional Canarian dishes. Service is friendly. Limited wine selection. Closed Mon.

FRONTERA El Pollo Asado *Tapas* 🕭 🖩 €€€

C/Las Lajas 4B, 38911 **Tel** *922 555 051*

This cheap and cheerful bar-restaurant offers a rustic dining experience with great local cooking. Simple Canarian tapas include goats' cheese, flaming sausages and sweet black pudding. The real speciality is roast chicken, flavoured with a "secret" blend of local herbs and spices. Terrace seating available. Closed Mon.

LA RESTINGA Casa Juan *Tapas* 🕭 €

Juan Gutiérrez Monteverde 23, 38915 **Tel** *922 557 102*

Located 23 km (14 miles) from Valverde, this hugely popular restaurant always seems packed with local families, especially at weekends. Although the simple, unfussy furnishings match the style of cooking, the food is exceptional. Try the fresh fish of the day, usually *vieja* or *cherne*, served with the ubiquitous spicy *mojo* sauce. Closed Jan and Wed in winter.

LAS PLAYAS Parador del Hierro *Tapas* 🗏 🕭 🖩 🖫 €€€€

Las Playas s/n, Valverde 38900 **Tel** *922 558 036*

In an unbeatable setting, sitting on top of a hill overlooking the crashing Atlantic Ocean, this restaurant offers elegant dining, suitable for a special occasion. It specializes in local cuisine and has a sizeable collection of good local and national wines. Unusual dishes include fish rissoles in limpet and sea urchin sauce, and cheese soup.

VALVERDE El Mirador de la Peña *Tapas* 🖫 €

Ctra. General Norte 40, Guarazoca, 38900 **Tel** *922 550 300*

This house hanging from a rock on the north coast of the island with spectacular views of the Valle del Golfo was designed by celebrated Canarian architect César Manrique. It serves typical El Hierro food such as *ensalada templada de ventresca de bonito* (warm tuna salad) and *mousse de gofio*, made with the typical Guanche cereal.

VALVERDE La Higuera de la Abuela 🕭 🖩 €€€

C/Tajaniscaba 10, Echedo, 38900 **Tel** *922 551 026*

Some 10 km (6 miles) to the north of Valverde, in a low-lying building with colourful walls and a courtyard planted with cactuses, sits La Higuera de la Abuela. It serves no-frills traditional, home-made island cooking, notably *cordero herreño a la herreña* (El Hierro lamb in El Hierro style) and a variety of local fish. Closed Thu.

VALVERDE La Taberna de la Villa *Tapas* 🗏 🖫 €€€

Ctra. General Rodriguez y Sanchez Espinola, 10 **Tel** *922 551 907*

This lively rustic-style restaurant located in the pedestrian area of Valverde turns into a "pub" after midnight, often with live music. Italian is the theme in the kitchen with good quality fresh pasta, but international dishes are also on offer. Good wine list and excellent choice of beers. Closed Sun.

Key to Price Guide *see p171* **Key to Symbols** *see back cover flap*

LA PALMA

BARLOVENTO La Palma Romántica
Tapas 🚻 🔲   €€€€

Ctra. General Las Llanadas s/n, 38726 **Tel** *922 186 221*

The elegant signature restaurant of the Hotel La Palma Romántica is located half an hour's drive from Santa Cruz de La Palma. Surrounded by lush tropical gardens, the restaurant serves a wide range of good quality Canarian and international dishes. The service is pleasant and relaxed.

BREÑA ALTA Las Tres Chimeneas
🚻 🔲   €€

C/Buenavista de Arriba 82, 38710 **Tel** *922 429 470*

Situated on the main road from Santa Cruz to Los Llanos, this is a pleasant little restaurant but with pretensions of grandeur, both in décor and price. The menu offers a wide range of Canarian meat and fish dishes and a splendid assortment of desserts – the chocolate cake is highly recommended. Closed Mon dinner, Tue.

BREÑA ALTA La Fontana
🔲 🔲   €€€

Los Cancajos, 38710 **Tel** *922 434 729*

This beachside restaurant offers good value for money meat and fish dishes. Try the catch of the day served with a home-made coriander sauce, or Canarian specialities such as *rancho Canaria* – a thick vegetable stew – or *cabrito al horno* – roast baby goat. There's a terrace for al fresco dining. Closed Mon.

EL PASO Franchipani
Tapas   €€€

Ctra. General Empalma Dos Pinos 57, 38750 **Tel** *922 402 305*

The all-girl staff create a cheery ambience in this stylish yet homely restaurant. Most of the ingredients in the international dishes are organic, and the cuisine is creative and well-presented. Try the pork tenderloin in a blue cheese and fig sauce for both a flavourful and a visual treat. Separate vegetarian menu. Closed Thu, Fri.

LOS LLANOS DE ARIDANE El Bernegal
€€€

C/Díaz Suárez 5, Santo Domingo, Garafia, 38760 **Tel** *922 400 480*

This restaurant, sited in an old house with an inner patio on the west coast of the island, serves traditional Canary Islands' cuisine and vegetarian dishes, notably *potaje de berros* and, if you like kid, *cabrito palmero*. For dessert there is *delicias con naranja* (a kind of biscuit with orange). Closed mid-May–early Jul. Closed Mon.

LOS LLANOS DE ARIDANE San Petronio
🔲 🚻 🔲 🍷   €€€

C/Pino de Santiago 4, 38760 **Tel** *922 462 403*

Although not easy to find, this chalet-style restaurant and guest house is worth the hunt. Italian is the principle theme of the cuisine, but reasonably priced international dishes are also served. Garden and terrace tables are available and car parking is provided for clients. Closed Mon, Sun & Jun.

SANTA CRUZ DE LA PALMA Chipi Chipi
Tapas 🚻 🔲 🍷   €

C/ Velhoco 42, 38700 **Tel** *922 411 024*

Around 6 km (4 miles) out of the island capital, this good-value restaurant with a pretty patio adorned with tropical plants specializes in grilled meats and local dishes such as chickpea soup, roasted cheese with *mojo verde* and kid. It offers a good selection of wines from the island. Private room available. Closed Wed, Sun, Oct–mid-Nov.

SANTA CRUZ DE LA PALMA Pizzeria Alameda
🔲 🔲 🍷   €

C/Perez Camacho, 38700 **Tel** *922 420 865*

Situated in the old quarter of the town, this authentic Italian restaurant offers fresh pasta dishes plus an array of other Italian and international meals, served with a good selection of Italian and Canarian wines. For dessert, the apple strudel is highly recommended. There's a children's menu. Closed Thu.

SANTA CRUZ DE LA PALMA La B del M
Tapas   €€

Álvarez de Abreu 58, 38700 **Tel** *922 415 912*

The name stands for "La Bodeguita del Medio", and this lively bar and restaurant is popular with both locals and tourists alike. Depending on your level of hunger, you can opt for tapas or order off the full menu, which has an assortment of simple but filling Canarian specialities. Closed Sun.

SANTA CRUZ DE LA PALMA La Placeta
🔲 🍷 🎵   €€€

Plazoleta de Borrero 1, 38700 **Tel** *922 415 273*

Athough it is renowned for its vegetarian options, this popular restaurant, located in an 18th-century house, is also a fine place to just sit with a drink and listen to music. A terrace and garden adds to its appeal. The menu also has an appealing selection of fish and rabbit dishes and a good selection of wines. Open for lunch and dinner.

TAZACORTE Playa Mont
Tapas 🚻 🔲 🍷   €

El Puerto, s/n **Tel** *922 480 045*

A hugely popular and award-winning terrace restaurant situated just behind the sweeping black sandy beach of Tazacorte. Fish is the speciality, with the menu boasting a wide choice of seafood. The extensive wine menu is equally impressive. Closed Wed dinner, Thu & Jul.

SHOPPING IN THE CANARY ISLANDS

A s with Spain's other regions, the Canary Islands boast their own culinary specialities. Many tourists buy local delicacies including goat's cheese, rum, wine, palm mead and the delicious *mojo* (ready-made sauce). Potted plants have also recently become popular presents from the islands. These may even include small banana trees, palms and dragon trees. Other souvenirs, such as

Label for Malvasía wine

handicraft products, embroidery and lace, leather goods and pottery, are likewise snapped up as mementos. Some visitors notice a price difference – a remnant of the days when the islands were a duty-free zone. Products such as alcohol, cigarettes, perfumes, sunglasses and electronic equipment are generally cheaper than in mainland Europe and are among the most easily purchased items.

Entrance to the shopping centre at Playa de las Américas

WHERE TO BUY

There are many shopping centres in large towns and around resorts. They offer practically every essential food product and manufactured item, and are less imposing than the megastores you find in Spain and elsewhere. They often include bars and restaurants.

Apart from the large department stores, the resorts have many small shops, offering souvenirs, clothes and cosmetics. They can be found along the main streets and seafront boulevards. There are many electronic equipment shops too. Fixed prices are not set in stone on the islands and it is well worth haggling. Just as numerous as the electronic shops are the *artesanía*

shops, selling souvenirs and handicraft items. Here, too, haggling over the price is almost expected. The local shops in smaller towns and villages are worth checking out, particularly when shopping for food, as they may sell products that do not reach larger towns.

Those wishing to buy local handicraft products can try buying directly from the local artists, at lower prices than at the seaside shops.

OPENING HOURS

Large shopping centres in big towns are generally open from 9am until 9pm Monday to Saturday. Some of the smaller ones may close for siesta, i.e. between 2pm and 5pm and then stay open for another few hours. Many

Traditionally decorated pot from La Orotava

shops, particularly food stores in tourist centres, are open non-stop, until late at night.

Most smaller shops and boutiques do not have such regular opening hours and may close without warning. Also, afternoon closing hours are not fixed. In small towns and villages, where the pace of life is slower, siesta breaks are longer, and shops may close earlier.

HOW TO PAY

Most shops accept major credit cards. The most popular are Visa and MasterCard. When shopping in small provincial shops and bazaars, you should bear in mind that credit cards may be of no use. When venturing outside large towns it is best to carry a certain amount of cash.

African carvings on sale at Teguise market

MARKETS AND BAZAARS

Markets and bazaars are an inherent feature of the Canary Islands' scenery. Markets are held at regular intervals in small towns and generally serve the local population. The articles on offer include food and items of everyday use (at home and on the farm). Prices are usually low; the olives and cheeses are exceptionally tasty.

Bazaars are organized in larger towns, with tourists in mind. They sell mainly handicraft products and island souvenirs. Prices are relatively high, but you can always haggle. A number of the bigger towns also have flea markets once a week, which can sometimes be a good place to pick up a curiosity.

In Gran Canaria and Lanzarote, the bazaar vendors include African traders. They sell goods that have nothing to do with the islands, but are attractive and eye-catching nevertheless.

ART AND HANDICRAFTS

Among the most popular island handicraft products has been the Canary knife (*Cuchillo Canario*). It is not advisable to purchase these, however, as increased airport security means you may not be able to take them home.

The most popular product made of wood is undoubtedly the *timple* – a kind of ukulele. It is also worth taking a look at other products made of wood, such as small boxes, bowls and smoking pipes. Wooden castanets are an especially popular souvenir. Wickerwork is also worth seeking out. Traditional woven baskets and other knick-knacks are on sale virtually everywhere.

Ceramic items on sale are often based on traditional Guanche designs. They include statuettes, beads and countless vessels, including bowls, pots, jugs and vases. They are often decorated in traditional geometric patterns,

Stalls at a weekly bazaar in Puerto de Mogán

typical of the first inhabitants of the islands.

Popular among textiles are embroidery, woollen hand-woven cloths and lace. Many shops offer textile products such as tablecloths, shawls and napkins, which can also be found in bazaars. Some shops have their own workshops, where you can see the products being made. Those interested in ethnography can take home the traditional folk costume.

A jar of palm honey

FOOD AND DRINK

Goat's cheese is one of the traditional Canary food items. The best known are *majorero*, from Fuerteventura, and *herre*, from El Hierro. In small villages you can often buy

Main shopping precinct in Las Palmas

locally made cheese. Here, preference is given to neighbours, with tourists only being offered the surplus.

Popular among alcoholic beverages are rum and its mead version – *ron miel* – as well as sweet Malvasía. Other wines have not gained such recognition with the Spaniards, although the locals are very keen on wines made on Tenerife and Lanzarote.

Another speciality is palm mead, known as *guarapo*, from La Gomera. It is made from palm juice, thickened through boiling.

Many tourists like to take home Canarian sauces – *mojos*. There are several types of them and they can be found in every supermarket.

The Canary Islands are also famous for the production of *puros palmeros* – cigars from La Palma. Although not as well known as the Havana cigars, they are nevertheless highly valued for their flavour and are even purchased for the Royal Court in Madrid.

Supermarkets are often the best place to buy food. They offer a wide variety, at moderate prices.

Another popular gift item is flowers, especially *estrelitsia*, the bird-of-paradise plant. You can buy them on departure ready-packed, from a flower shop or at the airport.

ENTERTAINMENT
IN THE CANARY ISLANDS

Logo of Parque
Las Aguilas

The Canary Islands offer seemingly endless forms of entertainment to tempt tourists. There are plenty of demonstrations of traditional skill on offer, from Spanish and local dancing, to the old custom of *lucha canaria* – wrestling. Typical modern attractions, including bars, nightclubs, casinos, cinemas, theatres and concerts, are likewise much in evidence. A wide variety of holiday entertainment is also on offer. The islands feature many small parks and botanical gardens, with tropical plants and wild animals. A trip in a glass-bottomed boat to see the marine fauna, including dolphins and whales, is a memorable experience, while the many water-parks, with their slides and splash pools, will have children squealing with delight.

Casino in Santa Catalina hotel

INFORMATION

Information regarding cultural events and concerts may often be found in the local press, which advertises them some days in advance. Keep your eyes peeled, too, as many interesting events are advertised on street posters. Other good sources of information are hotel reception foyers and tourist information centres.

NIGHTLIFE

There is a vast selection of nightclubs. Discos, pubs, bars, karaoke bars and casinos tempt visitors with their neon signs and music. The resort areas on the islands have severe night-time noise level restrictions in place, but this has done little to curb the number of pubs, clubs and bars.

There is a basic difference between bars and pubs on the islands. Bars *(tabernas)* are open all day, serving mostly beer and wine as well as snacks. This is often the first stop before the evening "ruta", where you can have a drink and a quiet conversation. They close around 1am.

Pubs *(cervecerías)* provide more typical evening entertainment. They also serve alcohol, but wine is not very common. The music is loud, and those wishing to dance can do so. Discos open late and close around 5am. They become crowded around 1am, or later, when other places close.

DAYTIME ENTERTAINMENT

During the daytime the entertainment on offer includes glass-bottomed boat and submarine trips. There are also dolphin and whale-watching trips (prices usually include lunch on board).

For the benefit of younger guests, the islands have developed numerous water-parks with merry-go-rounds, slides and swimming pools. Gardens such as **Palmitos Parque** and **Loro Parque** stage parrot and dolphin shows, specifically aimed at children. Another fun way to spend the day is to take one of the numerous safaris over wilderness areas, on camel-back or by jeep.

THEATRE AND CINEMA

It is only the large towns that have cinemas, theatres and concert halls. New films come to the screen with minimum delay. However, films are usually dubbed (except for a few cinemas) and therefore incomprehensible to non-Spanish speakers.

Trained sea-lion show in Loro Parque on Tenerife

Las Palmas Film Festival

MUSIC AND CONCERTS

The biggest musical event on the islands is the annual **Womad** concert. This ethnic music extravaganza is organized by former Genesis band member, Peter Gabriel, in Las Palmas de Gran Canaria. Gran Canaria is also the venue of **Atlantida** – a lively annual pop music concert that takes place in February on Playa del Inglés.

Fans of jazz music can enjoy the **International Canarias Jazz & Heineken** festival. It is organized each year, with concerts held on all the islands, except La Gomera and El Hierro.

Lovers of classical music can visit the concert halls in Las Palmas de Gran Canaria and Santa Cruz de Tenerife. At the end of January and the beginning of February there is a classical music festival. Concerts are held in the **Auditorio Alfredo Kraus** in Las Palmas de Gran Canaria, and the **Auditorio de Tenerife** in Santa Cruz de Tenerife, as well as on other islands.

Hotels often organize their own concerts and shows of flamenco dancing, as well as Spanish and local folk dances. These shows are very popular with tourists.

FESTIVALS

The best-known event on the Canary Islands is, of course, the carnival (Feb/Mar). The biggest and wildest one, held in Santa Cruz de Tenerife, is often compared to the famous carnival that takes place in Rio de Janeiro.

The theatre festival in Agüimes on Gran Canaria is the only one of its kind in Spain. This prestigious event is held in September and it attracts a wide range of theatre groups from Europe, Latin America and Africa.

The film festival held on Gran Canaria (Oct/Nov, every two years) includes works of international cinema, with special emphasis placed on European, African and Latin American movies. One category is reserved for Canary films, or films thematically linked with the archipelago.

Tiles commemorating the 1981 carnival

FIESTAS

As a rule, the religious festivals are an opportunity for the islanders to let their hair down. The central activity of most fiestas is the statue-carrying processions but they may also include fancy-dress parades and street decorations. Fiestas can easily last several days, during which time town life comes to a virtual halt: all public places, including shops, bars and restaurants, are closed.

Folk dancers on Gran Canaria

DIRECTORY

THEATRES

Teatro Pérez Galdós
Plaza Stagno, s/n. Las Palmas de Gran Canaria. **Tel** 928 433 805.
www.teatroperezgaldos.es

Teatro Guimerá
Marco Redondo, 2. Santa Cruz de Tenerife. **Tel** 922 606 265.
www.teatroguimera.es

Teatro Casa de la Cultura
C/Comodoro Rolin, 1. Santa Cruz de Tenerife.
Tel 922 202 202.

CONCERT HALLS

Auditorio Alfredo Kraus
Avda. Principe de Asturias, s/n. Las Palmas de Gran Canaria.
Tel 928 491 770.
www.auditorio-alfredokraus.com

Auditorio "Teobaldo Power"
C/Calvario, La Orotava.
Tel 922 330 224.
www.la-orotava.salir.com

Auditorio de Puerto del Rosario
Puerto del Rosario.
Tel 928 532 186.
www.auditorio.puertorosario.net

Auditorio de Tenerife
Parque Maritima, Santa Cruz de Tenerife. **Tel** 922 568 600.
www.auditoriodetenerife.com

OUTDOOR ACTIVITIES

Because of their superb climate, the Canary Islands are an excellent place for all types of sport. Visitors seeking to combine lounging on the beach with something more strenuous can come here at any time of the year, sure to find professional help and guidance. The most popular are, of course, water sports. Pozo Izquierdo on Gran Canaria is one

Windsurfer on Fuerteventura

of the world's best beaches for windsurfing. The coastal waters are considered some of the most attractive diving sites. Tenerife and the remaining islands offer excellent conditions for paragliding and hang-gliding. Anyone interested in golf, tennis, horse riding, hiking or cycling will also find plenty of opportunities to indulge in their favourite pastimes.

JOGGING

There are excellent conditions for running. Seaside promenades and sandy beaches, such as the ones on Fuerteventura, are ideal places for burning off the calories.

In the rugged central regions of the islands, small villages offer less favourable conditions for jogging. The best times to take a run are mornings and evenings, when temperatures are lower and the crowds thinner.

HIKING

The islands, with their pleasant climate, diverse landscape and numerous national parks and nature reserves, present many opportunities for hikers. Tourist offices on all the islands can offer advice as to the best walking trails.

Hikers on La Gomera

The national park areas, including Garajonay on La Gomera, are particularly attractive and feature many marked trails, but walkers should bear in mind the obligatory rules and restrictions. Walking trips around the islands are often the best method of exploring. The routes are not too difficult or arduous, though most footpaths are rocky.

Many routes lead over high ground along mountain ridges. Temperatures here can be low, even in the summer when the sun's rays still do not generate much heat. You should always make sure to bring warm clothing and do not forget to pack sunscreen, water and something to eat.

TENNIS

Good quality tennis courts, some of them floodlit, can be found in the grounds of many hotels and apartments. These can often be hired out, even if you are not a resident. Instructors and equipment hire are easy to organize. More information about holidays combined with tennis lessons can be obtained from the Real Federación Española de Tenis. Those longing for a game of squash will also find appropriate facilities, mainly within the hotel complexes.

Riders at sunset on Valle Gran Rey beach

HORSE RIDING

There are several riding centres on the islands, offering facilities for beginners as well as for advanced riders.

In the main, however, the islands do not offer attractive riding opportunities. The rocky and uneven terrain and the hard surfaces mean that there is a lack of routes suitable for galloping. The latter can only be enjoyed on some sandy beaches.

Among the most interesting trips on horseback are the organized sightseeing tours of the islands' national parks, including Garajonay on La Gomera.

All horse-riding outings, whether performed individually or in groups, are always supervised by the owner of the stable or an instructor who knows the area well.

Cyclists by Castillo Santa Barbara, near Teguise

CYCLING

The mountainous character of the islands creates excellent conditions for riding mountain bikes or racers. On steep, winding roads you can often encounter groups of cyclists whizzing past. Cycling, however, given the nature of the terrain you are likely to encounter, requires much care. Traffic, too, presents a serious danger.

More ambitious cyclists can undertake a guided tour. These usually lead over areas of wilderness and require a lot of stamina. The best places for this type of adventure are the national parks. There are many agents offering such tours. They organize transport for cyclists and their equipment to the starting point and collect them at the end. Some firms also include a picnic lunch in the price of the outing.

Bicycles are an excellent means of transport around the islands. Many tourists use touring bikes to reach distant beaches, for shopping trips or just to escape from the crowds.

FISHING

The Canary Islands' waters are packed with different varieties of fish that attract anglers, but due to depleted stocks there are now more restrictions in place. Almost every island offers sea trips combined with marlin fishing. One of the best places for trying to catch this fish are the waters around Isla

Graciosa, off the north coast of Lanzarote.

Tourists can hire a boat or join an organized expedition. Fishing equipment is generally provided by the organizer.

Yachts moored in Puerto de Mogán harbour

SAILING

Almost every large coastal town or village has a marina. These have been an important call for transatlantic sailors since the time of Columbus, and are visited by

yachts from all over Europe. Modern marinas have facilities for yacht repair. Food supplies are available in local shops, while the many harbour restaurants tempt hungry sailors. In smaller places, yacht harbours are usually combined with fishing harbours.

Conditions for sailing are good the whole year through, and you can charter a yacht or catamaran for a day or longer, provided you have the relevant qualifications. Those who do not can go on a cruise. These, too, can last a day or longer. Many of the cruises offer food, and even drink, as part of the price.

Everybody has the chance to learn the basic skills of sailing in the Canary Islands. All islands have sailing centres, offering short sailing courses for all ages.

NATURISM

Naturism is "officially" legal on all of Spain's beaches, including the Canary Islands' sandy swathes, though discretion is advised when stripping off completely in the more populated family resorts. Some beaches are more popular with nudists, such as Le Tejita to the south east of Tenerife, and Playa Guasimeta near Arrecife airport in Lanzarote. In Gran Canaria, the Maspalomas dunes provide plenty of privacy for naturists. All these beaches may also be used by non-nudists.

For those seeking more than nude sunbathing, Lanzarote and Gran Canaria both offer "clothing-optional" resorts.

Fishing at Puerto de las Nieves, Gran Canaria

HANG-GLIDING AND PARAGLIDING

Hang-gliding and paragliding (similar to hang-gliding but using a parachute-type wing) offer an unforgettable way to see the islands. The large islands, such as Gran Canaria, have particularly favourable weather for this sport. Tenerife alone has more than 40 centres for hang-gliding.

Many centres offer hang-gliding courses. They are held in the island's interior regions, which feature the best lifting currents. When the weather is right, it is possible to fly over an entire island by hang-glider. Those wanting a less risky taste of gliding can try their hand at parascending behind a motorboat.

WATER MOTORSPORTS

Motorboat races and other similar events are a rare sight on the islands. However, many people take the opportunity to try jet-ski rides. Equally popular are water-skiing and bumping along in rubber rafts towed by a speeding boat.

DIVING

Snorkelling and scuba diving are both well catered for on the islands and provide the opportunity to see rays, barracuda, turtles and a variety of tropical fish. You might even see a shark! There are many diving centres *(centro de buceo)* where you can hire equipment, go for a test dive with an instructor or join

Parachute towed by a motorboat near Los Gigantes cliffs

courses, for all levels of proficiency. In order to go scuba diving in Spain, you must have a proper diving certificate. The recognized ones include PADI, CUC, CMAS/FEDAS and SSI.

Holders of these certificates can join underwater expeditions. Diving around Famara, on Lanzarote, or La Restinga on El Hierro, provides an unforgettable experience. Underwater spearfishing is permitted only to snorkellers.

WINDSURFING

Hitching yourself to a windsurfing board is undoubtedly one of the islands' most popular sports. The strong winds on many beaches, combined with the sunshine, create excellent conditions for this sport.

There are several schools that can teach you how to do it. They also rent sailboards to stronger swimmers.

Advanced windsurfers (or *windsurfistas* as they are known to the locals) should definitely try the beaches at El Medano on Tenerife, Playa de Sotavento on

Fuerteventura and Pozo Izquierdo on Gran Canaria. These also play host to a number of international windsurfing events.

It should, however, be remembered that along beaches where top international events take place, the conditions can be very treacherous. Winds are strong and variable and the waves are big. The winds are particularly strong from April until the end of summer, while in the winter months the Atlantic waves are bigger and more dangerous to inexperienced windsurfers.

Windsurfer off the coast of Fuerteventura

SURFING

You will find surfers or people playing with boogie boards on practically all Canary Island beaches. Surfing schools are thin on the ground, however, but there are a number of hire shops in places that have particularly favourable sea conditions such as Gran Canaria's Maspalomas Beach.

Surfing is popular with the locals but it can be extremely dangerous and you should exercise great caution, particularly around the northern shores, where waves are much stronger than they seem from the shore. In many places, eddies and currents make the conditions even more treacherous. Another hazard is the rocky seabed, so before entering the water you should find out whether the beach is safe.

Diving – one of the most popular island sports

DIRECTORY

HORSE RIDING

Association of Gran Canaria Riding Clubs
C/León y Castillo, 47.
Las Palmas de Gran Canaria.

Centro Hípico del Sur
Camino Los Migueles 82,
Buzanada, Tenerife.
Tel 922 720 643.
www.centrohipicodelsur.
com

Círculo Hípico Manivasán
C/Terra, 5. El Paso.
Tel 922 460 316.

Lanzarote a Caballo
Ctra – Arrecife – Yaiza,
17 km.
Tel 928 830 038.
Fax 928 813 995.

Mamio Verde
Cuadras de Pino Alto, 39.
La Orotava.
Tel 922 322 059.

Sociedad Hípica Miranda
Miranda de Abajo.
Breña Alta.
Tel 922 437 696.
Fax 922 181 392.

CYCLING

Bike Station Gomera
Avda. Maritima, 10. Valle
Gran Rey, La Gomera.
Tel 922 805 082. **www**.
bikestationgomera.com

Bike'n Fun
C/Calvo, 20.
Los Llanos de Aridane.
Tel 922 401 927.

La Palma mtb
www.la-palma-mtb.com

SAILING

Club de Deportes Naúticos Barlovento
Puerto Deportivo "San
Miguel", San Miguel.
Las Palmas de Gran Canaria.
Tel 922 691 482.
Fax 922 691 492.
@ barlo@idecnet.com

Club de Mar de Radazul
Avda.Marítima, Radazul
– El Rosario.
Tel 922 681 099.
@ radazul
@clubmradazul.com

Real Club Náutico de Gran Canaria
C/León y Castillo, 308.
Las Palmas de Gran Canaria.
Tel 928 234 566.
Fax 928 246 324.
www.rcngc.com

Real Club Náutico de Tenerife
Avda. Francisco La Roche,
s/n. Santa Cruz de Tenerife
Tel 922 273 700.
www.rcnt.es

FISHING

Fishing Club Alegranza
C/Orchilla, 34.
La Restinga, El Hierro.
Tel 922 557 038.

NATURISM

Charco de Palo
(Naturist bungalow
complex)
Charco Natural,
Calle Montaña Redonda,
Lanzarote.
Tel 928 529 595.
www.charconatural.com

Federación Española de Naturismo
(Nudist beach listings)
www.naturismo.org

Magnolias Natura
(Naturist bungalow
complex)
Maspalomas,
Gran Canaria.
Tel 928 770 122.
www.canariasnatura.com

Monte Marina Apartments
(Naturist apartment
complex)
Jandia,
Fuerteventura.
Tel 928 544 052.
Fax 928 544 976.
www.montemarinaplaya.
com

International Naturist Federation
(Protecting the rights of
naturists)
www.inffni.org

Puerto Palace Hotel
(Naturist-friendly hotel)
C/Dr. Cobiella Zaera, s/n,
Puerto de la Cruz,
Tenerife.
Tel 922 372 460.
Fax 922 373 523.
www.puertopalace.com

HANG-GLIDING AND PARAGLIDING

Escuela de Parapente "IZAÑA"
Güimar.
Tel 619 073 210.

Escuela Parapente Palmasur
C/La Cruz, 2. Los Quemados.
Tel 609 647 103.

Guellillas del Hierro
C/Doctor Quintero, 23.
Valverde.
Tel 922 551 824.

Libertad Tacoronte
Pabellón de Deportes.
C/Perez Reyes, Tacoronte.
Tel 922 563 251.

Paraclub of Gran Canaria
Aerodrome El Berriel, Ctra.
General Del Sur, 46.5 km,
San Bartolome de Tirajana.
@ office@
paraclubgrancanaria.com

Real Aeroclub Gran Canaria
Tel 928 157 147.
www.aeroclubgran
canaria.com

DIVING

Blue Explorers Dive Centers
Paseo Maritimo, 4.
Playa de Taurito.
Tel 928 565 795.
www.blue-explorers.com

Centro de Buceo las Toninas
Aptos. Playa Flamingo,
Playa Blanca.
Tel 902 363 318.
Fax 928 517 490.
@ divingtoninas@
lanzarote.com

Club Barakuda
Playa Paraíso. Adeje.
Tel 922 741 881.
www.buceo-tenerife.com

Dive Center
C/Nuestra Señora
del Pino, 22.
Corralejo.
Tel 928 535 906.
www.divecenter
corralejo.com

El Submarino
Avda. Marítima, 2.
La Restinga.
Tel 922 557 075.

WINDSURFING

Centro Insular de Deportes Marítimos de Tenerife
Ctra. a San Andrés.
Tel 922 240 945.

Fanatic Fun Center
Caleta de Fuste.
Tel 928 866 389.

Flag Beach Windsurf Centre
General Linares, 31.
Corralejo.
Tel 609 029 804.
www.flagbeach.com

Pro Center René Egli – Windsurf & Kiteboarding
Hotel Sol Los Gorriones.
Sotavento.
Tel 928 547 483.
www.rene-egli.com

Sport Away Lanzarote
C/de las Olas, 18.
Costa Teguise
Tel 928 590 731.
www.sportaway-
lanzarote.com

Golfing in the Canary Islands

Previously known for attracting neon-seeking party-goers, the Canary Islands have recently become a Mecca for a different breed of clubber. It is clear that in recent years, the lucrative golf market has been a target for the region's local tourist authorities, keen to grab a slice of the Algarve's visiting golf fraternity. There are currently 23 courses, divided between five of the seven islands, with several more in the pipeline. Lured by a sub-tropical climate, ocean-side fairways and award-winning designs, golfers of all abilities come to lap up the greens and the year-round sunshine.

Spectacular view of the Atlantic at Buenavista golf course, Tenerife

GENERAL INFORMATION

All of the Canary Islands' golf courses, with the exception of the **Real Club de Golf de Tenerife**, are open to the public. Some offer facilities for non-golfing companions, such as swimming pools, tennis courts and restaurants. All have driving ranges, pro-shops and buggy rentals. Golf packages are offered at dozens of hotels and resorts. These usually include discounts on green fees and tee-time booking facilities. Green fees vary, with October through April being the peak season, and May to September affording lower rates. A "bono" discount is available at many courses if a number of rounds are booked at once.

PGA Spanish Open golf at Abama Golf, Tenerife

TENERIFE

Tenerife is golf central in the Canary Islands with nine courses already in place and a handful of others in the pipeline. There are courses for every level, from an easy par-27, to the challenging championship fairways of 27-hole **Golf del Sur**. Several legs of the PGA Spanish Open have been held on the island's courses over the years, with **Abama Golf** being the newest venue to join **Golf Costa Adeje** as championship hosts. Also in the south is **Golf Las Américas**, a green jewel located between the resorts of Las Americas and Los Cristianos. The legendary Seve Ballesteros designed **Buenavista Golf**, which is the most environmentally-friendly course on the island, boasting a minimal negative impact on the environment. Although it is the second oldest golf club in Spain, the **Real Club de Golf de Tenerife** still holds a distinctly British feel.

GRAN CANARIA

The eight courses of Gran Canaria offer an array of backdrops, from the smooth sandy dunes looming over the fairways of **Campo de Golf de Maspalomas** to the craggy volcanic scenery surrounding the **Real Club de Golf de Las Palmas**. Inaugurated in 1891, the latter stakes a claim as being the first golf club in Spain, although it moved to a different site in 1956. Another club in the north, **El Cortijo Club de Campo** has been the venue for several international championships including the Canaries Open of Spain. **Las Palmeras Golf** is an 18-hole par-3 course located close to the city centre, with a spa, gym, swimming pool, nursery and restaurant on-site. The neat, trimmed greenery of **Salobre Golf** stands in stark contrast to the wild moonscape edging its fairways. This demanding 18-hole course is set amongst volcanic cones and cacti-studded brushland. A similar landscape of lakes and volcanic mountains sur-rounds the 9-hole course at **Anfi Tauro Golf**. **Meloneras Golf** near Maspalomas is unique on Gran Canaria as it's the only course where several holes can be played right beside the sea.

Real Club de Golf de Las Palmas on Gran Canaria

LANZAROTE

Although golf has been played in Lanzarote for three decades, the choice is still limited to two golf courses, **Lanzarote Golf**, near Puerto del Carmen, and **Costa Teguise Golf**. The latter was designed by British land-scape architect John Harris. This 18-hole par-72 course runs along the side of an old volcano with stunning views of the ocean. In addition to the dramatic scenery, the course also has all the amenities you would expect from a top class club, including buggies, pro-shop, clubhouse, golf school and restaurant. Due to the dry nature of the island's climate, providing the necessary resources has always been a challenge. However, the introduction of de-salination plants has made it possible to provide the moisture necessary to grow the premium quality grass that is vital for playing top-level golf. With this in mind, the local authorities are looking to expand golf tourism with a number of courses planned near the resort areas of Playa Blanca and Puerto Calero.

Players enjoy sea views from Tecina golf course, La Gomera

FUERTEVENTURA

It is no surprise to find that the relatively flat topography of Fuerteventura is a feature on the island's three golf courses. Only the 17th and 18th holes are elevated on **Fuerteventura Golf Club** near Caleta de Fuste, but this does not detract from its demanding nature. Three lakes and a handful of dog-legs usually add a few unwanted numbers to the scorecard. Covering more 1,500,000 square metres, it is the largest expanse of

green on the whole of the island. In 2004 it was also the home of the Spanish Open. The newer par-70 **Salinas de Antigua** is equally level, but pock-marked with an assortment of low-lying volcanic cones. Another course, Jandia Golf, has been built but is closed indefinitely.

LA GOMERA

Until 2003 La Gomera was more famed for its walking than its sports facilities. Now, thanks to a combination of the two, the island can boast

an outstanding course that draws plenty of enthusiasts from Tenerife, a 45-minute ferry ride away. **Tecina Golf** is an outstanding course. Perched on a cliff, overlooking the Atlantic Ocean, this challenging 18-hole course has great views. Lush. tropical vegetation lines the fairways, tall palm trees stretch from the bright green baize into the azure-blue sky and greens seem to balance precariously above the crashing waves below. The stunning design is by Donald Steel, the architect behind the New St. Andrews course in Scotland.

DIRECTORY

TENERIFE

Abama Golf
Ctra. Gral TF-47, 9 km.
Playa San Juan. **Tel** 922
126 700. **www**.abama
hotelresort.com

Buenavista Golf
Buenavista del Norte.
Tel 922 129 034.
www.buenavistagolf.es

Golf Costa Adeje
Finca de los Olivos s/n.
Adeje. **Tel** 922 710 000.
www.golfcostaadeje.com

Golf del Sur
Urb. Golf del Sur. San
Miguel de Abona. **Tel** 922
738 170.
www.golf delsur.net

Golf las Américas
Playa de las Américas.
Tel 922 752 005.
www.golf-tenerife.com

**Real Club de Golf
de Tenerife**
C/ Campo de Golf, 1.
Tacoronte. **Tel** 922 636
607. **www**.realclubgolf
tenerife.com

GRAN CANARIA

Anfi Tauro Golf
Valle de Tauro s/n. Mogán.
Tel 928 560 462.
www.anfitauro.es

**Campo de Golf de
Maspalomas**
Avda. Touroperadores
Neckermann, s/n.
Maspalomas. **Tel** 928 762
581. **www**.maspalomas
golf.net

**El Cortijo Club de
Campo**
Autopista Sur GC-1, 6.4
km. Telde. **Tel** 928 711
111. **www**.elcortijo.es

Las Palmeras Golf
Avda. Doctor Alfonso
Chiscano Diaz s/n.Las
Palmas. **Tel** 928 222 333.
www.laspalmerasgolf.com

Meloneras Golf
C/ Gánigo 6, Plaza Ansite.
Playa Meloneras. **Tel** 928
145 309.

**Real Club de Golf
de Las Palmas**
Ctra. De Bandama. Santa
Brígida. **Tel** 928 350 104.
www.realclubdegolfdelas
palmas.com

Salobre Golf
Autopista GC-1, 53 km.
Maspalomas. **Tel** 928 010
103. **www**.salobregolf
resort.com

LANZAROTE

Costa Teguise Golf
Urb. Costa Teguise.
Tel 928 590 512.
www.lanzarote-golf.com

**Lanzarote Golf
Resort**
Carreterra del Puerto de
Carmen, Tias. **Tel** 928 514
050. **www**.lanzarotegolf
resort.com

FUERTEVENTURA

**Fuerteventura Golf
Club**
Ctra. De Jandía, 11 km.
Caleta de Fuste.
Tel 928 160 034.
www.fuerteventura
golfclub.com

Salinas de Antigua
Ctra. Jandia 12 km.
Antigua.
Tel 928 877 272.
www.salinasgolf.com

LA GOMERA

Tecina Golf
Playa de Santiago.
Tel 922 145 950.
www.tecinagolf.com

SURVIVAL
GUIDE

PRACTICAL INFORMATION

The Canary Islands' warm climate means that the tourist season here lasts the whole year. The huge investment in the tourist infrastructure means that the islands are well prepared to receive multitudes of visitors and have extensive hotel and catering facilities, as well as numerous attractions and things to do. Frequent charter flights to the islands plus a very well-developed information

service, particularly on the Internet, makes planning a holiday here a reasonably straightforward business. Those intending to visit can easily find all the necessary information and organize the necessary hotel bookings in advance. This is important since, particularly in summer and winter, the islands can get extremely crowded (although no longer so busy that you can't find accommodation without booking in advance).

Logo of the island of Lanzarote

WHEN TO VISIT

The holiday season lasts practically all year round on the Canary Islands. Thanks to their magnificent weather, the beaches can be used almost from January until December. The islands are particularly popular with visitors during winter months. Many decide to spend a balmy Christmas on the islands, rather than huddled round a fire in Europe.

The second most popular season is summer, particularly July and August, when the islands are packed, and early spring is also very busy. Late autumn has fewer visitors.

The islands are not only attractive for their sunshine and beaches. One local event that attracts crowds of tourists is the carnival. Visitors from Spain, and further afield, come mainly to Santa Cruz de Tenerife or Las Palmas de Gran Canaria to join the carnival celebrations. Magnificent fiestas, including

the Bajada de la Virgen de las Nieves in Santa Cruz de La Palma, provide another reason to visit the islands.

VISAS

Regulations covering admission to the Canary Islands are exactly the same as for the rest of Spain. Nationals of all the European Union member states do not require a visa to enter the Canary Islands for tourist visits of up to 90 days. Other non-EU countries including Australia, Canada, Israel, Japan, New Zealand and the USA are likewise not required to obtain a visa before entry. When in doubt, you should contact the Spanish Embassy or seek advice from a travel agent. Anyone who does require a visa must apply in person at the consulate in their own country.

Tourists at a viewpoint

CUSTOMS REGULATIONS

When Spain joined the European Union, the Canary Islands lost their status as a duty-free zone. For customs purposes, however, the islands are still not considered to be part of the EU and there are detailed regulations as to the amount of goods permitted for export. They include 200 cigarettes or 50 cigars, two litres of wine and one litre of alcohol over 22 per cent or two litres of sparkling wine.

In addition, visitors are allowed 250 ml of eau de toilette and up to €162 worth of souvenirs. Tobacco and alcohol allowances apply only to adults.

Specific cases may be referred to the *Departamento de Aduanas e Impuestos Especiales* (Customs and Excise Department) in Madrid. Travel agents and tour operators can provide further information.

Resting on a colourful bench in Santa Cruz de Tenerife

◁ **Bathers at a beach in Maspalomas, Gran Canaria**

Maspalomas' centre, on Gran Canaria, at night

LANGUAGE

The official language of the Canary Islands is Spanish. Local accents differ from those of mainland Spain, but apart from this and a few words particular to the islands, there are no major differences.

Apart from Spanish, it is possible to communicate in various foreign languages in all the tourist resorts, where you could get by without any Spanish at all. The second language is German, but most people also speak English. Information signs and restaurant menus are generally multilingual. The most frequent combination is Spanish, German and English.

Communication problems may arise while away from the major tourist centres. Here most people speak only Spanish, though the younger population may be able to understand German or English.

TOURIST INFORMATION

Tourist information on the Canary Islands is a well-oiled machine. Bigger towns and tourist centres have an *oficina de turismo* (information office). These provide information about the locality, accommodation (including staying on a farmstead or in a converted village house), events and tourist attractions.

Tourist offices can also provide visitors with free information packs and maps and can offer advice regarding the best walking routes, nearby historic sights and a variety of day trips.

The information packs are an excellent point of reference. They are illustrated with colour photographs and issued in several languages.

Outside Spain, there are plenty of Spanish information offices, which are usually attached to the embassies, where you can obtain all the necessary information prior to visiting the islands.

The Internet is another free source of information, but often official sites are not updated as often as they should be. Every island and many individual regions have their own websites that are nevertheless worth visiting. The Spanish Tourism Institute – *Turespaña* – has its own site (www.tourspain.es), which provides information about hotels, camping sites and tourist attractions throughout Spain. Various travel agents, hotels, restaurants, car hire firms and other establishments also advertise their services on the Internet. Their pages generally include many photographs, which can be helpful when choosing a hotel.

Information packs promoting tourism

DIRECTORY

TOURIST INFORMATION

United Kingdom
22/23 Manchester Square,
London W1M 5AP.
Tel 020 7486 8077
www.tourspain.es

Gran Canaria
Las Palmas de Gran Canaria.
Tel 928 219 600.
www.grancanaria.com

Playa del Inglés, Avda. España and
Avda. EE.UU.
Tel 928 771 814.
Fax 928 767 848.

Fuerteventura
Puerto del Rosario. Avda. Primero
de Mayo, 33.
Tel 928 851 024.
www.fuerteventuraturismo.com

Lanzarote
C/Blas Cabrera Felipe 3.
Tel 928 811 762.
www.turismolanzarote.es

Tenerife
Santa Cruz de Tenerife. Plaza de
España, s/n – Palacio Insular.
Tel 922 239 592.
www.webtenerife.com

Aeropuerto Reina Sofía.
Tel 922 759 000.
Fax 922 759 247.

La Gomera
San Sebastián de La Gomera.
C/Del Medio, 20.
Tel 922 141 512.
Fax 922 140 151.
www.lagomera.es

El Hierro
Valverde. C/Dr Quintero, 4.
Tel 922 550 302.
www.elhierro.es

La Palma
Santa Cruz de La Palma.
Plaza de la Constitucion.
Tel 922 412 106.

TOURIST INFORMATION ON THE INTERNET

www.canarias-saturno.org
www.canarias24.com
www.canary-guide.com
www.gobcan.es
www.mytenerifeinfo.com
www.situr.org
www.tourspain.es
www.vivecanarias.com

Paseo de las Canteras in Las Palmas de Gran Canaria

YOUTH/STUDENTS

Holders of the International Student Identity Card (ISIC) and the Euro under-26 card are entitled to many benefits when visiting the Canary Islands. They can get discounts on ferry travel, entrance charges to museums and galleries, and tickets to many other tourist attractions. Many travel agents also offer cheaper flights to holders of these cards.

Under-26 cards can be obtained on Tenerife or Gran Canaria with a passport. To get an ISIC card you will need to provide proof that you are a full-time student.

CHILDREN

The Canary Islands are geared up for family holidays and, as with most of Europe, children are welcome almost everywhere. The beaches provide a safe playground all year round. The numerous water parks and the zoos, which stage trained parrot and dolphin shows, are a big draw and are aimed, to a large extent, squarely at kids.

Many travel agents specialize in arranging family holidays. They provide all-day childcare, giving parents a chance to take a well-earned rest. They also organize competitions, games and trips for their younger guests.

There is no problem feeding young children. Children's portions, high-

chairs, activity packs and outside seating are the norm rather than the exception in most restaurants.

FACILITIES FOR THE DISABLED

The islands are not particularly hospitable to disabled people. The majority of restaurants and hotels are not adapted to serve guests who use wheelchairs. Moving around some of the towns is also very difficult, and taking part in events or going on organized trips is practically impossible.

When planning a visit to the islands, a disabled tourist should check the travel

Parking for the disabled sign

conditions and hotel facilities with their travel agent. The organization which helps disabled people to plan their holiday on the Canary Islands is the Confederación Coordinatora Estatal de Minusválidos Físico de España (COCEMFE) – The Spanish Association for the Disabled. There are also special guides published. Another helpful agency is Viajes 2000.

SIGHTSEEING TOURS

A wide range of sightseeing tours are is available for tourists throughout the islands. Most organizers and travel agents offer a variety of types. These may include desert safaris by jeep or on the back of a camel, fishing trips, organized walks, submarine cruises, trips in a glass-bottomed boat, and visits to one of the islands' parks, including Palmitos Parque or Loro Parque. People tend to see only one or two islands when they visit the Canaries but there are day trips to small islands, such as the Isla de Lobos, close to Fuerteventura.

Those not wishing to join a trip organized by a hotel or travel agent can find many other alternatives. Hotel reception desks and tourist offices carry a range of colourful leaflets with relevant information. The tours are mainly reasonably priced daytrips though some can last overnight or even longer. Most of them start after breakfast and the price includes lunch on board a boat or in a friendly restaurant catering for groups of tourists. Visitors living away from the large towns are offered trips to city nightclubs. Shows, dancing and karaoke are the most common features of these forms of evening entertainment.

Minigolf for children and adults

OFICINA DE TURISMO

Tourist information sign

TIME

The Canary Islands are on GMT, the same as the UK and Ireland, and an hour behind mainland Spain. In summer, to make better use of the sunshine, the clocks go an hour forward. The changeover takes place on the last Sunday in March. The clocks are put back again on the last Sunday in October.

Road sign for visitors to Parque Nacional de Garajonay

ELECTRICAL EQUIPMENT

The mains voltage on the islands is generally 220 V. A readily available three-tier standard travel converter will enable you to use foreign equipment. Mains sockets require round-pin plugs.

RELIGION

Like the rest of Spain, the Canary Islands are largely Roman Catholic. Religion plays an important role in community life. All religious festivals are lavishly celebrated, and many **fiestas** are of religious origin. Most of the islands' churches are Roman Catholic. Their opening hours differ; some are open only during services.

There are also churches of other denominations. Services are held in various languages, and their times change frequently. Hotel reception desks and tourist information centres can usually provide details. A multi-denominational church – Templo Ecuménico – has recently opened on Gran Canaria, in Playa del Inglés. A similar one can be found in Puerto de la Cruz, on Tenerife.

OPENING HOURS

Most monuments and museums are open from Tuesday to Sunday. The hours are generally from 10am to 2pm. They close for the siesta and reopen from 5pm to 8pm. They generally close for public holidays and fiestas, similar to all offices. The hours for museums in smaller towns are more unpredictable and it is best to phone ahead. Outside of the major tourist resorts, shops close on Sundays. Church opening hours also vary. The best time to visit is during morning or evening services.

Theme parks and gardens are generally open seven days a week, but even these close for public holidays.

WATER

Tap water on the Canary Islands is suitable for drinking, although it is usually heavily treated and can upset the stomach if you are not used to it. It is generally recommended that you drink bottled water and use tap water for cooking. You should remember to drink a lot of liquid, to prevent dehydration.

Shops offer a large variety of bottled waters, mainly from local wells. Particularly good are the sparkling waters, including those from Firgas, on Gran Canaria.

Sign for Gran Canaria's botanical garden

DIRECTORY

EMBASSIES ON MAINLAND SPAIN

Australia
Plaza del Descubridor Diego de Ordás 3,
38003 Madrid.
Tel 91 441 61 80 or 913 536 600.
@ information@embaustralia.es

United Kingdom
Calle de Fernando El Santo 16,
28010 Madrid.
Tel 91 700 82 00.
www.ukinspain.com

CONSULATES IN THE CANARY ISLANDS

Ireland
Calle del Castillo 8,
Santa Cruz de Tenerife.
Tel 922 245 671.

USA
C/Martinez de Escobar 3,
Las Palmas de Gran Canaria.
Tel 928 271 259.

United Kingdom
C/Luis Morote, 6,
Las Palmas de Gran Canaria.
Tel 928 262 508.
Plaza de Weyler, 8,
Santa Cruz de Tenerife.
Tel 922 242 000.
Fax 922 289 903.

YOUTH/STUDENTS

Instituto Canario de la Juventud Gobierno Canarias
C/Profesor Agustín Millares Carlo, 18,
Las Palmas de Gran Canaria.
Tel 928 306 397.

Edificio el Cabo
C/Leoncio Rodriguez, 7,
Santa Cruz de Tenerife.
Tel 922 208 800.
C/Wenceslao Yañez, 8, La Laguna.

ORGANIZATIONS FOR THE DISABLED

COCEMFE
C/Luis Cabrera, 63, Madrid.
Tel 917 443 600.
Fax 914 131 996
www.cocemfe.org

Viajes 2000
Paseo de la Castellana, 228–230,
Madrid. *Tel 913 231 029.*
www.viajes2000.com

Personal Security and Health

Visitors to the Canary Islands can generally feel safe. Thefts do occur in the most crowded places and even in hotels, but they can be minimized by taking sensible precautions. Credit cards and money are best hidden away or carried in a belt. Never leave anything visible in your car when you park it. It is also advisable to avoid carrying excessive amounts of cash. When in need, you can always ask a policeman for help. Basic medical help and advice is usually provided by a pharmacist. Holders of valid medical insurance can receive treatment in public hospitals and clinics.

PERSONAL PROPERTY

Before going away it is necessary to make sure you have adequate holiday insurance in order to protect you financially from the loss or theft of your property.

Even so, it is advisable to take common-sense precautions against loss or theft in the first place. Traveller's cheques are a far safer option than cash. If you have two credit cards, do not carry them together. Particular care should be exercised in crowded places, such as airports or bus stations, as well as inside tourist attractions, which are always full of people. Patrolling policemen often remind visitors about the need to be careful. There are also cases of tourists falling victim to theft when drunk. Never leave a bag or handbag unattended and do not put down a purse or wallet on the tabletop in a café. The moment you discover a loss or theft, report it to the local police station. The police will give you a *denuncia* (written statement), which you will need to make an insurance claim. If you have your passport lost or stolen report it to your consulate.

SPANISH POLICE

In the Canary Islands, as in the rest of Spain, there are essentially three types of police. The *Policía Nacional* (state police), the *Policía Municipal,* also known as the *Policía Local* (local police), and the *Guardia Civil* (National Guard).

The *Policía Nacional* wear blue uniforms and drive white cars with navy-blue doors. These operate in towns with a population of more than 30,000.

The uniform of the *Policía Local* varies depending on the locality. Their officers are mostly encountered in small towns, and patrol the streets of crowded tourist resorts; they have a separate branch for traffic.

The *Guardia Civil* wear green uniforms and generally drive white-and-green four-wheel drive vehicles. They mainly patrol the open roads.

The islands' police are friendly towards tourists. They are, however, very firm with those who commit traffic offences. All three services will direct you to the relevant authority in the event of an incident requiring police help.

Uniform of the Guardia Civil

Local police four-wheel drive car, a common sight on the islands

Information board at Amadores beach on Gran Canaria

SUNSHINE

Though it is, of course, one of the attractions, the sun should be taken seriously in the Canary Islands. The archipelago lies in the tropical zone where the sun is much stronger that in the rest of Spain. People with pale skin should always use sun block creams to avoid burning. Many people tend to forget that creams do not remain active throughout the entire day and should be reapplied every few hours.

When going to the beach try to avoid the hottest hours of the day. Between 1pm and 4pm it is best not to stay in the sun for too long. The sun is also strong in the mountains, above the clouds. The somewhat cooler air makes it feel less hot, but the results can be just as unpleasant. When sitting out in the sun you should remember to wear a hat, to prevent sunstroke.

OUTDOOR HAZARDS

Another potential problem on the islands, besides the sunshine, is the ocean. Many people do not realize the strength of the ocean waves.

In order to avoid any unpleasant surprises, you should always swim where there are lifeguards. Always take note of warning signs. The currents can be particularly powerful around the Canary Islands. If you cannot see plenty of other people swimming in the water then the chances are that it may not be safe. Never bathe where there are surfers or windsurfers. These are a potential hazard, especially when beginners come too close to the shore. Surfers and divers using unguarded beaches should be aware of the rocky ocean bottom. A violent wave can sometimes throw a person against the rocks, causing serious injuries.

When diving near the shore, it is always advisable to have another person with you for protection. The marine fauna do not present a danger to swimmers, although jellyfish can inflict a painful sting.

MEDICAL CARE

Both national and private healthcare is available in Spain. Visitors from EU countries are entitled to free national health treatment. They must, however, remember to travel with a certified copy of a European Health Insurance card (EHIC). These can be obtained in the UK before you travel by filling in an application form on either the EHIC website or at a post office. Please note that Spanish healthcare does not cover all expenses, such as the cost of dental treatment. Visitors from outside the EU should always carry valid insurance.

In case of illness, you should report to the nearest hospital or clinic. At night, you should contact the emergency service *(Urgencias)* and in case of an accident call for a Red Cross ambulance *(Cruz Roja).*

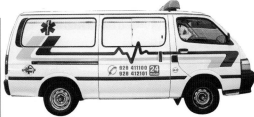

Ambulance in Las Palmas de Gran Canaria

PHARMACIES

Pharmacists can offer help and advice. In some cases, they can also prescribe medicines. If you have a non-urgent medical problem the *farmacia* is a good place to start. Most pharmacists will speak English. They are open during the same hours as other shops and carry a green cross sign, often with the word *farmacia.* Details about those open at night and on public holidays can be found in the windows of all pharmacies.

Illuminated Spanish pharmacy sign

FIRE HAZARDS

The high temperatures on the islands make them very dry. This should be remembered, particularly when travelling by car. At woodland camp sites and picnic spots, great care must be taken to prevent fire. When leaving, check carefully the remains of any bonfires and pick up glass, particularly empty bottles, which can cause fires. It goes without saying that you should be especially careful with cigarettes.

OUTDOORS

Visitors touring the islands may see various signs written only in Spanish, as well as warning and information notices.

Coto de caza or vedat de caça means a hunting ground. *Camino particular* means a private road, while *privado* informs you that the area is private property.

Hiking routes on the islands can be difficult. When setting off you should take the right equipment and plenty of water. Tell someone where you are going and when you intend to return.

DIRECTORY

EMERGENCY NUMBERS

Police, ambulance, fire brigade
Tel 112.

Policía Nacional.
Tel 091.

Policía Municipal
Tel 092.

Guardia Civil
Tel 062.

Ambulance
Tel 061.

Sea Rescue
Tel 928 467 955.

Fire Brigade
Tel 080 (Gran Canaria).
Tel 112 (Tenerife).

INFORMATION ON MEDICAL CARE

www.ehic.org.uk
Tel 0845 606 2030 (from UK).
Tel +44 191 203 5555 (from outside UK).

Sign warning of the risk of forest fires

Communication and Banks

Logo of a local bank

Most public telephones are served by the Spanish company Telefónica. There are plenty of public telephones and no problems in finding them. Thanks to the transfer to digital technology in 1998, the line quality is generally good. The Spanish postal system is not among the best. When exchanging messages with Spanish firms it is best to use fax or e-mail. There are several banks on the islands. These generally offer the best exchange rates. The major Spanish and foreign banks, including Deutsche Bank and Banesto, have branches here. There are also many local banks.

Typical post box belonging to the Spanish *correos*

TELEPHONING

There are two types of payphone on the island: card- and coin-operated, and card-operated (which do not accept coins). Some phones are equipped with multi-lingual electronic displays.

Phonecards are very convenient and can be purchased at newsstands and estancos (tobacconists). There are two types of telephone cards. One has a magnetic strip with an encoded value, the other has a PIN number that is entered before a connection is made.

When dialling a number you should remember that in Spain the area code is a permanent part of the number, which consists of nine digits in total. For Tenerife and its dependent islands, El Hierro, La Palma and La Gomera the area code

is 922. For Gran Canaria province and islands, Lanzarote and Fuerteventura, the number is 928. Calls between islands of the same province are charged at the same rate as long-distance calls within the island. Other calls are charged at the inter-provincial rate.

When calling Spain from abroad you should dial 34, followed by the subscriber's number, including the area code. When calling a mobile phone number you should dial the country code followed by the subscriber's number.

International calls are cheapest at night (after 8pm) and on Sunday. A call from a public telephone box costs 35

One of the many Spanish phonecards

per cent more than one made from a private phone in someone's home. Using public telephones is always cheaper than making calls from a hotel, however.

POSTAL SERVICE

Post offices are open between 9am and 7pm. Postage stamps can be bought at post office desks or any of the kiosks displaying the word *timbre*. Letters should be posted in yellow post boxes, marked *correos*. The Spanish *correos* (post office) is the only institution authorized to handle mail, so it is not recommended that you leave your letters in shops or hotels, which sometimes offer this service.

The postal system works at its own pace. You should therefore not be surprised if a letter or postcard takes a week or more to reach its destination.

Postal charges depend on where the item is being sent and fall into bands that include the EU, the rest of Europe, the USA and the rest of the world. Post offices also accept telegrams, registered mail and parcels.

CURRENCY

In March 2002, the Spanish peseta was fully replaced by the common EU currency – the euro. Notes have several denominations, ranging from €5 to €500.

USING A COIN AND CARD TELEPHONE

1 Lift the receiver and wait for the dialling tone and for the display to show *Inserte monedas o tarjeta*.

2 Insert either coins *(monedas)*, using the button on the top if there is one or a card *(tarjeta)*.

3 Key in the required number firmly, but not too fast – Spanish phones require a slight pause between each digit.

4 As you press the digits, the number you are dialling will appear on the display. You will also be able to see how much money or how many units are left.

5 When you finish your call, replace the receiver. The phonecard will re-emerge or any excess coins will be returned.

CHANGING MONEY

All major currencies can be exchanged without any problems in bureaux de change or banks.

Bureaux de change charge higher rates than banks, but even banks charge a few per cent commission. You can draw up to €300 on major credit cards at a bank.

In smaller towns and on islands, such as El Hierro, you may have problems with exchanging money. When travelling to some of the more remote places you should carry enough cash. *Cajas de Ahorro* (savings banks) can also exchange money. They open from 8:30am to 2pm on weekdays and also on Thursday afternoons from 4:30pm to 7:45pm.

Logo of one of the islands' most popular banks

BANKS AND CASH DISPENSERS

It is usually easy enough to find a bank or cash dispenser on the islands. Most banks are open from 9am until 1pm or 2pm. Some change their opening hours once a week and open in the afternoon instead.

Cash dispensers can be found on almost every street corner. They all dispense money and accept all major credit cards. Some charge a commission on withdrawals

Popular dailies published on the Canary Islands

with cards issued by other banks. If you want to avoid this, you should find out if any Spanish bank has an agreement with your own bank before travelling.

CREDIT CARDS

Credit cards are generally accepted, particularly in the tourist resorts, where every effort is made to make it easy for visitors. In less-frequented places, small shops and local bars it is sometimes necessary to pay in cash, and it is always worth carrying some cash to pay for small items. The most widely accepted card in Spain is Visa. MasterCard and American Express are also generally accepted. When you pay with a card, cashiers will ask for ID and usually pass your card through a reading machine. Sometimes you may be asked to punch in your PIN number.

NEWSPAPERS

Each of the islands of the archipelago publishes its own newspaper, dealing mainly with local issues. These are an excellent way to find out about any local events. There are also newspapers common to all the islands, including *Canarias 7* and *Island Connections*.

In many towns, kiosks and hotels sell Spanish national papers and also foreign newspapers, including a number of German and English language titles.

RADIO AND TELEVISION

There are several local radio stations on the Canary Islands. Reception quality varies because of the mountainous character of the area. Similar to the mainland stations they broadcast mainly Spanish music and news. There are also a number of foreign language stations.

You can receive Spanish television programmes, such as TVE1, without any problem. Foreign satellite channels such as Sky, CNN and Eurosport are also accessible.

One of the cash dispensers available on the islands

DIRECTORY

LOST OR STOLEN CREDIT CARDS

Visa
Tel 902 114 400/ 900 991124.

American Express
Tel 902 375 637/ 915 720 303.

MasterCard
Tel 902 192 100/ 900 971 231.

Diners Club
Tel 901 101 011/ 915 474 000.

POST OFFICES

Gran Canaria
C/Primero de Mayo, 62,
Las Palmas de Gran Canaria.
Tel 928 361 320.

Fuerteventura
C/Primero de Mayo, 58–60,
Puerto del Rosario.
Tel 928 850 412.

Lanzarote
Avda del Marino 8,
Arrecife.
Tel 928 800 673.

Tenerife
Plaza de España,
Santa Cruz de Tenerife.
Tel 922 259 605.

La Gomera
C/Real 60,
San Sebastián de La Gomera.
Tel 922 871 081.

El Hierro
Correo 3,
Valverde.
Tel 922 550 291.

La Palma
Plaza de la Constitución,
Santa Cruz de La Palma.
Tel 922 411 702.

TRAVEL INFORMATION

Air links with most of Europe and the Canary Islands are extremely efficient. Each island has an airport. Tenerife, Gran Canaria and Lanzarote take in most of the international flights as well as those from mainland Spain, while the other smaller airports are principally for hopping from island to island. Most of the air transport to and from the islands is by charter flights. Air links between the islands are provided mainly by Binter Canarias Airlines. You can also travel to the Canary Islands by ship. Most boats sail from harbours on mainland Spain or the West African coast. Ferries and fast catamarans provide regular links between the islands.

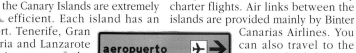

Airport sign

Attended car park at Gran Canaria airport

GETTING THERE

There are scheduled flights to the islands from all major Spanish towns. Flights from Madrid to Gran Canaria run almost every hour. These routes are served by three airlines: Iberia, Spanair and Air Europa. Iberia planes fly to all the islands of the archipelago, while the other two airlines fly only to Tenerife, Gran Canaria and Lanzarote.

The Canary Islands also have scheduled flights to and from many European cities. Air links with Africa are provided by three airlines – Air Maroc, Air Mauritanie and Air Atlantic. These connect the islands with the towns of Morocco and the former Spanish Sahara.

Apart from scheduled flights, all airports operate hundreds of charter flights. These are used mostly by German and British tourists, although holidaymakers come from all over Europe.

Charter flight tickets were once only bought as part of a package tour. Now visitors can travel independently, making a ticket-only purchase and booking their accommodation separately.

When buying an air ticket you should always enquire about current offers. Occasionally, some airlines offer very good bargains. Bargains are also to be had if you book your ticket on the Internet. However, it is difficult to find a bargain during the high seasons, such as the school summer holidays, Christmas or during the carnivals, which take place in February and March. Information can be found on the Internet or obtained from travel agents.

You can also travel to the islands by ship (the only option if taking a motorbike or car).

There are weekly departures from Cadiz to Tenerife and Gran Canaria. The voyage takes one-and-a-half to two days, depending on the destination.

Brochure for Binter Canarias

FLIGHTS BETWEEN THE ISLANDS

All the islands of the archipelago now have their own airports. Nevertheless, not all of them offer flights to all the other islands. For example, La Gomera only has flights to Tenerife and Gran Canaria. Most routes are served by Binter Canarias Airlines.

When hopping between the islands, it is a good idea to find out which airline provides the service. It is not a cheap option and some aircraft are very small, with a dozen or so seats. Often, the airline will not allow you to take large hand luggage. Travelling in a small, packed and stuffy aircraft can be a little unpleasant for people who suffer from claustrophobia or other health problems.

Flights between the islands are short. The shortest, between La Palma and El Hierro, takes 20 minutes; the longest – from La Palma to Lanzarote – 70 minutes.

Gran Canaria airport, next to the sea

Lineas Fred Olsen ferry

AIRPORTS

Tenerife has two airports – **Los Rodeos** in northen Tenerife and **Reina Sofia** in southern Tenerife. Flights from Tenerife Norte go to all the other islands of the archipelago and the airport handles most of the scheduled flights to Tenerife. Reina Sofia is a more modern airport, and caters mainly for the heavier load of charter traffic.

El Hierro has a small airport – **El Llano del Cangrejo**. It is situated 12 km (7 miles) from the island's capital – Valverde, but it is difficult to get there by bus. It handles flights to Tenerife, La Palma and Gran Canaria.

La Gomera's airport, **Punta del Becerro**, is situated not far from Playa de Santiago. The island has flights to Tenerife (Los Rodeos) and Gran Canaria only.

La Palma's airport is situated near Santa Cruz de La Palma. It handles flights to Gran Canaria, Lanzarote, Tenerife and El Hierro.

Gran Canaria has only one airport, situated between Las Palmas and Maspalomas. The airport has good bus links with both of the largest towns on the island. Gran Canaria has flights to all the other islands of the archipelago.

The **Arrecife** airport on Lanzarote handles flights to Gran Canaria, Tenerife and La Palma. It is situated not far from the town of Arrecife, which also has a bus station.

Fuerteventura has air links with Gran Canaria and Tenerife. A bus runs from the airport to Puerto del Rosario, 6 km (4 miles) away.

FERRIES

Ferries provide an alternative form of inter-island transport, although crossings are not always direct and might require a change. Direct crossings to all the other islands, or crossings with a single change, run only from Tenerife, which is the hub of island-hopping by sea *(see inside back cover)*. The most popular tourist resorts provide several daily crossings, by ferry or large, fast catamarans. These carry cars, buses and lorries as well as foot passengers. They also have bars, restaurants and cabins.

Logo for the Trasmediterranea line

When planning a tour around the archipelago you should remember that travelling by ferry is always much cheaper than flying. Although it takes longer it can be a very pleasant option.

Ticket prices for crossings offered by the two biggest companies serving inter-island routes – **Trasmediterranea** and **Lineas Fred Olsen** – are broadly similar. Slightly cheaper tickets are offered by **Naviera Armas** lines.

DIRECTORY

AIRPORTS

Gran Canaria
Tel 928 579 000.

Fuerteventura
Tel 928 860 500.

Lanzarote – Arrecife
Tel 928 846 000.

Tenerife – Los Rodeos
Tel 922 635 635.

Tenerife – Reina Sofía
Tel 922 759 000.

La Gomera – Punta del Becerro
Tel 922 873 000.

El Hierro – Llano del Cangrejo
Tel 922 553 700.

La Palma
Tel 922 426 100.

AIRLINES

Binter Canarias Airlines
Tel 902 391 392.
www.bintercanarias.com

Iberia
Tel 902 400 500.
www.iberia.com

FERRY LINES

Trasmediterranea
Tel 902 456 456.
www.transmediterranea.net

Líneas Fred Olsen
Tel 902 100 107.
www.lineasfredolsen.es

Naviera Armas
Tel 902 456 500.
www.navieraarmas.com

Ferry harbour in Las Palmas de Gran Canaria

Getting Around the Islands

Depending on your plans for visiting the islands, you can choose one of many forms of transport. The bigger islands, such as Tenerife, Gran Canaria and Lanzarote, have efficient buses. Here you can travel by bus to almost any point on the island. Exploring some of the smaller islands means hiring a car, motorbike or bicycle. However, some places are best visited as part of an organized tour, with an experienced guide and driver.

Winding roads in the vicinity of Masca

ROADS

Visitors touring the Canary Islands by car cannot but be impressed by the state of the roads. Many are newly built and smoothly surfaced. All major towns and villages can be reached by road, without any problem. Larger islands have their own motorways *(autopistas)*, running along the coast, which connect with the airports and major resorts.

Roads in the central, mountainous regions, on the other hand, are narrow and winding. They often lead through narrow tunnels. Problems can arise when two vehicles try to pass each other, particularly when one of them is a bus or a lorry. Sometimes a hidden oncoming vehicle signals its approach by blowing its horn.

Driving conditions may become dangerous in some areas when it is raining or foggy, as the roads can become slippery and the visibility limited.

Many scenic spots are accessible only by rough tracks or unmade roads, requiring a four-wheel-drive vehicle. The best way to visit them is to join an organized tour. A heavy rainfall can make these roads impassable.

The islands' roads are, in the main, well signposted, with clear signs for towns, major tourist attractions and viewpoints. El Hierro is the exception and you may have problems spotting the small, wooden signposts from a distance. In town, the well-signposted streets make historic sites and museums easy to find.

BUSES AND TAXIS

On larger islands, such as Gran Canaria and Tenerife, there are no problems travelling by bus. You should, however, bear in mind that buses to some smaller towns or villages may run only once or twice a day and you might have problems finding a bus to get you back to your hotel or apartment.

Travelling from a small town or village to a major nightlife centre later in the evening may also be something of a problem.

Large towns have their own bus networks. These serve the town and its immediate environs.

Smaller islands have infrequent bus services, which, although sufficient for the locals, make it difficult to explore these places.

In towns and major tourist resorts it is easy to get a taxi. They are a much more convenient, although more expensive, form of transport than buses. Taxi drivers are obliged to turn on the meter at the start of the journey, and the sum displayed is the one you pay. Only when travelling to and from an airport is there an additional airport fee as well as a small luggage charge.

TOWN DRIVING

If at all possible, you should avoid driving in the capital cities. Las Palmas and other cities often experience traffic jams during the rush hours, and at other times. Cars parked by the pavements make driving conditions more difficult. It is also very difficult to find a parking space, particularly in city centres. Most car parks charge fees, and there are fines for non-payment.

Advertisement for one of the numerous car hire firms

CAR HIRE

On all the islands you can easily find a car hire firm. Major companies, including **Avis** and Hertz, as well as the local ones, including **Cicar**, have their desks at the airports. Car hire is generally very reasonable, but the price depends on many factors,

Tourist coach on La Gomera

An unorthodox form of transport on the islands

including the time of year, the size of the car and the length of hire. Advance booking also affects the price. It is worth comparing the prices quoted by various agencies and checking exactly what the quote includes.

When hiring a car you should carefully inspect its condition, as you will have to return it in the same state or pay a fine.

The terms and conditions of hire vary according to individual companies. There are no established rules regarding insurance, mileage or petrol. Check carefully before signing any contract. For an ordinary car the terms will probably include a provision ensuring that you do not drive on unmade roads, or take the car by ferry to another island. Hire cars must be returned to where they were collected, or to another agreed place.

Firms offering motorbikes for hire are few and far between. Crash helmets are obligatory, and for anything over 50cc you'll need to produce a driving licence.

BUYING PETROL

Petrol (gasoline) on the islands is cheaper than on mainland Spain. Petrol stations offer all types of fuel, but most cars use unleaded petrol.

Petrol station pumps are generally operated by the staff. Only a few are automatic and open 24 hours. When touring the small islands, such as El Hierro, you

should remember that there are very few petrol stations, and that a car uses more fuel on mountainous terrain than on a flat road. It is therefore worth filling the tank before setting off.

RULES OF THE ROAD

The traffic regulations on the islands are generally the same as those of other European countries. Vehicles drive on the right-hand side of the road and there are few road signs specific to Spain or the islands. Speed limits, though not always obeyed by the Spaniards, are legally binding. On motorways the speed limit is 120 km/h (74 mph), on major roads, 90 km/h (55 mph) and in towns, 50 km/h (30 mph).

The fines for exceeding the speed limit are high, just as they are for drunken driving. The highest permitted blood alcohol level is 0.05 per cent (random breath testing is carried out). Safety belts are obligatory for passengers as well as drivers.

Road breakdown help point

DIRECTORY

CAR HIRE

CICAR
Tel 928 822 900.
www.cicar.com

Europcar
Tel 922 791 154.
www.europcar.es

Avis
Tel 902 180 854.
www.avis.com

BUS STATIONS

Gran Canaria
Tel 928 361 956.

Fuerteventura
Tel 650 532 866.

Lanzarote
Tel 928 811 522.

Tenerife
Tel 922 236 582.

La Gomera
Tel 922 141 101.

El Hierro
Tel 922 550 729.

La Palma
Tel 922 411 924.

MAPS

When buying a map you should first check if it is up to date. This is important, in view of the continuing local road development programme. Should you fail to buy maps before leaving, you can always get the island's map from each car hire firm. Street maps can be obtained from tourist offices.

Cavalcade of jeeps at a mountain road stopping point

General Index

Acknowledgments

Wiedza I Życie would like to thank the following people for their contribution to the preparation of this guide: Jürgen Bingel, Magdalena Borzęcka, Zbigniew Dybowski, Joanna Egert-Romanowska, Daniel Poch, Javier Lopez Silvosa, Damian Sosa.

Additional Contributor
Joe Cawley

Additional Photography
Antony Souter

For Dorling Kindersley
Publishing Manager: Helen Townsend
Managing Art Editors: Kate Poole and Ian Midson
Senior Editor: Jacky Jackson
Editorial and Design Assistance: Claire Baranowski, Jill Benjamin, Marian Broderick, Jo Cowen, Maite Lantaron, Jude Ledger, Carly Madden, Kate Molan, Helen Peters, Lucinda Smith, Susana Smith, Stewart Wild, Hugo Wilkinson
Additional Picture Research: Rachel Barber, Rhiannon Furbear
DTP: Vinod Harish, Azeem Siddiqui, Vincent Kurien
Cartography: Uma Bhattacharya, Mohammed Hassan, Jasneet Kaur

The Publisher would also like to thank all those who gave permission to reproduce photographs of their property and for allowing the use of photographs from archives.

AFP (Piotr Ufnal); Casa de Colón – Las Palmas de Gran Canaria; (Elena Acosta Guerrero, Ramon Gil); Casino Las Palmas – Las Palmas de Gran Canaria (Victoria Rivero); CORBIS (Małgorzata Gajdzińska); Fundacíon Césare Manrique (Bianca Visser); Hotel Rural Finca de Salinas – Yaiza; Hotel Santa Catalina– Las Palmas de Gran Canaria (Kati von Poroszlay); Loro Parque (Grettel Pérez Darias); Museo Arqueológico de Tenerife – Santa Cruz de Tenerife (Néstor Yanes); Museo de Cerámica – Casa Tafuriaste – La Orotavie (Antonio Cid Menchen); Museo de Historia de Tenerife – La Laguna (Ana Moreno, Jorge Gorrin Morales); Museo Etnografico Tanit – San Bartolomé (Remy de Quintana); Museo Municipal de Bellas Artes (María del Carmen Duque Hernández); Museo Néstor – Las Palmas de Gran Canaria (Pedro Luis Rosales Pedrero); Patronato de Turismo de Fuerteventura; Patronato de Turismo de Gran Canaria (Alfonso Falcón); Sociedad de Promocion de Las Palmas de Gran Canaria (Candelaria Delgado); ZEFA (Ewa Kozłowska); ZOOM s.c.

Picture Credits

t=top; tl=top left; tc=top centre, tr=top right; c=centre; cl=centre left; cr=centre right; cb=centre below; ca=centre above; clb=centre below left; crb=centre right below; cla=centre left above; cra=centre right above; b=bottom; bl=bottom left; bc=bottom centre; br=bottom right; bca=bottom centre above; bla=bottom left above; bra=bottom right above; blb=bottom left below; bcb=bottom centre below, brb=bottom right below, l=left; lc= left centre, r=right; ra=right above, rb=right below.

Works of art have been reproduced with the permission of the following copyright holders: *Sculpture Monumento*

al Campesino in Mozaga 90c, *Logo (sculpture)* of *National Park Timanfaya* 92tr, *sculpture of cactus in Jardin de Cactus in Guatiza* 86tl; *Logo (sculpture)* of *Mirador del Rio* 88c, *Room in the Artist's House, Tabiche* 85, Mosaics from artist's house, Tahiche 82clb all works by Cesar Manrique ©DACS, London 2006.

4Corners Images: SIME/Schmid Reinhard 11tr, 44br. Alamy Images: Alan Dawson Photography 53tl, 190cr; FAN travelstock/Katja Kreder 10bl; Eddie Gerald 45br; LOOK Die Bildagentur der Fotografen GmbH/Juergen Richter 11bl, 44cla; Nicholas Pitt 10cra; Profimedia International s.r.o. 170cl; David Robertson 11cr; Peter Titmuss 182cl. Buenavista Golf: 190cl. Carnaval Las Palmas de Gran Canaria: www.laspalmascarnaval.com 45tc; Corbis: 12t, 25b, 28, 71tr; Jack Fields 11b; Robert Holmes 192–193; Robert Krist 25c; José F. Poblete 199b,; Roger Ressmeyer 150b; Nik Wheeler 24b, 122, 132, 137t. www.designhotels.com: 169C; DK Images: 5cr, 18b, 19tl, 35bl, 40; 196c, 188c; Max Alexander 197t, 198c; Philip Gatward 121cb; Sven Larrson 56t; Neil Lukas 199c, 200tr; Ian O'Leary 5ca, 170tr, 170crb, 170bl, 170br; Brian Pitkin 188b; Kim Sayer 10tc, 14bl, 24cr, 26b, 39tl, 41t, 62t, 81b; Tony Souter 187br; Linda Whitwam 19tr. Fundacíon Césare Manrique: 85b. Getty Images: Stuart Franklin 190bl. Hacienda del Buen Suceso: 154br; Hotel San Roque: 155bc; José Miquel Hernández Hernández: 100br; Hotel Santa Catalina – Las Palmas de Gran Canaria: 184c. Andrzej Lisowski 120b, 123b. Loro Parque: 114t, 114c, 114b, 115t, 115ca, 115cb, 115b, 184b. Mary Evans Picture Library: 37ca. Carlos Minguel:18t, 18lt, 18lc, 18lb, 19c, 19bl, 19br. Paweł Murzyn: 36–37. Museo Arqueológico de Tenerife – Santa Cruz de Tenerife: 30cb, 31br. Museo Néstor – Las Palmas de Gran Canaria: 46bl. Oronoz: 30–31, 35t. Robert G. Pasieczny: 17tc, 17tr, 17bl, 17the 31tl, 32ca, 38ca, 52t, 64b, 65b, 67t, 68t, 69t, 70c, 71tl, 72c, 74t, 75c, 76b, 77br, 78t, 78c, 81t, 82t, 94c, 95b, 97t, 100c, 106t, 108t, 117t, 119t, 119bl, 137b, 138c, 140t, 141t, 143t, 154t, 168t, 168b, 169b, 186t, 186cr, 188t, 194c, 204b. Piotr Paszkiewicz: 26t, 54t, 54b, 123t. Patronato de Turismo de Gran Canaria: 185b. Ángel Gómez Pinchetti: 48t, 48c, 48b, 49t, 49cb, 49b. Magdalena Polak: 130t, 149cl, 149cr, 149b; Punchstock: Digital Vision/Manchan 50–51. Maria Ángeles Sanchez: 22c, 23b, 27b, 128b, 149t, 150c. Sociedad de Promocion de Las Palmas de Gran Canaria: 4b, 22t, 22b, 23t, 23c, 185t. Tecina Golf: 191tr.

Jacket
Front – DK Images: Pawel Wojcik clb; Photolibrary: Mitterer Mitterer main image.
Back – Corbis: Zefa/Karl Kinne clb; DK Images: Pawel Wojcik bl, cla, tl. Spine – DK Images: b; Photolibrary: Mitterer Mitterer t.
All other images © Dorling Kindersley.
For further information see:
www.DKimages.com

SPECIAL EDITIONS OF DK TRAVEL GUIDES

DK Travel Guides can be purchased in bulk quantities at discounted prices for use in promotions or as premiums. We are also able to offer special editions and personalized jackets, corporate imprints, and excerpts from all of our books, tailored specifically to meet your own needs.

To find out more, please contact:
(in the United States) **specialsales@dk.com**
(in the UK) **travelspecialsales@uk.dk.com**
(in Canada) DK Special Sales at **general@tourmaline.ca**
(in Australia)
business.development@pearson.com.au

Phrase Book

In an Emergency

Help!	¡Socorro!	soh-**koh**-roh
Stop!	¡Pare!	pah-reh
Call a doctor!	¡Llame a un médico!	yah-meh ah oon meh-dee-koh
Call an ambulance!	¡Llame a una ambulancia!	yah-meh ah oonah ahm-boo-**lahn**-thee-ah
Call the police!	¡Llame a la policía!	yah-meh ah lah poh-lee-**thee**-ah
Call the fire brigade!	¡Llame a los bomberos!	yah-meh ah lohs bohm-beh-rohs
Where is the nearest telephone?	¿Dónde está el teléfono más próximo?	dohn-deh ehs tah ehl teh-leh-foh-noh mahs prohx-ee-moh
Where is the nearest hospital?	¿Dónde está el hospital más próximo?	dohn-deh ehs tah ehl ohs-pee-**tahl** mahs prohx-ee-moh

Communication Essentials

Yes	Sí	see
No	No	noh
Please	Por favor	pohr fah-**vohr**
Thank you	Gracias	**grah**-thee-ahs
Excuse me	Perdone	pehr-**doh**-neh
Hello	Hola	**oh**-lah
Goodbye	Adiós	ah-dee-ohs
Good night	Buenas noches	**bweh**-nahs noh-chehs
Morning	La mañana	lah mah-**nyah**-nah
Afternoon	La tarde	lah tahr-deh
Evening	La tarde	lah tahr-deh
Yesterday	Ayer	ah-yehr
Today	Hoy	oy
Tomorrow	Mañana	mah-**nya**-nah
Here	Aquí	ah-**kee**
There	Allí	ah-yee
What?	¿Qué?	keh
When?	¿Cuándo?	**kwahn**-doh
Why?	¿Por qué?	pohr-**keh**
Where?	¿Dónde?	**dohn**-deh

Useful Phrases

How are you?	¿Cómo está usted?	koh-moh ehs-**tah** oos-**tehd**
Very well, thank you.	Muy bien, gracias.	mwee behr-**ehn grah**-thee-ahs
Pleased to meet you.	Encantado de conocerle.	ehn-kahn-**tah**-doh deh koh-noh-**thehr**-leh
See you soon.	Hasta pronto.	ahs-tah **prohn**-toh
That's fine.	Está bien.	ehs-**tah** bee-**ehn**
Where is/are ...?	¿Dónde está/están ...?	**dohn**-deh ehs-**tah**/ehs-**tahn**
How far is it to ...?	¿Cuántos metros/ kilómetros hay de aquí a ...?	**kwahn**-tohs meh-trohs/kee-**loh**-meh-trohs **eye** deh ah-**kee** ah
Which way to ...?	¿Por dónde se va a ...?	pohr **dohn**-deh seh bah ah
Do you speak English?	¿Habla inglés?	ah-blah een-**glehs**
I don't understand	No comprendo	noh kohm-**prehn**-doh
Could you speak more slowly please?	¿Puede hablar más despacio por favor?	pweh-deh ah-**blahr** mahs dehs-pah-thee-oh pohr fah-**vohr**
I'm sorry.	Lo siento.	loh see-**ehn**-toh

Useful Words

big	grande	**grahn**-deh
small	pequeño	peh-**keh**-nyoh
hot	caliente	kah-lee-**ehn**-teh
cold	frío	**free**-oh
good	bueno	**bweh**-noh
bad	malo	**mah**-loh
enough	bastante	bahs-**tahn**-teh
well	bien	bee-**ehn**
open	abierto	ah-bee-ehr- toh
closed	cerrado	thehr-**rah**-doh
left	izquierda	eeth-key-ehr-dah
right	derecha	deh-**reh**-chah
straight on	derecho	toh-doh **rehk**-toh
near	cerca	**thehr**-kah
far	lejos	**leh**-hohs
up	arriba	ah-**ree**-bah
down	abajo	ah-**bah**-hoh
early	temprano	tehm-**prah**-noh
late	tarde	**tahr**-deh
entrance	entrada	ehn-**trah**-dah
exit	salida	sah-**lee**-dah
toilet	lavabos, servicios	lah-**vah**-bohs sehr-**bee**-thee-ohs
more	más	mahs
less	menos	**meh**-nohs

Shopping

How much does this cost?	¿Cuánto cuesta esto?	**kwahn**-toh kwehs-tah ehs-toh
I would like ...	Me gustaría ...	meh goos-ta-**ree**-ah
Do you have?	¿Tiene?	tee-**yeh**-nehn
I'm just looking.	Sólo estoy mirando, gracias.	soh-loh ehs-**toy** mee-**rahn**-doh **grah**-thee-ahs
Do you take credit cards?	¿Aceptan tarjetas de crédito?	ah-**thehp**-tahn tahr-**heh**-tahs deh **kreh**-dee-toh
What time do you open?	¿A qué hora abren?	ah keh oh-rah **ah**-brehn
What time do you close?	¿A qué hora cierran?	ah keh oh-rah thee-**ehr**-rahn
This one.	Éste.	**ehs**-teh
That one.	Ése.	**eh**-seh
expensive	caro	**kahr**-oh
cheap	barato	bah-**rah**-toh
size, clothes	talla	**tah**-yah
size, shoes	número	**noo**-mehr-oh
white	blanco	**blahn**-koh
black	negro	**neh**-groh
red	rojo	**roh**-hoh
yellow	amarillo	ah-mah-**ree**-yoh
green	verde	**behr**-deh
blue	azul	ah-**thool**
antiques shop	la tienda de antigüedades	lah tee-**ehn**-dah deh ahn-tee gweh-**dah**-dehs
bakery	la panadería	lah pah-nah-deh-**ree**-ah
bank	el banco	ehl **bahn**-koh
book shop	la librería	lah lee-breh-**ree**-ah
butcher's	la carnicería	lah kahr-nee-theh-**ree**-ah
cake shop	la pastelería	lah pahs-teh-leh-**ree**-ah
chemist's	la farmacia	lah fahr-**mah**-thee-ah
fishmonger's	la pescadería	lah pehs-kah-deh-**ree**-ah
greengrocer's	la frutería	lah froo-teh-**ree**-ah
grocer's	la tienda de comestibles	lah tee-**yehn**- dah deh koh-mehs-**tee**-blehs
hairdresser's	la peluquería	lah peh-loo-keh-**ree**-ah
market	el mercado	ehl mehr-**kah**-doh
newsagent's	el kiosko de prensa	ehl kee-**ohs**-koh deh **prehn**-sah
post office	la oficina de correos	lah oh-fee-**thee**-nah deh kohr-**reh**-ohs
shoe shop	la zapatería	lah thah-pah-teh-**ree**-ah
supermarket	el supermercado	ehl soo-pehr-mehr-**kah**-doh
tobacconist	el estanco	ehl ehs-**tahn**-koh
travel agency	la agencia de viajes	lah ah-**hehn**-thee-ah deh bee-**ah**-hehs

Sightseeing

art gallery	el museo de arte	ehl moo-**seh**-oh deh **ahr**-teh
cathedral	la catedral	lah kah-teh-**drahl**
church	la iglesia	lah ee-**gleh**-see-ah
	la basílica	lah bah-**see**-lee-kah
garden	el jardín	ehl hahr-**deen**
library	la biblioteca	lah bee-blee-oh-**teh**-kah
museum	el museo	ehl moo-**seh**-oh
tourist information office	la oficina de turismo	lah oh-fee-**thee** nah deh too-**rees**-moh
town hall	el ayuntamiento	ehl ah-yoon-tah-mee-**ehn**-toh
closed for holiday	cerrado por vacaciones	thehr-**rah**-doh pohr bah-kah-thee-**oh**-nehs
bus station	la estación de autobuses	lah ehs-tah-thee-**ohn** deh owtoh-**boo**-sehs
railway station	la estación de trenes	lah ehs-tah-thee-**ohn** deh **treh**-nehs

Staying in a Hotel

Do you have a vacant room?	¿Tiene una habitación libre?	tee-**eh**-neh **oo**-nah ah-bee-tah-thee-**ohn** lee-breh
double room	habitación doble	ah-bee-tah-thee-**ohn doh**-bleh
with double bed	con cama de matrimonio	kohn **kah**-mah deh mah-tree-**moh**-nee-oh
twin room	habitación con dos camas	ah-bee-tah-thee-**ohn** kohn dohs **kah**-mahs
single room	habitación individual	ah-bee-tah-thee-**ohn** een-dee-vee-doo-**ahl**
room with a bath	habitación con baño	ah-bee-tah-thee-**ohn** kohn bah-nyoh
shower	ducha	**doo**-chah
porter	portero	ehl boh-**toh**-nehs
key	la llave	lah **yah**-veh
I have a reservation.	Tengo una habitación reservada.	tehn-goh **oo**-na ah-bee-tah-thee-**ohn** reh-sehr-**bah**-dah

Eating Out

Have you got a table for …?	¿Tiene mesa para …?	tee-**eh**-neh meh-sah pah-**rah**
I want to reserve a table.	Quiero reservar una mesa.	kee-eh-roh reh-sehr-**bahr oo**-nah **meh**-sah
The bill please.	La cuenta por favor.	lah **kwehn**-tah pohr fah-**vohr**
I am a vegetarian	Soy vegetariano/a	soy beh-heh-tah-ree-**ah**-no/na
waitress/	camarera	kah-mah-**reh**-rah
waiter	camarero	kah-mah-**reh**-roh
menu	la carta	lah **kahr**-tah
fixed-price menu	menú del día	meh-**noo** dehl **dee**-ah
wine list	la carta de vinos	lah **kahr**-tah deh **bee**-nohs
glass	un vaso	oon **bah**-soh
bottle	una botella	oo-nah boh-**teh**-yah
knife	un cuchillo	oon koo-**chee**-yoh
fork	un tenedor	oon teh-neh-**dohr**
spoon	una cuchara	oo-nah koo-**chah**-rah
breakfast	el desayuno	ehl deh-sah-**yoo**-noh
lunch	la comida el almuerzo	lah koh-**mee**-dah/ ehl ahl-**mwehr**-thoh
dinner	la cena	lah **theh**-nah
main course	el primer plato	ehl pree-**mehr plah**-toh
starters	los entremeses	lohs ehn-treh-**meh**-sehs
dish of the day	el plato del día	ehl **plah**-toh dehl **dee**-ah
coffee	el café	ehl kah-**feh**
rare (meat)	poco hecho	**poh**-koh **eh**-choh
medium	medio hecho	**meh**-dee-oh **eh**-choh
well done	muy hecho	mwee **eh**-choh

Menu Decoder

al horno	ahl **ohr**-noh	baked
asado	ah-**sah**-doh	roast
el aceite	ah-**thee-eh**-teh	oil
las aceitunas	ah-theh-**toon**-ahs	olives
el agua mineral	**ah**-gwa mee-neh-**rahl**	mineral water
sin gas/con gas	seen gas/kohn gas	still/sparkling
el ajo	**ah**-hoh	garlic
el arroz	ahr-**rohth**	rice
el azúcar	ah-**thoo**-kahr	sugar
la carne	**kahr**-neh	meat
la cebolla	theh-**boh**-yah	onion
el cerdo	**thehr**-doh	pork
la cerveza	thehr-**beh**-thah	beer
el chocolate	choh-koh-**lah**-teh	chocolate
el chorizo	choh-**ree**-thoh	spicy sausage
el cordero	kohr-**deh**-roh	lamb
el fiambre	fee-**ahm**-breh	cold meat
frito	**free**-toh	fried
la fruta	**froo**-tah	fruit
los frutos secos	froo-tohs **seh**-kohs	nuts
las gambas	**gahm**-bahs	prawns
el helado	eh-**lah**-doh	ice cream
el huevo	oo-**eh**-voh	egg
el jamón serrano	hah-**mohn** sehr-**rah**-noh	cured ham

el jerez	heh-**rehz**	sherry
la langosta	lahn-**gohs**-tah	lobster
la leche	**leh**-cheh	milk
el limón	lee-**mohn**	lemon
la limonada	lee-moh-**nah**-dah	lemonade
la mantequilla	mahn-teh-**kee**-yah	butter
la manzana	mahn-**thah**-nah	apple
los mariscos	mah-**rees**-kohs	seafood
la menestra	meh-**nehs**-trah	vegetable stew
la naranja	nah-**rahn**-hah	orange
el pan	pahn	bread
el pastel	pahs-**tehl**	cake
las patatas	pah-**tah**-tahs	potatoes
el pescado	pehs-**kah**-doh	fish
la pimienta	pee-mee-**yehn**-tah	pepper
el plátano	**plah**-tah-noh	banana
el pollo	**poh**-yoh	chicken
el postre	**pohs**-treh	dessert
el queso	**keh**-soh	cheese
la sal	sahl	salt
las salchichas	sahl-**chee**-chahs	sausages
la salsa	**sahl**-sah	sauce
seco	**seh**-koh	dry
el solomillo	soh-loh-**mee**-yoh	sirloin
la sopa	**soh**-pah	soup
la tarta	**tahr**-tah	pie/cake
el té	teh	tea
la ternera	tehr-**neh**-rah	veal
las tostadas	tohs-**tah**-dahs	toast
el vinagre	bee-**nah**-greh	vinegar
el vino blanco	**bee**-noh **blahn**-koh	white wine
el vino rosado	**bee**-noh roh-**sah**-doh	rosé wine
el vino tinto	**bee**-noh **teen**-toh	red wine

Numbers

0	cero	**theh**-roh
1	uno	**oo**-noh
2	dos	dohs
3	tres	trehs
4	cuatro	**kwa**-troh
5	cinco	**theen**-koh
6	seis	says
7	siete	see-**eh**-teh
8	ocho	**oh**-choh
9	nueve	**nweh**-veh
10	diez	dee-**ehth**
11	once	**ohn**-theh
12	doce	**doh**-theh
13	trece	**treh**-theh
14	catorce	kah-**tohr**-theh
15	quince	**keen**-theh
16	dieciséis	dee-eh-thee-**seh-ees**
17	diecisiete	dee-eh-thee-see-**eh**-teh
18	dieciocho	dee-eh-thee-**oh**-choh
19	diecinueve	dee-eh-thee-**nweh**-veh
20	veinte	**beh**-een-teh
21	veintiuno	beh-een-tee-**oo**-noh
22	veintidós	beh-een-tee-dohs
30	treinta	**treh**-een-tah
31	treinta y uno	treh-een-tah ee **oo**-noh
40	cuarenta	kwah-**rehn**-tah
50	cincuenta	theen-**kwehn**-tah
60	sesenta	seh-**sehn**-tah
70	setenta	seh-**tehn**-tah
80	ochenta	oh-**chehn**-tah
90	noventa	noh-**vehn**-tah
100	cien	**thee**-ehn
101	ciento uno	thee-**ehn**-toh **oo**-noh
102	ciento dos	thee-**ehn**-toh dohs
200	doscientos	dohs-thee-**ehn**-tohs
500	quinientos	khee-nee-**ehn**-tohs
700	setecientos	seh-teh-thee-**ehn**-tohs
900	novecientos	noh-veh-thee-**ehn** tohs
1,000	mil	meel
1,001	mil uno	meel **oo**-noh

Time

one minute	un minuto	oon mee-**noo**-toh
one hour	una hora	**oo**-na **oh**-rah
half an hour	media hora	meh-dee-a **oh**-rah
Monday	lunes	**loo**-nehs
Tuesday	martes	**mahr**-tehs
Wednesday	miércoles	mee-**ehr**-koh-lehs
Thursday	jueves	hoo-**weh**-vehs
Friday	viernes	bee-**ehr**-nehs
Saturday	sábado	**sah**-bah-doh
Sunday	domingo	doh-**meen**-goh

Canary Island Ferry Routes

LA PALMA

•Santa Cruz
de La Palma

LA GOMERA

San Sebastián
de La Gomera

Los Cristianos

TENERIFE

•Santa Cruz
de Tenerife

•Puerto de la Estaca

EL HIERRO

Atlantic Ocean

FERRY LINES

Trasmediterranea
www.trasmediterranea.es
Tel 902 454 645.

Líneas Fred Olsen
www.fredolsen.es
Tel 902 100 107.

Tenerife
Santa Cruz de Tenerife
Tel 922 628 200.
Los Cristianos
Tel 922 790 215.

La Gomera
San Sebastián de La Gomera
Tel 922 871 007.

La Palma
Santa Cruz de La Palma
Tel 922 415 433.

Naviera Armas
www.navieraarmas.com

Gran Canaria
Las Palmas de Gran Canaria
Tel 928 300 600.

Fuerteventura
Puerto del Rosario
Tel 928 851 542.
Morro Jable
Tel 928 542 113.
Corralejo
Tel 928 867 080.

Lanzarote
Arrecife
Tel 928 824 931.
Playa Blanca
Tel 928 517 912.

Tenerife
Santa Cruz de Tenerife
Tel 922 534 050.

La Palma
Santa Cruz de La Palma
Tel 922 411 445.

Líneas Marítimas Romero
www.lineas-romero.com
La Graciosa
Tel 928 842 070.

| | 0 km | 30 | |
| 0 miles | | | 30 |

KEY

— Ferry route

▬ Motorway/Highway

▬ Major road

═ Other road

• Major ferry port

✈ Airport